Praise
High Co[nflict]

"Insightful and enthralling . . . with a scrupulous eye for scientific evidence that is rare in a book this entertaining, Ripley also explains how it is possible for hardened combatants to leave behind the conflicts that once defined the core of their identity."

—*The New York Times Book Review*

"Amanda Ripley has combined skilled reporting, deep research, and riveting storytelling into a stellar work about an urgent topic. At a moment when too many Americans are at each other's throats, this is the book our country needs."

—Daniel H. Pink, author of
When, Drive, and *To Sell Is Human*

"Rarely have I read a book as downright clairvoyant as *High Conflict.* While most of us were raging at the rage in our culture, Amanda Ripley composed a lucid, compulsively readable roadmap to a world in which we can live with one another again. Honestly, I'll never argue the same way again."

—Evan Osnos,
National Book Award–winning author of
Joe Biden

"Ripley brilliantly illuminates the forces driving us to build impenetrable walls between ourselves and differing others, as well as the forces empowering us to build bridges over those walls. The lessons couldn't be more captivating or timely."

—Robert Cialdini, author of
Influence and *Pre-Suasion*

"This is one of the most important books that will be published in 2021. The COVID vaccine will soon free humanity from a biological pandemic, and this book, if widely read, could free humanity from an equally deadly scourge—high conflict."

—Jonathan Haidt, Thomas Cooley Professor of
Ethical Leadership, NYU-Stern School of Business,
author of *The Righteous Mind*, and
coauthor of *The Coddling of the American Mind*

"The unforgettable stories in this book show how even people who disagree profoundly can still connect with one another and make progress. A book to give you confidence in the future."

—Omar Epps

"A brilliant book that reveals how poisonous showdowns work. But more than just highlighting the problems, Ripley's book also provides solutions. Equally valuable in our personal lives as in navigating the polarized time we're living in."

—Jonah Berger, *New York Times* bestselling author of
The Catalyst and *Contagious*

"Amanda Ripley shows that the same minds that get us into bitter tribal battles can get us out of them. Via riveting stories in diverse settings—urban gangland, a war-torn South American nation, fractious municipal politics—Ripley proves that happy endings can happen in real life."

—Robert Wright, *New York Times* bestselling author of
Why Buddhism Is True

"The fascinating stories, global history, and dialogue from local politics Ripley includes keep the book moving at a brisk pace. . . . Readers interested in conflict management and negotiation and the decision-making process will be intrigued as Ripley thoughtfully explains the intensities and nuances of conflict, and the crux of high conflict in any setting."

—*Booklist*

"A revealing study of 'high conflict,' the intractable sort that seems to be running like a virus through American society . . . Ripley's observations are provocative, and she introduces us to ideas of mediation and problem-solving that would make many people less miserable if put into practice. . . . Students of mediation, social psychology, and conflict resolution will find much of value here."

—*Kirkus Reviews*

"Illuminating. Amanda takes us around the world to understand how people learn to stop demonizing the other side and start agreeing to disagree productively. I think it should be required reading for everyone in politics and the media—and for anyone who's had a squabble with a colleague or a blowup at a family gathering."

—Adam Grant, LinkedIn

also by amanda ripley

The Smartest Kids in the World: And How They Got That Way
The Unthinkable: Who Survives When Disaster Strikes—and Why

High Conflict

WHY WE
GET TRAPPED
and HOW
WE GET OUT

Amanda Ripley

Simon & Schuster Paperbacks

new york   london   toronto   sydney   new delhi

for max

Simon & Schuster Paperbacks
An Imprint of Simon Schuster, Inc.
1230 Avenue of the Americas
New York, NY 10020

First Simon & Schuster trade paperback edition April 2022

SIMON & SCHUSTER PAPERBACKS and colophon are registered trademarks
of Simon & Schuster, Inc.

For information about special discounts for bulk purchases,
please contact Simon & Schuster Special Sales at 1-866-506-1949
or business@simonandschuster.com.

To book this speaker at your event, contact tom@brightsightspeakers.com
or check out Amanda Ripley's speaker page at www.brightsightspeakers.com.

Manufactured in the United States of America

10 9 8 7 6 5

The Library of Congress has cataloged the hardcover edition as follows:

Names: Ripley, Amanda, author.
Title: High conflict : why we get trapped and how we get out / Amanda Ripley.
Description: New York : Simon & Schuster, [2021] | Includes bibliographical references
    and index. | Summary: "In the tradition of bestselling explainers like The Tipping
    Point, the first popular book based on cutting edge science that breaks down the idea
    of extreme conflict, the kind that paralyzes people and places, and then shows how to
    escape it"— Provided by publisher.
Identifiers: LCCN 2020043664 | ISBN 9781982128562 (hardcover) |
    ISBN 9781982128586 (ebook)
Subjects: LCSH: Social conflict. | Interpersonal conflict. | Conflict management.
Classification: LCC HM1121 .R57 2021 | DDC 303.6—dc23
LC record available at https://lccn.loc.gov/2020043664

ISBN 978-1-9821-2856-2
ISBN 978-1-9821-2857-9 (pbk)
ISBN 978-1-9821-2858-6 (ebook)

"Out beyond ideas of wrongdoing and rightdoing, there is a field. I'll meet you there."

—*Sufi poet Jalal al-Din Muhammad Rumi, 13th century*

contents

glossary

Confirmation bias. The human tendency to interpret new information as confirmation of one's preexisting beliefs.

Conflict entrepreneurs. People who exploit high conflict for their own ends.

Conflict trap. A conflict that becomes magnetic, pulling people in despite their own best interests. Characteristic of high conflict.

Contact theory. The idea that people from different groups will, under certain conditions, tend to become less prejudiced toward one another after spending time together.

Crock pot. A shorthand term for the issue that a conflict *appears* to be about, on the surface, when it is really about something else.

Cyberball. A simple online ball-tossing game created by researchers to study the effect of social exclusion.

Fire starters. Accelerants that lead conflict to explode in violence, including group identities, conflict entrepreneurs, humiliation, and corruption.

Fourth way. A way to go through conflict that's more satisfying than running away, fighting, or staying silent, the three usual paths. Leaning into the conflict.

Good conflict. Friction that can be serious and intense but leads somewhere useful. Does not collapse into dehumanization. Also known as healthy conflict.

High conflict. A conflict that becomes self-perpetuating and all-consuming, in which almost everyone ends up worse off. Typically an us-versus-them conflict.

Humiliation. A forced and public degradation; an unjustified loss of dignity, pride, or status. Can lead to high conflict and violence.

Idiot-driver reflex. The human tendency to blame other people's behavior on their intrinsic character flaws—and attribute our own behavior to the circumstances we find ourselves in. Also known as the fundamental attribution error.

Illusion of communication. The extremely common and mistaken belief that we have communicated something, when we have not.

La Brea Tar Pits. A place in Los Angeles where natural asphalt has bubbled up from below the ground's surface since the last Ice Age. A metaphor for high conflict.

Looping for understanding. An iterative, active listening technique in which the person listening reflects back what the person talking seems to have said—and checks to see if the summary was right. Developed by Gary Friedman and Jack Himmelstein and detailed in their book *Challenging Conflict*.

Magic ratio. When the number of everyday positive interactions between people significantly outweighs the number of negative, creating a buffer that helps keep conflict healthy. (In marriage, for example, the magic ratio is 5 to 1, according to research by psychologists Julie and John Gottman.)

Paradox No. 1 of High Conflict. We are animated by high conflict, and also haunted by it. We want it to end, and we want it to continue.

Paradox No. 2 of High Conflict. Groups bring obligations, including the duty to harm—or, at other times, the obligation to do *no* harm, to make peace.

Paradox No. 3 of High Conflict. No one will change in the ways you want them to until they believe you understand and accept them for who they are right now. (And sometimes not even then.)

Power of the binary. The dangerous reduction of realities or choices into just two. For example: Black and White, good and evil, Democrat and Republican.

Saturation point. The point in a conflict where the losses seem heavier than the gains; an opportunity for a shift.

Telling. The use of superficial shortcuts (like clothing or hair color) to quickly figure out who belongs to which group in a given conflict. A term used in Northern Ireland.

Understory. The thing the conflict is really about, underneath the usual talking points (see *Crock pot*).

principal characters

oxford, england

Mark Lynas. Environmentalist and author. Formerly an activist against genetically modified crops.

muir beach, california

Gary Friedman. Conflict mediator, author, and former trial lawyer. Ran for local office in his town of Muir Beach, California.

Tanya. Labor organizer, author, and neighbor of Gary's. Served as Gary's political strategist in his campaign.

Hugh. Businessperson, current and former board member, and neighbor of Gary's. Member of the "Old Guard" in Gary's conflict.

Elizabeth. Designer, former board member, and neighbor of Gary's. Member of the "New Guard."

chicago, illinois

Curtis Toler. Violence interrupter, actor, and a former leader in the Black P Stone gang.

Benji Wilson. A star high school basketball player in Chicago in the 1980s.

Billy Moore. Violence interrupter, author, and a former member of the Gangster Disciples, a rival gang to the Black P Stones.

bogotá and medellín, colombia

Sandra Milena Vera Bustos. Social justice advocate and former guerrilla fighter. Voluntarily exited Colombia's civil war.

Diego. A police officer and old friend of Sandra's, who accompanied her on the day she turned herself in.

Juan Pablo Aparicio. A graduate student who investigated whether soccer-related propaganda helped to nudge people out of high conflict in Colombia.

new york city, new york

José Rolando "Roly" Matalon. The senior rabbi at the Manhattan synagogue B'nai Jeshurun, known as "BJ" to its members.

Caleb Follett. A conservative, Christian corrections officer who lives in central Michigan.

Martha Ackelsberg. A liberal, Jewish academic who lives in New York City.

introduction

Police arrest protesters raiding a field of genetically modified crops outside Oxford, England, in 1999.
Nick Cobbing

As a rule, Mark Lynas did not enjoy upsetting people. He liked to read history books and play ultimate frisbee. He had a job editing a small charity network website. The son of a scientist, he was passionate about protecting the environment. But he preferred to write his arguments rather than scream them.

And yet, one night in 1999, Mark found himself trespassing on a farm near his home in the east of England, dressed all in black, carrying a machete. It felt like the absolutely right thing to do to bring that machete down hard, cracking through one healthy corn stalk after another.

He worked methodically, thrashing his machete up one row and down the other, taking care to avoid hitting his fellow activists. The air smelled of moist soil and freshly ruptured roots. He stopped to adjust his glasses every so often.

It had started, as these things do, quite reasonably. A few years earlier, Mark had attended a get-together of young environmentalists like himself in a seaside town in England. There he'd learned about something

called "genetic engineering." A giant chemical company named Monsanto had begun altering the DNA of seeds in order to grow better crops.
It sounded fairly creepy to Mark. Why would they do such a thing?

For profit, of course. Their new, bioengineered plants had a super-
power. They could survive the application of Monsanto's own noxious
weed killer, known as Roundup.

Mark leaned forward. Was he hearing this right? Monsanto was
the same company, he learned, that had helped manufacture Agent
Orange, a mixture of toxic weed killers that the U.S. military had used
during the Vietnam War. Now the company was apparently creating
an entire ecosystem in which only its own sci-fi seeds could survive
the storm of poison to come.

Hearing this, Mark recognized a pattern. This was around the same
time as the controversy over mad cow disease was roiling England.
Thousands of cows had gotten sick with a fatal brain infection. For
years, British officials had insisted there was no evidence humans could
be harmed by contaminated beef. Everything was fine! Carry on! But
then, it turned out, they'd been totally wrong. A human variant of the
disease did seem to be linked to the beef products. The government was
forced to recant. Eventually, more than two hundred people would die.

It was proof that the government could not be trusted, not when
it came to protecting the public against huge corporations. And now,
it seemed, it was happening all over again. A giant multinational
company was meddling in the food supply, playing God with nature.

The more Mark learned, the more outraged he got. He had to do
something. So he wrote a screed, one of the first-ever articles warning
of the danger of genetically modified crops. "In the great global genetic
experiment, which is being pursued by chemical and food multina-
tionals in their search for greater profit, we—the consumers—are the
guinea pigs," he wrote in *Corporate Watch* magazine. He warned that if
companies "win their battle to force us to accept genetically engineered
produce . . . the course of life on planet earth may be changed forever."

The threat was existential and urgent. "These are dangerous times ahead." The piece was compelling, and it got people talking. So he wrote another and another. Then he started participating in "decontaminations," like the one on the field that night.

Later, Mark would wonder when he'd started missing things. It wasn't right away, he knew. He'd had good reason to be suspicious of Monsanto. But somewhere along the way, he'd started making mistakes. It was astonishing really, looking back on it. But that was later.

The police appeared suddenly across the open field that night. Mark dropped to the ground, heart hammering in his chest. This had not happened to him before. The beams of their flashlights arced across the field. He could hear the pop and static of their radios and, as they got closer, the panting and whimpering of their dogs. Lying there, he remembered something he'd heard about police dogs. That they are trained to bite and not let go. He hoped it was not true.

It occurred to him then how strange it all was. "I'm quite law abiding. You know, I wear glasses. I don't want to get hit in the face with a truncheon. I'm not really into confrontational situations at all." And yet here he was, spectacles pressed into the freshly turned soil, hunted by dogs.

high conflict

This is a book about the mysterious force that incites people to lose their minds in ideological disputes, political feuds, or gang vendettas. The force that causes us to lie awake at night, obsessed by a conflict with a coworker or a sibling or a politician we've never met.

High conflict is different from the useful friction of healthy conflict. That's what I like to call *good conflict*, in homage to what the civil rights leader John Lewis called "good trouble." Good conflict is a force that pushes us to be better people. Good conflict is not the same thing as forgiveness. It has nothing to do with surrender. It can be stressful and heated, but our dignity remains intact. Good conflict can lead to radical change, tectonic shifts in how societies operate. But it does not collapse into caricature. We remain open to the reality that none of us has all the answers to everything all the time, and that we are all connected. We need healthy conflict in order to defend ourselves, to understand each other and to improve. These days, we need much more of it, not less.

High conflict, by contrast, is what happens when conflict clarifies into a good-versus-evil kind of feud, the kind with an *us* and a *them*.

In high conflict, the normal rules of engagement no longer apply. In this state, each encounter with the other side, whether literal or virtual, becomes more charged. The brain behaves differently. We feel increasingly certain of our own superiority and, at the same time, more and more mystified by the other side. When we encounter *them*, in person or on a cable news channel, we might feel a tightening in our chest, a dread mixed with rage, as we listen to whatever insane, misguided, dangerous thing the other side says. The conflict feels like an existential threat, even if it isn't.

Both sides often feel this same emotion, interestingly, although they don't discuss it with each other. Whatever we do to try to end the conflict—calling someone out on social media or complaining to HR about an obnoxious coworker—only makes things worse. That's because, as we'll see, any intuitive thing you do in high conflict usually backfires. You have to do counterintuitive things, and do them with great care.

Some people are more susceptible to high conflict than others. They are what therapists call "high conflict personalities." These people are quick to blame, certain they are right, always on guard. Most of us know someone like this. Someone for whom the fault lines are clear and always lead away from themselves. Most of us are not like this. Most of us try to avoid high conflict whenever possible. This avoidance brings its own problems, as we'll see.

Eventually, high conflict affects all of us, one way or another. Either we get drawn into high conflict ourselves, or we watch people or communities we care about get trapped by it, sometimes for generations.

Again and again, in research spanning different continents, people in high conflict explain their frustrations as a justifiable response to the other side's initial aggression. Regardless of the facts, *both sides* are convinced they are reacting defensively—somehow. They find themselves returning to the feud over and over, itemizing the indignities, tending to it like a fire.

How does this happen? In theory, most people appreciate the danger of demonizing their siblings or neighbors. Very few of us actually want to live in perpetual tension with other people. So why do we continue to do it? Why can't we get back to good conflict, even when we want to?

That is the first mystery of this book, which begins in a paradise on the coast of Northern California. Here, we meet Gary Friedman, a world-renowned conflict expert who decides to enter local politics, in hopes of changing it for the better.

We start small, focusing on a conflict that escalated quietly in an unexpected place, to understand the layers of this phenomenon. Us-versus-them conflict is rarely about what it seems to be about. It has an understory, which is the most interesting part. The corn plants are never just corn plants.

Then we'll investigate how conflicts explode. Why do some conflicts ignite, becoming violent and lasting for generations while others just simmer or fade away altogether? We'll meet Curtis Toler, a former gang leader who spent years transfixed by a vendetta in Chicago, to learn about the four accelerants that inflame conflict, all over the world.

The goal is to understand high conflict better, so we can see it coming—and help ourselves or other people shift out of it, if we want to. Which leads to the most interesting mystery of all.

People *do* escape high conflict. Individuals—even entire communities—find ways to short-circuit the feedback loops of conflict. They don't suddenly agree, and this is important: they don't surrender their beliefs. Nor do they defect, switching from one position to the opposite extreme.

Instead, they do something much more interesting: they become capable of comprehending that with which they *still* disagree. Like someone who learns a second language, they start to hear the other side without compromising their own beliefs. And that changes everything. Curiosity returns. Humanity revives. IQs go back up. Conflict becomes necessary and good, instead of just draining.

How does this happen—this shift from high conflict to healthy conflict? What are the patterns? What needs to happen first, second, and third? And can the process be nudged along? The short answer is Yes. I've now seen this shift happen—and felt it occur in myself—again and again. But it won't happen on its own; it requires us to take a series of steps, none of which feel natural at first.

Can entire towns or even countries follow these unintuitive steps to prevent or disrupt high conflict, at scale? To find out, we'll go to Bogotá, Colombia, to meet Sandra Milena Vera Bustos, a guerrilla fighter who chose to take a formal, legal, and optional path out of civil war—and who understands what needs to happen to help many thousands of other people make that journey.

Finally, we'll see what it looks like to inoculate a place against high conflict from the beginning. We'll return to the United States, to an unusual synagogue just outside of Central Park in New York City. This congregation learns to handle conflict differently, investigating it with curiosity and conviction, even when it's deeply uncomfortable. We will follow along as a group of liberal Jews travel from this synagogue to rural Michigan and spend three days in the homes of conservative Trump supporters who work in their local prisons. It is a bewildering and provocative scene: two groups going against most of their instincts to try to make political conflict healthy again, instead of high.

This phenomenon of high conflict is fascinating and misunderstood. If we don't learn to recognize, navigate, and even prevent it, we will all be in its thrall, sooner or later. As we'll see, we can get so mesmerized by high conflict that we don't realize we have somehow started fighting on the wrong side—against our own cause. We can end up sacrificing what we most treasure.

the invisible hand

I grew up around a fair amount of conflict. It wasn't extreme. I got plenty of food, love, and second chances. But my mom struggled with bouts of depression and anxiety, and she reverted to anger and blame when she felt threatened, which was often.

So I spent a lot of time sitting on the stairs of our New Jersey home, drawing shapes with my index finger into the moss-green 1980s carpet, listening to my parents fight. I'd listen for content but mostly for tone. My father was plenty culpable, too, of course, but all I could hear from upstairs was my mother's voice. As it got higher and louder, my stomach would fill with dread.

My brother closed his bedroom door and played with his Star Wars action figures when this happened. A wise move. But back then, I wanted to listen. For some reason, it felt important to monitor what was happening, to surveil the conflict. Maybe I thought it would help me predict what was going to happen next, or even prevent it.

As I got older, I found a way to witness conflict for a living. As a journalist for *Time* magazine, I covered crime, disasters, terrorism, all manner of human misery. Then I covered education, which, despite all the pretty talk of children and learning, is its own high conflict in America. (Out of all the hate mail I've received, the only person who's ever called me the c-word was a teacher responding to a story I'd written on education reform.)

There was a strange kind of comfort in this role. Subconsciously, I was still that kid, believing that I could somehow protect myself and everyone else by chronicling conflict, never letting it out of my sight.

After the 2016 U.S. presidential election, I had to admit my master plan had failed. I couldn't predict conflict. I couldn't even understand it. Not even in my own country. How could so many people be perceiving the world so differently, with such utter conviction? Half of Democrats and Republicans saw members of the opposing party as not just ill-informed but actually frightening. Even as Americans continued to agree on many policy matters, we began to dehumanize one another based on our political affinities. By some estimates, 38 million Americans stopped talking to a family member or friend because of that election.

It felt like curiosity was dead. What was the point of telling stories in such a time? Of painstakingly reporting and fact-checking every detail, only to be speaking to the same shrinking choir of partisans? Two out of three Americans said they didn't really trust the news media to report the news fully, accurately, and fairly. Many actively avoided the news, because it was so depressing. Others were addicted to it, because it was so enraging.

For a while, I blamed America's unique pathologies. Maybe our history of racism, combined with extreme economic inequality, had created a perfect storm of political polarization. That was part of the answer. But looking around, it was plain to see that these problems weren't limited to America.

In other countries, people were storming out of family dinners because of differences over refugees or Brexit or fuel prices. In Argentina, nine out of ten people said their country was very or fairly divided. In Norway and Denmark, there was a major schism over how to handle wild wolves. In New Zealand, it was cats (yes, cats!). Half of Europeans said their society was less tolerant than it was a decade ago. "We are experiencing permanent indignation, a kind of social rage," Frank-Walter Steinmeier, the president of Germany, said. "Germany does not talk. Germany shouts and screams."

Surely the explanation had something to do with YouTube, Facebook, and Twitter, which fueled endless conflict loops by design. And media sensationalism, which converted outrage into profit. Attention economies rewarded our worst instincts, at a massive scale. On TV and online, we were greeted by a chorus of trolls, goading us on, hissing that we were right.

All of this mattered. But none of these explanations felt quite adequate. There were lots of people who weren't spending much time on social media but were still at each other's throats. Something else was happening, too. Something that had not been named.

So I tried to find what I'd missed. I spent time with people who have worked on raging conflicts of other kinds, in other places, from Rwanda to Colombia to Israel. I completed eighty hours of conflict mediation training, focused on interpersonal conflicts like divorce, and workplace and custody battles. I started to see how similarly people behave in very different conflicts.

Five years later, here is what I've learned. Lots of forces got us to this place. Technological change, demographic shifts, globalization, badly regulated markets, and rapid social change have caused waves of anxiety and suspicion. Humans are not wired to manage change at this pace. It feels disorienting at best, threatening at worst. So we hunt for a story to explain our unease, a way to claw back some control over the chaos. That desperate search for a storyline (and a scapegoat) makes it easy for opportunistic leaders, pundits, and platforms to exploit our most reliable social fissures, including prejudices of all kinds.

But there is another invisible force that, like gravity, exerts its pull on everything else. When conflict escalates past a certain point, the conflict itself takes charge. The original facts and forces that led to the dispute fade into the background. The us-versus-them dynamic takes over. Actual differences of opinion on health care policy or immigration stop mattering, and the conflict becomes its own reality. High conflict is the invisible hand of our time.

Postcard of the swimming pool at Oak Park, in Montgomery, Alabama. Alabama Department of Archives and History

closed

In the 1930s, the city of Montgomery, Alabama, built a public rec-
reational facility called Oak Park. It featured a large swimming pool
with a modern filtration system and a smaller wading pool for little children. There were six clay tennis courts and a merry-go-round.
They even built a zoo, complete with a bear, alligators, and monkeys.
It was a municipal wonderland.

But there was an *us* and a *them* in Montgomery and all over the
United States, a high conflict that dated back hundreds of years. Oak
Park was for White people only.

One fall day in 1957, a young Black man named Mark Gilmore
took a shortcut home from work through Oak Park. He got arrested
for violating the segregation policy. When he challenged the policy
in court, a federal judge ruled that the city's Whites-only policy was
unconstitutional. All the citizens had paid for the park to be built,
including Black taxpayers, and so it had to be open to all.

It was a huge victory for equality and justice, or so it seemed. But
what happened next? Instead of integrating, the city shuttered *all* of
its parks. If White people couldn't swim without Blacks, then no one
could swim at all. The Oak Park pools were drained and filled with
dirt; the bear, alligators, and monkeys given away or sold. The pools
have never been reopened. Everyone lost, Black and White.

This is a sure sign of high conflict. Every attempt to make things
better seems to make it worse. The losses accumulate.

Good conflict is vital. Life would be much worse without it. It's a
lot like fire. We need some heat to survive—to illuminate what we've
gotten wrong and protect ourselves from predators. We *need* turbu-
lent city council meetings, strained date-night dinners, protests and
strikes, clashes in boardrooms and guidance counselor offices. People
who try to live without any conflict, who never argue or mourn, tend
to implode sooner or later, as any psychologist will tell you. Living
without conflict is like living without love: cold and, eventually, un-

bearable. But if conflict shifts into high conflict, it can burn down the whole damn house. The distinction matters.

I'd spent my life monitoring conflict, but like most journalists, I was missing the understory, the most interesting part. It was a revelation. I started to see that political polarization is not its own special category of problem. People behave very similarly in all kinds of high conflict, from neighborhood feuds to divorce courts to labor strikes.

High conflicts are magnetic. Until we understand this, our differences will feel bigger and more inevitable than they are. Wicked feuds have a way of luring us in, driving us to act in ways that go against our own best interests. We've all felt this at some level. Once we're drawn into a conflict like this, our field of vision narrows. Matters become very clear, too clear. We *think* we are acting on our own volition—making judgments based on hard facts and deeply held values. But are we?

doubt

That dark night in England, the police dogs did not find Mark lying in the field. He made a run for it, just in time, sprinting over a barbed wire fence to a nearby field, where he hid in the undergrowth until dawn.

So he carried on, campaigning against genetically modified crops in all kinds of creative ways. In 2001, Mark walked into a Borders bookstore in Oxford and threw a supermarket sponge cake into the face of a Danish statistics professor with whom he disagreed. The professor was promoting his book, in which he detailed why he'd abandoned some of his more extreme views on the environment.

"That's for everything you say about the environment which is complete bullshit!" Mark yelled, in an unnaturally high voice.

It was all very awkward. Not at all like he'd imagined. The statistics professor quietly wiped the whipped cream from his face. The audience, waiting for the reading to begin, stared at Mark, confused.

He paced back and forth by the book-signing table, wondering why no security guard had arrived to haul him away. He had not planned to give a speech, so he improvised.

"That's for lying about climate change," he said. "That's what you deserve for being smug about everything to do with the environment."

He was finally escorted out a few moments later, which came as a relief. He felt embarrassed. Confrontation just wasn't his kind of thing. But he still believed he was fighting the good fight.

And it was working! As the years went by, his side registered a series of stunning victories. Governments in Europe, Asia, Africa, and Australia banned most genetically modified crops, persuaded by the arguments of environmentalists like him. It was one of the most impactful leftist opposition campaigns in his lifetime.

And yet. Every now and then, Mark would experience a tremor of doubt. One day, rioting broke out at protests he'd helped organize in London. Windows were smashed. Nine police officers were injured. Afterward, as his fellow activists celebrated at a pub, he felt sick to his stomach.

These moments crept up on him suddenly, like vertigo. He was in this fight in order to protect the environment and help the most vulnerable among us. He was standing up to big corporations, rightly demanding that they be held accountable. And yet, something else was happening, too.

In 2002, a severe drought and famine spread across Africa. Millions of people went hungry. But the government of Zambia turned away all imports of genetically modified corn, citing the alleged dangers of the food. Zambians had been eating this same kind of corn for years. So had Americans. But now, when it was needed most, the corn was deemed impure. In thrall to high conflict, Mark and his fellow activists had helped turn much of the world against genetically modified crops, based on very little scientific evidence, and now people were dying.

"Simply because my people are hungry, that is no justification to give them poison, to give them food that is intrinsically dangerous to their health," Zambian president Levy Mwanawasa said. The United Nations World Food Program began removing the food aid it had delivered. It was a tragedy layered on top of a catastrophe. Zambian leaders' distrust of foreign aid had long and complicated roots, but the crusading of activists like Mark was making a terrible situation worse.

For years, Mark managed to avoid reckoning with his doubts. Humans are very good at this. When new scientific studies came out showing that genetically modified food could be safe and even life-saving, there was always a reason to dismiss them. It wasn't hard.

Until it was.

the world as it is

Let's just acknowledge that high conflict can be useful. It feels good. It gives life meaning. But these days, high conflict has reached the upper limit of its usefulness. Again and again, the problems we face as a civilization seem to be made worse—not better—by high conflict.

The challenge of our time is to mobilize great masses of people to make change *without* dehumanizing one another. Not just because it's morally right but because it works. Lasting change, the kind that seeps into people's hearts, has only ever come about through a combination of pressure *and* good conflict. Both matter. That's why, over the course of history, nonviolent movements have been more than twice as likely to succeed as violent ones.

High conflict is extremely flammable. It can easily tip into violence, which leads the opposition to respond with more violence, in an ever-escalating spiral of harm. Very quickly, the most helpful people flee the scene, and the extremists take over.

Any modern movement that cultivates us-versus-them thinking tends to destroy itself from the inside, with or without violence. High conflict is intolerant of difference. A culture that sorts the world into good and evil is by definition small and confining. It prevents people from working together in large numbers to grapple with hard problems.

The coronavirus pandemic drove this lesson home like a jackhammer. On December 31, 2019, Chinese health officials reported a cluster of pneumonia cases in Wuhan City, Hubei Province, to the World Health Organization. Two weeks later, a Washington State resident returned to America from Wuhan, arriving at the airport with no symptoms at all. Four days after that, he sought medical attention for what turned out to be Covid-19. Meanwhile, Chinese authorities downplayed the severity of the threat to the public, and the World Health Organization repeatedly assured the world that the situation was under control.

In New York, the first official Covid-19 positive test was announced on March 1, 2020. But the virus had been spreading silently through the city for weeks, if not months, largely through travelers from Europe—not China. Before that first positive test, an estimated eleven thousand New Yorkers may have already contracted the virus.

By the end of April, the global economy had shuddered to halt, and over 26 million Americans had filed for unemployment benefits. At that point, more than three million people were confirmed to have been infected with the virus worldwide.

Overnight, the human species was threatened by a common enemy, a new, wickedly contagious virus. It was an unprecedented opportunity to link arms with one another, regardless of party affiliation, race, or citizenship.

And at first, most people did exactly that, all over the world, even in hyperpolarized nations. In late March, 90 percent of Americans said they believed that "we're all in it together," up from 63 percent in the fall of 2018. The U.S. Senate passed a massive federal stimulus bill by a vote of 96 to 0, a consensus that would have been unimaginable just a month earlier.

People are wired to sort the world into *us* and *them*, but we are also wired to expand our definition of *us*, under certain conditions. Big shocks like a pandemic can make *us* encompass the entire world, overnight.

But high conflict is magnetic. It is very hard to resist, especially for people who have, in the past, found great meaning, camaraderie, and power in perpetuating high conflict. In India, a majority Hindu country, news outlets began blaming Muslims for spreading the coronavirus after an early outbreak was traced back to an Islamic missionary gathering. "Coronajihad" started trending on Twitter.

In the United States, President Donald Trump blamed China, correctly criticizing Chinese authorities for suppressing information about the virus in the beginning of the outbreak. Then he blamed the World Health Organization, declaring that the U.S. would withdraw funding and cut ties to the organization because of its slowness to react to the pandemic. Here again, he had a point. The World Health Organization had made mistakes and should be held accountable.

But a pandemic is a global emergency. Managing it requires collaboration. Blame is self-defeating. Cutting funding to the world's only central fire department in the middle of a rip-roaring nine-alarm fire made a terrible situation a little worse. Suddenly essential workers at the World Health Organization and the White House were managing politics instead of public health.

Meanwhile, thousands of American schools reopened—or stayed shuttered—based on politics, not science. Children and families suffered unnecessarily. People died who did not have to die. The habits of high conflict are hard to break. But they self-destruct in the modern world, where there are few bright lines dividing *us* and *them*. Today, an outbreak can travel from a remote village to any major city in the world in less than a day and a half. Between 1980 and 2013, there were 12,012 recorded outbreaks of infectious diseases, affecting 44 million people and nearly every country in the world. That was all *before* the coronavirus pandemic. Over half of the world's population now lives in dense, urban cities, making it easy for viruses to spread. And the globalized economy has captured us like a spiderweb, intertwining our financial futures, even if we manage to protect our physical health.

"Rivalries and hatreds between groups are nothing new," the psychologist Gordon Allport wrote in the 1954 preface to his classic book *The Nature of Prejudice*. "What is new is the fact that technology has brought these groups too close together for comfort. . . . We have not yet learned how to adjust to our new mental and moral proximity."

We are all connected. We have to adapt. This is the central challenge of our time. To create institutions and societies designed for good conflict, not high conflict. Built to respond to problems without collapsing into dehumanization. We know this is possible because people have done it, in big and small ways, all over the planet, as we'll see.

On May 25, 2020, a forty-six-year-old Black man named George Floyd was killed by a White Minneapolis police officer, who knelt on Floyd's neck for almost nine minutes, even as Floyd said repeatedly that he could not breathe. The killing, much of which was captured on video, sparked protests across Minneapolis and around the world. The scale of the response created a historic opening for serious conversations about race and justice and major policy changes. In many places, the conflict was intense but healthy.

But not everywhere. In some places, people committed acts of violence against the police and against one another. Police officers and federal agents used tear gas and weapons on peaceful demonstrators in some cities. Certain politicians demonized protesters, and some activists vilified the police, generalizing wildly and unfairly. At least a dozen additional Americans died in the unrest, most from gunshot wounds. The violence led people to come up with justifications for more violence in response. Which is what usually happens in high conflict.

Then came the 2020 election and the storming of the Capitol by a mob of Trump supporters on January 6, 2021. Here again, there was a golden opportunity to shift into good conflict, in the pause created by this shock. But the country, battered by division and disease, manipulated by conflict entrepreneurs, remained its own worst enemy. Even when evidence accumulated that masks and ventilation reduced the threat, that schools could safely reopen, that vaccines were very safe for most people, the high conflict raged on. Many thousands of people were going to die from the pandemic, no matter what. But at least 163,000 Americans died who did not have to die—casualties not just of the virus, but of high conflict itself.

Mark Lynas. Robert Stone

an escape

One summer day in 2008, *The Guardian* asked Mark Lynas to write a quick piece attacking genetically modified crops, as he'd done many times before. In under an hour, he knocked off a story warning that genetically modified superweeds, bacteria, or viruses could "run rampant and breed," contaminating other fields. It was an argument he'd made before.

But after the piece appeared, something strange happened. He glanced at the comments underneath, and he felt unsettled. One person complained that Mark lacked "any kind of scientific knowledge and understanding." The criticism stung in a way it hadn't in the past.

So Mark decided to defend himself. He began searching around for empirical evidence backing up his argument. He clicked through page after page, scanning journal articles and books. He scrolled and scrolled, his heart rate rising. He could not find anything credible. The scientific evidence to date did not support his fears and long-standing claims. To the contrary, what he saw was a pretty clear consensus in the opposite direction.

Genetically modified crops could, in some cases, *benefit* the environment and alleviate suffering. They didn't require as much pesticide, because they were bred to be resistant to pests. In countries that used genetically modified crops, pesticide use had declined by about 30 percent. *Thirty percent.* That's a huge decrease.

Nothing was simple. Monsanto and other companies had made mistakes. They could have done a much better job introducing their genetically modified crops. But rather than wrecking the planet, these crops could help save it. With the best of intentions, Mark had worked to block immense progress from happening across Africa and Europe, for years.

He sat back in his seat, feeling suddenly warm. The realization was physical, not just intellectual, like leaning over an abyss. "A crack had opened up in my worldview, and I didn't know what I would find on the other side."

Many people had accused Mark of ignoring the science before. He'd debated scientists and rejected their arguments for years. There were no new facts in this scenario. So why did this time feel different?

A series of experiences had shifted Mark's loyalties and opened his mind, as we'll see. He could not easily close it again. Five years later, Mark stood up before thousands of farmers at a conference in England and gave a speech no one there would ever forget.

"Now my lords, ladies and gentlemen, I want to start with some apologies," he said. "For the record, here and upfront, I want to apologize for having spent several years ripping up GM [genetically modified] crops."

He'd written down every word of the speech in advance, knowing he'd be nervous. He looked up through his glasses every ten seconds or so to make eye contact with the audience.

"I am also sorry," he went on, "that I assisted in demonizing an important technological option which can and should be used to benefit the environment."

This was not a defection. Mark remained obsessed with fighting climate change and exploitive corporations. "It wasn't that I'd stopped believing in climate change," he told me. "It was that I started realizing that what we were doing wasn't working." He wrote three books on climate change *after* giving this speech. But from that day onward, he told a more sophisticated and precise story. He continued to publicly criticize businesses and politicians, but he did it with less contempt. As he shifted out of high conflict, he became more effective, not less. He was no longer wasting so much time, fighting battles against people who wanted many of the same things he did.

There are other people like Mark, some of whom we'll meet in this book. People who understand the lure of high conflict, the enormous toll it takes—and who appreciate what it takes to break free.

To thrive in the modern world, we need to understand how this happens. We need to step back from high conflict and marvel at its contours. Then we can recognize the way it warps our vision and imagine another way to live.

Wishing your opponent will finally see the light is a fool's errand. It will only lead to heartbreak. Counting up the other side's wrongs is a hobby that can last a lifetime. Obsessing over the next election is a delay tactic. Telling people to reject hate and choose love will not work. Because people swept up in high conflict do not think of themselves as full of hate, even if they are. They think of themselves as *right*.

Hate is an important emotion. But it's a symptom; *high conflict* is the cause. And high conflict is a system, not a feeling.

part I

into conflict

Gary Friedman. Laurie Phuong Ertley

chapter 1

the understory of conflict

When they asked to meet with Gary Friedman, they didn't say why. But Jay and Lorna were old friends, so Gary invited them to come by his law office in a leafy neighborhood in Northern California. They showed up at the appointed time and told him their news: they wanted to get divorced. And they wanted Gary to help them. Both of them, at once.

Gary was stunned. Not so much by their decision to get divorced; Gary knew they had been struggling. Jay had been having an affair. They had three young children and not enough steady income. All that Gary knew already. No, what surprised him the most was that they wanted him to be their lawyer. Their only lawyer.

"I could only represent one of you," he said gently, looking back and forth between them.

Hearing this, Lorna's face fell. Gary tried to explain: "To try to represent you both would result in a conflict of interest." They were dear friends but for some reason he found it hard to talk to them that way in this moment.

"Although I support your desire to keep the divorce amicable, to fully protect your interests you really are going to need separate lawyers." The more he talked, the less he liked himself.

"Even representing one of you would be hard to do, since I'm a friend to you both."

Lorna interrupted him. "We don't want you to take sides. We just want you to help us make decisions. Why can't you just help us—and not be on either side?"

The truth is, it had never occurred to Gary that he could be on both sides—or neither side. That such a thing was even possible. It was the late 1970s, and the legal profession just didn't work that way.

"The law is much more complicated than you think," Gary said, and he knew he was right. But something else bothered him, even as he spoke. He'd been railing against "the law" for years now. His profession was excessively adversarial, as he'd told everyone who would listen, including these same friends. He'd wanted to find a new way to practice law, one that left his clients better off. So why was he now reciting the platitudes of the profession as if he believed them?

Sitting there, Gary felt as dismayed as Jay and Lorna did. So he paused. He allowed himself to contemplate, for a moment, what they were asking. Maybe this was the chance he'd been looking for, to do something different.

"You know what?" he said. "You're right. You should be able to do this. I want to help. I don't know how to do it, but I'm happy to try."

It was crazy, on its face. He had no experience doing divorces, he told them, let alone in this radical new way. But even as he issued these caveats, he saw his friends' expressions change. They looked hopeful for the first time in a while. And he felt the same way.

For four months, the three of them worked together, in the same room. It was uncomfortable. Sometimes, it was brutal, when Jay and

Lorna started yelling at each other about who got the house or custody of the children. Jay wanted more time with the kids, but Lorna
didn't want Jay's girlfriend around them. And on and on.

It felt, at these moments, like they were caught in a vortex. Jay
and Lorna hated the fact that they were fighting, but they couldn't
stop. Gary worried he was failing them. He felt like he was walking a
high wire without a safety net. But it also felt liberating, in a strange
way. Normally, his clients were on the outside of the arena, while he
fought on their behalf, using the blunt weapons of the law. Now he
was *with* them, accompanying them through their problems. This felt
right, because they understood their own problems better than anyone. Which meant they should understand how to solve their problems better than anyone. In theory.

One day, in a pause in the bickering, Gary made a suggestion.
He asked them to close their eyes and imagine their lives ten years
in the future. He asked them to visualize the kind of relationship
they wanted to have with their kids—and with each other—at that
point. He reminded them of the time horizon. They would be in one
another's lives forever. That was just the way it was. If their daughter
got married, they'd both be there. If their son had a child, they'd need
to deal with each other. He traveled through time with them, and for
a moment, Jay and Lorna went quiet. They were reminded that they
were stuck with each other, even after the divorce. So then what?

Jay and Lorna eventually came to an agreement about the house,
the kids, and everything else. And for Gary, it was proof. Proof that
there was another way to do conflict, one that honored the relationships between people. He knew he had a lot to learn. But it was possible! Just because people were getting a divorce didn't mean they
had to hate each other. After they signed the papers, Jay and Lorna
hugged Gary—and each other.

After that, Gary never practiced law the same way again. Hearing
about Jay and Lorna's divorce, other couples came to see him, wanting to try this thing he called "mediation." Establishment lawyers ad-

vised their clients not to go to Gary. People came anyway. Sometimes they came *because* their lawyers had told them not to. He never had trouble getting clients.

People are drawn to Gary because he seems to do the impossible—tap into our best selves at our worst moments. Because as much as humans like to fight, we also want, very badly, to find peace.

High conflict makes us miserable. It is costly, in every sense. Money, blood, friendships. This is the first paradox of conflict: we are animated by conflict, and also haunted by it. We want it to end, and we want it to continue. That's where Gary comes in.

When Gary started doing this work in the mid-1970s, the local bar association investigated him. It could not possibly be ethical for the same person to advise a husband and a wife together in the same room, or so the thinking went. But nothing came of it, and eventually, the legal profession came around to Gary's approach. By the 1980s, the American Bar Association was hiring Gary to teach other lawyers his new way of navigating all kinds of conflicts.

the conflict trap

In the Miracle Mile district of Los Angeles, there exists a prehistoric death trap, gurgling away, right off Wilshire Boulevard, a block from an International House of Pancakes restaurant. The La Brea Tar Pits, as this place is named, can look benign, like a small, dark lake, one which bubbles up occasionally.

But scientists have found more than three million bones trapped in the depths of these pits, including well-preserved, nearly complete skeletons of massive mammals. They've found mammoths, sloths, and more than *two thousand* saber-toothed tigers. How did this happen? How did thousands of the most powerful predators on the planet all get drawn into the same small pit? And why couldn't they get out?

The La Brea Tar Pits is a living quagmire, a place where natural asphalt has been gurgling up from the ground since the last Ice Age.

What may have happened, researchers believe, is a fairly diabolical cycle: one day, tens of thousands of years ago, a large creature like an ancient bison lumbered into the Tar Pits. It quickly became stuck, hooves anchored in the sludge of asphalt, and began grunting in distress. It only took a few centimeters of the muck to immobilize a large mammal.

The bison's alarm attracted the attention of predators like, say, the now extinct dire wolf (*Canis dirus*, "fearsome dog"). Dire wolves are social animals, like coyotes and humans. So a few of these wolves probably came trotting upon the scene together and, naturally, pounced on the trapped bison. What luck! Then the wolves themselves got stuck.

And so the dire wolves howled in frustration, attracting more attention. More creatures arrived. Eventually, the wolves died of hunger or other causes, and their rotting carcasses drew scavengers—some of whom also got stuck. The population of the doomed grew geometrically. A single carcass could remain visible for up to five months, attracting more unwitting victims, before finally sinking out of sight, into the murky, underwater crypt. To date, scientists have pulled the bones of four thousand dire wolves out of the Tar Pits.

In his mediation work, Gary refers to conflict as a "trap." That's a good description. Because conflict, once it escalates past a certain point, operates just like the La Brea Tar Pits. It draws us in, appealing to all kinds of normal and understandable needs and desires. But once we enter, we find we can't get out. The more we flail about, braying for help, the worse the situation gets. More and more of us get pulled into the muck, without even realizing how much worse we are making our own lives.

That's the main difference between high conflict and good conflict. It's not usually a function of the subject of the conflict. Nor is it about the yelling. It's about the stagnation. In healthy conflict, there is movement. Questions get asked. Curiosity exists. There can be yelling, too. But healthy conflict leads somewhere. It feels more interesting to get to the other side than to stay in it. In high conflict, the conflict *is* the destination. There's nowhere else to go.

In normal life, humans make many predictable errors of judgment. In high conflict, we make many more. It is impossible to feel curious while also feeling outraged, for example. We lose access to that part of our brain, the part that generates wonder.

High conflict degrades a full life in exchange for moments of fleeting satisfaction, and the implications are physical, measurable, and punishing. When they fight, couples experience spikes in cortisol, a stress hormone, as do political partisans after their candidate loses an election. In high conflict, cortisol injections can become recurring, impairing the immune system, degrading memory and concentration, weakening muscle tissue and bones, and accelerating the onset of disease.

Then there are all the people who do not actively participate in the high conflict, the bystanders. They are so distressed by the fight that they tune out altogether. And this category includes most people. About two thirds of Americans are fed up with political polarization and wish people would spend more time listening to one another, according to the nonpartisan organization More in Common, which labeled this group the "exhausted majority."

And who can blame them? Most of us avoid all kinds of conflict, often for very good reason. We eventually stop hanging out with that friend who complains incessantly about his ex-wife. Or we stop reading the news. We keep our heads down. This detachment is understandable, but it leaves high conflict untreated. The extremists take over.

Overnight, high conflict can shape shift into violence, as history keeps showing us. One isolated act of bloodshed leads to collective pain on the other side, and then a need for revenge. In war, the us-versus-them mindset is an essential weapon. It is much easier to kill, enslave, or imprison people if you are convinced they are subhuman.

This was the primordial force Gary was up against, as he tried to create a new way to navigate conflict. He had successes, like the one with Lorna and Jay, but it was difficult, risky work. He had to build a new boat, a kind that could skim the surface of the Tar Pits.

Over the next four decades, Gary mediated some two thousand cases this way. He got better at it over time. He handled corporate disputes, sibling feuds, neighborhood rifts, and many other unpleasant asphalt rescues. It was not until very recently that Gary got stuck in the Tar Pits himself. He got separated from his rescue boat for a time, as we'll see, without realizing it. And it did not go well.

Mostly, though, Gary managed to move just above the surface of the muck. He came to realize that human beings have two intrinsic capacities when it comes to solving problems: one is our capacity for adversarialism. The pursuit of mutually exclusive, selfish interests by groups working against one another. This is how the legal system traditionally operates. Husband versus wife. Prosecution versus defense.

Our other capacity, also evident throughout human history, is our instinct for solidarity. Our ability to expand the definition of *us* and work across differences to navigate conflicts. In fact, our evolutionary success as a species has depended more on this second capacity than the first.

During the first phase of the coronavirus pandemic, billions of people responded to a highly unfamiliar, ever-changing threat with breathtaking cooperation and selflessness. Citizens around the world began staying home days *before* official stay-at-home orders were issued by their governments. This happened in poor countries and rich. After the U.K.'s National Health Service put out a call asking for 250,000 volunteers to run errands for at-risk people in quarantine, three times that many signed up.

There were exceptions. Specific leaders and small numbers of regular people who scapegoated others and divided the world cleanly into us and them. But for months, the vast majority of people felt a visceral pull in the opposite direction, toward collective unity. Now imagine what might have happened had more of our traditions been designed to encourage that instinct for collaboration, rather than adversarialism?

Institutions can be designed to incite either version of human nature, to provoke adversarialism *or* unity. But in modern times, we've erred on the side of adversarialism. We see everything, from politics to business to the law, as a contest between winners and losers.

And yet, Gary and other mediation pioneers proved that there is another way. They built a nonadversarial option for resolving disputes, and it usually works more efficiently and fairly than the traditional system.

Even the U.S. Supreme Court has recognized the limits of adversarialism. "For many claims, trials by adversarial contests must in time go the way of the ancient trial by battle and blood," Chief Justice Warren Earl Burger said in his State of the Judiciary speech in 1984. "Our system is too costly, too painful, too destructive, and too ineffective for a truly civilized people."

Couldn't the same be said about politics today? It is too costly, painful, destructive, and ineffective for a truly civilized people.

So it made a certain kind of sense when, in 2015, one of Gary's neighbors asked him to run for local office in his small town of Muir Beach. The Community Services District Board of Directors, as it is known, is in charge of area roads and water management. Its five members are unpaid volunteers. The board is not a particularly powerful body, and the elections are nonpartisan. But somehow, the town meetings had become adversarial and draining. People were calling each other names—just like on cable news, just like on Twitter. There had been a nasty fight recently with the U.S. Park Service over the aesthetics of a proposed new bus stop, and it had nearly torn the community apart. Couldn't Gary, the godfather of mediation, help change the tone, and find some peace?

the michael jordan of conflict

"This is a terrible idea," Cassidy said, for the second or maybe the third time. Gary and his thirty-five-year-old son were hiking, following an eight-mile loop near Gary's house that rambles through old-growth redwood trees before breaking through to a ridge with wide-open views of the Pacific.

Gary's wife, Trish, had loved the idea of his running for office. She hadn't seen it as a political issue; in her mind, public office would be a gift, a natural way for him to give back to their community. Gary was seventy-one years old, and he'd been looking to travel less anyway, so he could spend more time with his grandchildren. This might be perfect timing. His daughter had been thrilled, too. Who better to bring the community together than her dad, America's conflict guru?

Cassidy was the only holdout in the family. He was now working as a documentary filmmaker, but years ago he'd been a small-town reporter. And so he thought he understood things that his father didn't.

"Politics can be horrible," he said. "Neighbors turn on neighbors. I've seen it happen."

They reached the ridge and stared out at the ocean. From here, they could see all the way to the San Francisco Bay and the peak of Mount Tamalpais. They'd had some of their most important conversations on this trail. They'd talked, decades earlier, about moving as a family to France for a year. More recently, they'd talked about what it was like for Cassidy to become a father himself.

Cassidy had a habit of asking Gary hard questions, which Gary appreciated. On that day, he tried to explain himself to his son. "The one frustration of my mediation life is that I'm always in the middle," he said. "I just sit on the sidelines."

He knew politics could be toxic, but that was the point: he wanted to repair the process, to help people get underneath their conflict to what really mattered. He'd seen the political polarization dividing the country, and he recognized the pathology. He'd spent his whole life treating it. Politicians were acting like feuding families: resentful, suspicious, unable to see how they were destroying the things they once held dear. That the name-calling had infected Muir Beach showed how bad things had gotten.

He'd helped create an alternative to the legal traditions, hadn't he? There was a time when no one had thought that could be done either.

"What if the model of mediation that I've been working on for so long, what if that could be applied to politics?"

His son looked alarmed. It sounded to Cassidy like his dad thought he could singlehandedly fix politics. He might as well have said he was thinking of swan-diving off the cliff in front of them. Gary could wreck his reputation and his peace of mind—and for what? The location of a bus stop?

This felt familiar to Cassidy, in a bad way. He'd seen his father let his ambition get away from him before. Despite his usual humility, despite his deep knowledge of the human psyche, his dad could suffer from visions of grandeur. He was doing it again, Cassidy saw, even now, a man in his seventies letting his ego run wild. It bothered him, to see this contradiction in his father and not be able to make him see it, too.

Maybe, Cassidy thought, he could use a sports analogy, something his dad could understand. He could appeal to the ego, rather than fighting it. "You have this incredible record. It's like when Michael Jordan tried to play baseball, remember? And everyone was like, 'Don't do it!'" he said, the pitch of his voice rising as he spoke.

Gary smiled.

Cassidy tried again, this time more directly. "Look at your personality. You're not a politician. You're not schmoozy. You don't even like small talk!"

Gary nodded. It was true. He hated superficial conversations. He didn't do pleasantries. He didn't even attend the community board meetings normally. They were tedious, he thought. But that was why he was exactly the right person for the job. "Maybe I could change politics," he said with a shrug and another smile, his wavy white hair blowing in the sea breeze.

His son sighed. Then something shifted in Cassidy's expression. It was difficult to tell, but Gary thought he looked angry.

"It's way more likely," Cassidy said, "that politics will change you."

false flags

Gary's craft has evolved since Lorna and Jay's divorce. If you go to him for a divorce today, he'll invite you and your spouse to tell him the story of your marriage. He sits in the middle, in every sense of the word. He listens intently, even when the two of you start arguing. Gary is okay with arguing. He has a kind face, like the uncle you wish you had at all your family dinners, someone who knows when to laugh, and when to listen. He might introduce you to his dog, a small brown mutt named Artie who is also fine with arguing; Artie will curl up at Gary's feet and observe the proceedings in Zen-like silence.

When you've finished your story, Gary will check to see if he has understood it. His questions might sound a little odd to someone trying to end a marriage. "What is one thing you understand about your husband's view?" or "What would change in your life if you got what you wanted?"

Gary tends to ask his questions with his head cocked to the side, eyes bright, as if he's hearing something he's never heard before. This posture communicates curiosity, which is contagious. When he does this, most people find themselves thinking before they answer. For all their years of fighting, they may never have articulated what their lives would be like if they won. Question by question, Gary helps people chip underneath layers of familiar, everyday grievances to find what they care about most. To get beyond conflict, you have to go through it; there's no other way.

Say a wife makes a demand: "I want four thousand dollars a month for spousal support." The husband recoils. "That's absurd!" he yells. "Never going to happen." It appears they're fighting about the money, and they are. But the more interesting conflict lies underneath this fight over money.

"Why *four thousand* dollars?" Gary asks, probing the specificity of the number. He could guess but he tries not to. He asks this question in a quiet voice, to show that he really wants to know the answer. "What does that amount of money mean to you?"

The wife pauses. Then she reveals that she is worried she won't be able to earn enough money on her own. She has this notion, this idea that she could go back to school and become a physician's assistant. She thinks she'd be good at it. So she wants the money to help cover her normal expenses plus tuition. That's where the figure comes from. Her husband has never heard this before.

Humans tend to interpret new information so that it fits into their existing beliefs, a well-studied phenomenon known as confirmation bias. The worse a conflict gets, the harder it is to disrupt. When the husband had initially heard the wife's request for money, he fit it into his narrative for their marriage: she was selfish, and he would never get out from under her control. Gary's questions interrupted that cascade of assumptions, just for a split second, which is sometimes enough.

Then Gary asks the husband how he felt when he heard his wife say the number four thousand. "What would it be like for you," he asks, tilting his head toward the husband, "if you agreed to the four thousand dollars?" The husband sighs. He wants to quit his job, he says, which he hates. His job has kept him from being the kind of parent he wants to be. He wants to do better before their thirteen-year-old son grows up. He'd stayed in that suffocating position for years in order to provide for his family—and now his family is falling apart. The threat of having to pay four thousand dollars a month makes him feel trapped, like he's losing his past *and* his future.

Hearing this, the wife's reaction is complicated: she'd pushed him to quit that job for years, and now he's going to do it, after all this time? It's bittersweet. But once she understands what's underneath his objection to the money, she can see it for what it is. It's not just that he resents her getting his money. It's also about his own future, his own dreams.

Eventually, both people feel more understood. Even as they continue to disagree about many things. At that point, Gary has found, they are able to stop defending their positions and make more thoughtful decisions about their futures and their children. And like Lorna and Jay, *they* will make the decisions, not a judge or some lawyers. Which means they probably will not need to relitigate their conflict anytime soon.

Since his first seminars for the American Bar Association, Gary has trained thousands of lawyers, judges, and therapists around the world and taught negotiation courses at Stanford and Harvard. He's published three books. While other people have popularized many different styles of mediation, Gary's approach remains unusual.

He insists on keeping everyone in the same room and, together, digging up what lies underneath the conflict. Other mediators separate the feuding parties into different rooms, because it's easier. They stay on the surface, focused on fixing the immediate problem and not much more. That surface-level work seems safer, and it is—in the short term. Going deep into conflict is risky; it can ignite latent resentments, fueling ever more conflict.

To do this, Gary trains mediators to ask specific questions and to check to make sure they understand each answer, a process he calls "going down the Why trail." If a couple is fighting over who gets the crock pot, he investigates why that crock pot matters so much. These questions help people lower their guard. Importantly, Gary trains his clients to do this *for each other*, in the same room. So the people with the problem also own the problem, not him. In this way, he helps everyone in the room come to understand the situation and one another a little better. *Even* as they continue to disagree. This understanding moves people from stuck to free. There is still conflict, but it's no longer a trap.

"There is nothing more important to a person who is undergoing a life crisis than to be understood," Gary likes to say. Being understood is more important than money or property. It's more important even than winning.

Consider the crock pot. Gary might ask the wife, with genuine curiosity, what it means to her. It was from the couple's wedding registry, she explains eventually. It was a shinier version of the one her own parents had used, in her childhood home, where as a little girl she could smell a pot roast cooking all Sunday afternoon.

She and her husband had not created that home in real life. They didn't even like to cook, let's be honest. But she wants the crock pot anyway.

Her husband, hearing this, feels a sadness, one he shares with his wife. He admits that he only wanted the crock pot because, well, she seemed to want it so much. This is hard to confess but it comes as a relief. She is the one who wanted the whole divorce, he says, and since he can't stop the divorce, he supposes he's trying to make her at least feel some of the pain he's feeling.

They start to see the understory of the crock pot. And that means they can loosen their grip on it. And on other things. They get unstuck, little by little.

"A man always has two reasons for what he does—a good one, and the real one," as the banker John Pierpont Morgan once said. Every mediator has a story like this—about some mundane object over which a couple clashes inexplicably. One California couple feuded so relentlessly over a broken Hibachi grill that the judge finally offered to bring them the broken Hibachi grill from his own garage, if they would just stop fighting. In another case, a set of Legos practically brought one divorce proceeding to a standstill. The husband wanted the Legos. The wife wanted the Legos. They were paying their lawyers in one hour enough to buy all those Legos many times over. It didn't matter. Because the Legos were not just Legos: they were their child's most precious toys. Where the Legos went, so went the child's affection, or so it seemed to them, quite naturally.

Most of the time, people trapped in conflict don't know the understory. They get so focused on false flags like the crock pot or the Legos that they get stuck. High conflict is like a trance in this way. It's hard to look away. So Gary helps people step back and look at the Legos from a small distance, with his questions and his listening, so they understand what lies underneath.

Because once people feel understood, they can relax their defenses. People can let many things go while holding fast to the things that matter most, once they know what those things are. "We are more willing and able to understand others when we feel understood ourselves," Gary and his coauthor Jack Himmelstein wrote in their book *Challenging Conflict*.

The traditional, adversarial legal system is designed to play into our worst conflict instincts, to go to war over Legos. Like cable TV news and many social media platforms, the law is designed mostly to perpetuate itself. Stock market millions have been made by inciting high conflict systematically, creating a vast conflict-industrial complex.

By offering a way to go through conflict, without making it worse, Gary and other pioneering mediators have done more to subvert this conflict-industrial complex than most people alive today. Mediation typically costs a fraction of what a traditional divorce would cost. In money and also in spirit.

If he could make divorce less toxic, how much harder could politics be?

trouble in utopia

The tiny, fogged-in village of Muir Beach (pop. 250) is only twenty minutes north of the Golden Gate Bridge, yet it feels like a secret—a velvet slip

The playground at Muir Beach, located just outside of the community center, where Gary's board meetings were held. Amanda Ripley

of sand, nestled up against Muir Woods, surrounded entirely by national park land. Gary had lived here for the past forty years. He and Trish had raised four children in the community.

Muir Beach is home to an unusual mix of people. There are the aging bohemians and beatniks who came here in the 1960s and still talk about the time the Grateful Dead played on the beach. These folks migrated over from Haight-Ashbury, in San Francisco, way before there was such a thing as Silicon Valley forty-five miles south of Muir Beach. After Janis Joplin died of a heroin overdose in 1970, her ashes were scattered here, or so the rumor goes.

Then there are the libertarians who moved here because it feels impossibly far from everything. There are no street lights or grocery stores; just over a hundred homes, perched above acres of swaying beachgrasses, and a small nude beach. In the early 1970s, a nostalgic British expat wanted to build a Tudor-style English tavern. It took him eight years to overcome the local opposition. The result, the Pelican Inn, remains the only commercial enterprise in town. In 1984, *The New York Times* described Muir Beach as a place of "unstrained, unlittered, Pacific isolation," and that still feels right.

The most recent arrivals are the opposite of the beatniks in many ways. They leave early in the morning to go to work in the city, and they come home late. You don't see them as much, but they tend to own the most expensive houses, the ones with the scorchingly modern architecture, high up on the cliffs.

It's hard to get beatniks, libertarians, and tech capitalists to agree on priorities, which was one of the reasons that local politics had become fraught in Muir Beach. Some neighbors wanted to invest in new roads and bridges, and others wanted to be left alone. Some were consumed with worries about climate change and wildfires, while others resented how much they paid in taxes. This discord made for some long, tortured public meetings.

Trish and Gary had arrived in 1976, after flirting with the New Age subculture but never really committing to it. They bought one of the last available parcels of land—which is to say they got very lucky—and managed to build a modest home in an achingly beautiful place that only multimillionaires can afford today. And they know just how lucky they are. They have both come to love the place, in different ways.

For Gary, living in Muir Beach made his work on conflict possible. He'd spend hours in his office in nearby Mill Valley, submerged in his clients' rage and blame. At the end of the day, he had to pull himself out, somehow. So Gary would bike home. His commute took him exactly forty-two minutes, beginning on steep hills, then rolling through the wet, dense shade of redwoods before emerging into the light of the beach and a long view of sparkling ocean or rolling fog, depending on the day's weather.

When he got home, he was ready to tend to his garden, which always took his mind to a better place. Later, he might put some meat on the grill while Trish made a salad. Before bed, they'd slip into the Jacuzzi out back, listening to the waves, talking about their days. Trish was a psychotherapist, and he learned from her stories, and she from his. In the morning, he'd meditate in a small lean-to he'd built next to his garden, overlooking the Pacific, readying himself for the turmoil that awaited him at work.

It was not lost on Gary that he lived in a utopia. He actually felt a little guilty about it. He worried a lot about economic inequality in the country, and yet here he was living in a place that was out of reach for most Americans. Maybe if he ran for office, he could change that, too, opening up some space for affordable housing. It was all starting to make sense, this politics idea.

Gary didn't socialize much in the neighborhood; that was Trish's role. She was the one who brought muffins to sick neighbors, who knew all the children's names. For Trish, Muir Beach was less a refuge than a community. It was a place of deep connections and long friendships.

Actually, she was the one, Cassidy had said on their hike, who should run for office. That made a lot of sense, Gary thought. Trish would be a wonderful public servant. But she didn't want to run, and he did.

Not long afterward, Gary drove his forest-green Mini Cooper to the county elections office and filed the paperwork to become a candidate.

the new guard

"Muir Beach is magic," Gary said, speaking before his neighbors at the candidates' debate in September 2015. "That was the first thought that my wife, Trish, and I had when we first saw it. And that's why we moved here." Gary and the other candidates were seated in a row behind a long table. The windows behind them overlooked the town playground and beyond it, the vast ocean.

The community center was packed, with an overflow crowd standing in the back. Cassidy had stayed home. But Gary's daughter, Sydney, was there, sitting next to Trish, who held Artie on a leash. It was exhilarating to see so many people assembled. Gary had attended some town meetings in recent weeks, in preparation for his campaign, and usually he saw just a handful of other people—often the same people, many of whom liked to hear themselves talk.

But this night was different. Gary was campaigning as an insurgent, running alongside Elizabeth, another political novice, against a group of incumbents who had been in charge for decades. (At Gary's request, I've changed the names of the neighbors involved in this story to protect their privacy. The names of Gary and his family are unchanged.) Jim, for example, had been on the board for the previous twenty-nine years. He *was* the board, in a way. Another neighbor named Hugh had spent four years on the board before becoming the district manager, a hired position charged with carrying out the board's decisions. For the past twelve years, Jim and Hugh had gotten used to working closely together in these roles, without much public interference. In private, Gary started referring to these incumbents and their backers as the "Old Guard." He and Elizabeth and their supporters were the "New Guard," in opposition to them.

That night, Gary seemed like the kind of politician we want but never get. His face lit up when he talked about the beach and his grandkids. He was warm and quick to laugh at himself. When people asked questions, he listened in ways that made them feel heard. He told them he wanted to reinvigorate democracy in the town.

"This is a chance for a real change," he said, "for everybody to be involved."

Gary's model of mediation was built on this idea that everyone needed to be in the room. In 1996, the San Francisco Symphony orchestra went on strike, walking out for sixty-seven days and canceling forty-three concerts. Gary worked with fellow lawyer Robert Mnookin and others to mediate the case, and they insisted on involving *all* 105 musicians—not just a handful of representatives. Normally, lawyers would deal with lawyers, shuttling back and forth, trading this for that. But they wanted everybody to understand the crock pot and everything it represented. Otherwise, the underlying conflicts would just resurface the next year.

The musicians had presented management with a list of sixty-five demands, including better pay and benefits. The musicians claimed that they were overworked and underappreciated. In response, management had insisted that the organization was running a deficit and could not afford such extravagances. Neither side believed the other.

In December of 1996, the musicians canceled a sold-out Mozart concert and took to the picket lines. Dressed in their elegant performance outfits, they played "Taps" on their instruments.

"It feels like we have to do this every three years. It's very discouraging," Mariko Smiley, a violinist, told the *San Francisco Examiner*.

"I'm sure there's a better way," said one of the dismayed ticketholders watching the surreal scene.

To push the musicians into negotiating, management withheld health insurance benefits. In protest, a bassoonist held up his sick toddler before TV news cameras. Concertgoers started demanding refunds and withholding donations. Everyone was losing, every day.

"A kind of desperation set in on both sides where each of us said to ourselves, 'We're not going to get anywhere with these people. They don't even hear what we are saying,' said Peter Pastreich, the executive director and chief negotiator on behalf of the symphony management. "And that turned into great anger."

By the time Gary and Mnookin, a Harvard law school professor, arrived on the scene, the walkout had ended, but the symphony was still trapped in conflict. The musicians had fractured into competing camps. Some felt they'd caved too soon. The string section felt particularly aggrieved. Violinists and cellists tended to play more than the others, and they were complaining of repetitive stress injuries. Another walkout seemed inevitable.

In this fog of hostility, Gary and his colleagues set up a series of workshops to train the musicians to extract themselves from the Tar Pits. First, they taught them a form of active listening Gary calls "completing the loop of understanding," or "looping." It's one of his most powerful tools as a mediator. Basically, it means to listen in ways people can see. *Show* them you're listening; don't *tell* them you are.

Most of us do not feel heard much of the time. That's because most people don't know how to listen. We jump to conclusions. We think we understand when we don't. We tee up our next point, before the other person has finished talking.

On average, doctors interrupt patients after only eleven seconds of listening to them explain what ails them. When doctors don't interrupt, patients stop talking on their own just six seconds later. That's all the time they need to explain themselves: just seventeen seconds. But almost none of them get it.

And there are real consequences to our bad listening, the kind you can measure. When people don't feel heard, they get slightly anxious and defensive. They say less, and whatever they do say tends to be oversimplified. The walls go up.

But when people do feel heard, magical things happen. They make more coherent and intriguing points. They acknowledge their own inconsistencies. Willingly. They become more flexible. Customers who feel heard by their financial advisors are more likely to trust them—and to pay for their services. Workers who feel heard perform better and like their bosses more. Patients, if they feel understood, leave the hospital more satisfied and more likely to follow their doctor's orders.

Among couples, people who feel more understood by their partners can make use of conflict without doing damage. Arguing actually seems to make them feel better, not worse, even as they continue to disagree. The conflict is healthy.

Gary knew there was no way to get out of a conflict trap without better listening skills. So he divided the musicians into pairs and had them practice looping. One person listened while the other explained why she'd joined the orchestra to begin with. When the talker said something that seemed important to her, the listener "played it back" to her to see if he'd understood. The listener didn't repeat what she'd said word for word, like a robot. He tried instead to distill what he thought she'd meant into the most elegant language he could muster. Then he asked if he'd gotten it right.

"So it sounds like you joined this symphony originally because you wanted to challenge yourself, to play alongside some of the greatest musicians in the world. Is that right?"

One of two things happened when the musicians did this. First, the listeners did not get it right as often as they'd expected. That's partly because we all make assumptions when we hear people talk, some of which are off base. And it's partly because it's hard for any human to convey exactly what she means the first time she's asked.

For example, the violinist might refine her point when it gets played back to her: "Actually, I was looking for inspiration, not just challenge. I wanted to feel that sense of wonder, I guess you'd call it, that I'd felt for music when I was younger." To grasp what someone *really* means, the musicians learned, requires both curiosity and double-checking.

Second, the listeners learned that people really, really appreciate being heard. When they'd looped the talker correctly, the talker almost always responded the same way: their eyes lit up, and they said, "Exactly!" For Gary, it was a lovely thing to see.

When people feel understood, they trust the other person to go a little deeper and keep trying to get it right. This iterative back-and-forth process helped the musicians identify what was really important to them *as a group*. The goal was to find what lay beneath their various contract demands. Why was the crock pot—or the vacation allowance—important to them?

"This was a fascinating exercise for me," one violinist said. "I've been playing alongside Phil for the last fifteen years, and we've talked about a number of things, but until now, we never talked about why we love doing what we do."

In this way, the musicians were able to identify their most important, shared concerns—and come up with a shorter list of priorities. They wanted better pay not just for the cash money but also because they worried about fairness and the future: they wanted to feel that their compensation was commensurate with other symphonies so they could attract new talent.

Management wanted those things, too, as it turned out. But there had been no opportunity to come to that realization, because neither side was really listening to each other. "I came to understand how important it was for me to listen," said Pastreich, the chief negotiator on the management side. "It became clear to me that one of the things that the musicians were angry with me about was they felt [that] I wasn't even listening to what they were saying. And I think it is true," he said. "Nor do I think they were listening to us."

Once we feel understood, we see options we couldn't see before.

We feel some ownership over the *search* for solutions. Then, even if we don't get our way, we are more accepting of the result because we helped build it.

It took many weeks, but the new contract provided a pay increase that made the San Francisco Symphony one of the best-paid symphonies in America. It also took some of the strain off the string section. And it didn't imperil the financial health of the organization. The musicians overwhelmingly ratified the new contract, which was set to last six years—twice the usual length. After a joint press conference announcing the agreement, the bassoonist kissed the board director on the cheek. It was like watching Jay and Lorna all over again.

winning

The night of the candidates' debate, Gary imagined that every town meeting could be just as crowded. The elected officials wouldn't own the problems or the solutions; the people would. Just like the musicians in San Francisco.

"Boy, has Muir Beach changed," Gary told the crowd. He knew, from decades of public speaking, how to connect with an audience. He smiled, making eye contact with his neighbors, taking his time. "We have many more pressures on us, on the land and the watershed, than we had any idea would come, back in those days."

He had their full attention, and it felt good. He may have been one of the oldest people running, but he really did feel like an up-and-comer. He was doing what he'd imagined he could do—bringing people together without putting anyone else down. Politics did not have to be ruthless. "I'm up for the challenge," he said, "to make the magic go on."

In the weeks before, Gary, Elizabeth, and Trish had gone door-to-door, talking to neighbors Gary had never met before, urging them to vote for change. A neighbor named Tanya had volunteered to be Gary's political adviser. Born into a family of politicians, she had spent her entire career as a labor organizer, writing articles and books about how to fight the powerful and help America's workers. So it came naturally to Tanya to draft talking points and create a strategic plan for Gary's campaign. She upped Gary's game, making it more like a traditional political campaign than the typical Muir Beach candidacy. "We knocked on all the doors three times," she told me. "That had never been done before."

With Tanya's advice, Gary adopted the campaign slogan, "Do you want to move forward or backwards?" Tanya talked a lot about winning. Soon Gary did, too.

At the candidates' forum, when someone asked him about his experience with managing water, the most important job of a community board in a remote, often drought-stricken place like Muir Beach, Gary responded with honesty. "I don't know that much about water, but I know I can learn," he said.

This was not what politicians were supposed to say; that's why he said it. Gary took pleasure in breaking the political mold, in proving that there was a way to do politics honestly—and inclusively.

After the debate, Gary's wife and daughter embraced him, their pride visible. People came up to shake his hand. The only criticism came from Tanya, who told him he should not have answered the water question so honestly. It was a mistake, she said, to reveal any weakness to his rivals.

In the following days, neighbors brought bottles of wine to the house, thanking him for what he was doing. In the *Marin Independent Journal*, Gary promised a new order, if elected: "I am committed to bringing a tone of respect, enthusiasm, and openness to meetings and to interactions with others."

On election day, November 3, 2015, the county posted the results online at 11 p.m. Gary received far more votes than any other candidate. Elizabeth won, too. Together, they'd defeated two members of the Old Guard—including Jim, who had been in office for nearly three decades. He had lost by just four votes. "We killed them," Tanya said later.

Gary felt euphoric. He had started his campaign because he'd believed it was possible to revive democracy, even now. That people will get involved if you listened to them, if you empowered them. It was the central contribution of his life's work, and now he was applying it to politics. And it was working, undeniably. Muir Beach reported the highest turnout for any race in Marin County that election cycle: a whopping 74 percent of residents had come out to vote. All was not lost, here or anywhere.

A neighbor and fellow board member named Joel told Gary he wanted to be board president—a position voted on by the rest of the board at their first meeting. But Gary gently convinced him not to do so; Gary wanted to be president himself. He thought it would be the best thing for the community. Joel agreed to step aside.

"We're going to come together," he told Trish. "We're gonna live up to the promise."

chapter 2

John Adams and Thomas Jefferson. National Portrait Gallery, Smithsonian Institution; Jefferson painting, created by Mather Brown, is a bequest of Charles Francis Adams. Adams painting created by John Trumbull.

the power of the binary

In 1775, American revolutionaries John Adams and Thomas Jefferson met as delegates to the Continental Congress, the body governing America's thirteen colonies. They could not have been more different, really. Adams was short and sarcastic. He talked a lot and lost his temper easily. Jefferson was tall and elegant. He remained silent in the public sessions, saving his voice for the smaller committees. He was amiable and diplomatic, reluctant to offend. And yet the two men became fast friends.

Adams came to see the younger Jefferson as a sort of protégé. The next year, he persuaded Jefferson to draft the Declaration of Independence, which both men signed. Their friendship deepened in the 1780s when they were posted to Europe on diplomatic missions.

Both men loathed the idea of political parties. Adams called them "the greatest political evil" imaginable. Jefferson thought party loyalty represented "the last degradation of a free and moral agent." They understood the danger of collapsing civilization into two sides.

Neither of them imagined that the country would be split apart by their own supporters.

But that was back when they were speaking to one another.

As time went on, Jefferson and Adams began to hold different views about the future of the new nation. Jefferson was suspicious of central government while Adams felt a strong government was necessary to get things done. Both opinions had merit. And they remained friends, able to disagree with warmth.

Then, in 1796, the Democratic-Republican party backed Jefferson for president, while the Federalists got behind Adams. It was the first contested presidential election in American history. There were two parties, dividing Americans, just as Jefferson and Adams had feared. The campaign got ugly, and the followers of both men used their writings against them. Adams won, in the end, but Jefferson had come uncomfortably close to beating him, falling just three electoral votes short of a victory. To Adams, this affront, from his protégé no less, felt like a humiliation, and it lingered in his heart and his head.

By its very nature, politics sorts us into binary categories: Democrats versus Republicans. Incumbents versus Upstarts. Old Guard versus New. Sorting almost guarantees conflict, as Jefferson and Adams had warned it would; there are, all of a sudden, two sides, and everyone must choose. It's not for nothing that the word *category* comes from the Greek word for "accusation."

After the election, Jefferson drafted a letter to Adams to smooth things over. He emphasized his continued friendship, loyalty, and respect. It was a good idea. He must have sensed that the campaign had left Adams feeling battered, and he wanted to repair their bond. But James Madison, the party leader who had convinced Jefferson to run, advised Jefferson against sending the letter. Adams might not respond well, he warned. And what if the letter got leaked somehow? Jefferson's supporters might feel betrayed by the conciliatory tone. So Jefferson never sent the letter, which is a pity.

The two men governed together, as expected in those days, with short, sarcastic Adams as president and the tall and elegant Jefferson as vice president. But they spoke less often. When they took different views on various issues, this distance made it easier for each man to assume the worst of the other.

In 1800, Jefferson ran for president again. The campaign was even nastier this time. Back then, individual candidates did not personally campaign; that was left to their followers. But it felt quite personal all the same, as both sides spread rumors and demeaned their opponents. Jefferson hired a journalist of dubious character to badmouth Adams in the press. It was fake news, nineteenth-century style.

Meanwhile, President Adams had assumed that he would be able to continue to hold office until he chose to leave, as George Washington had before him. There was no precedent for a new president being ousted in this way. But, caricatured by Jefferson's party as an out-of-touch monarchist, Adams lost his reelection bid.

It was a painful defeat for Adams. But there was a bigger picture to keep in mind: his old friend and protégé was taking his place, presiding over a new and unstable nation. For the sake of the country, there was much they should discuss, lessons they should share, alliances they could create. But that's not what happened.

On Jefferson's inauguration day, Adams left Washington in a stagecoach at four in the morning. He became the first American president not to welcome his successor.

History books focus on ideological differences between Adams and Jefferson. But ideology was just the crock pot. The understory of this conflict was betrayal, ostracism, and humiliation. About who belonged, and who did not.

With their own feud, Jefferson and Adams proved that they'd been right about the danger of parties. Any system that pits groups of people against each other can lead to high conflict. It doesn't have to, not if people talk about the conflict honestly, out in the open, and find ways to resist the power of binary thinking. What would have happened if Jefferson had mailed that letter to Adams, reminding them both that they were friends and fellow Americans before they were partisans?

As it was, Adams remained embittered, telling his son a year after the election that Jefferson was impulsive and unreliable. "His ambition and his cunning are the only steady qualities in him." He and Jefferson did not speak to one another for eleven years. Until, finally, someone else rescued them from the Tar Pits, sort of like Gary or another mediator might today. As we'll see, there was a way to transcend the false binaries of partisanship, even then.

categories and accusations

"Overcategorization is perhaps the commonest trick of the human mind."

—Gordon Allport, *The Nature of Prejudice*

Back in Muir Beach, during the run-up to the election, Gary stopped talking about "me" and "you" and started talking about "forward" and "backwards," *us* and *them*. He put himself in one category and other people in a separate category. A lesser category.

In regular life, we put people into categories all the time. That's how we navigate the world, as social animals who evolved in small groups. About 52 million years ago, scientists estimate, our ancestors stopped traveling through life alone. Groups, they discovered, offered a fantastic way to stay alive. This was especially true when primates started hunting during the day, which made them vulnerable to predators. In sunshine, groups mattered more than ever.

Categories save us time and energy, by allowing us to treat individuals the same way, so we don't have to look too closely or think too much. And categories also make us feel good about ourselves. The White woman who puts a Black Lives Matter sign on her front lawn feels like she is in the tribe of the woke. The French driver who puts a yellow vest on the dashboard of his car feels like he is in the tribe of the aggrieved workers, fighting the Establishment.

But categories blur out important details. They're efficient yet slippery. Once we have a *them* to contrast with *us*, we change. We know this from decades of research, all over the world. Under the influence of categories, we are less likely to cooperate with the other group and more likely to become hostile. We subtly adjust how we think and act in order to better fit our category.

This tendency is automatic, and it happens even when people are divided in an arbitrary way. On the set of the 1968 film *Planet of the Apes*, the actors playing chimps and the ones playing gorillas ate lunch in separate groups. They just felt more comfortable with people in their same costume category.

It takes shockingly little for groups to become tribes, for favoritism to emerge. It doesn't require competition, ritual, pep rallies, or financial incentives; it only requires a belief that you are in one group and others are in another.

In 1971, when social psychologist Henri Tajfel and his colleagues brought a group of forty-eight teenage boys together in a suburb of Bristol, England, they showed them six paintings by Paul Klee and six paintings by Wassily Kandinsky. The boys weren't told which paintings were by which artist, but they were asked which works they preferred. Then they were told that they'd been placed in groups based on their artistic preferences.

Now, these paintings were all abstract works, created around the same time period.

Senecio *by Paul Klee, 1922.* Kunstmuseum Basel, Sammlung Online

They were not particularly divisive or provocative, as artwork goes. And the boys already knew one another well from school, so they had many preexisting alliances among themselves. But once they were grouped by artistic preference, this new identity became salient. The boys immediately thought of themselves as fans of either Klee or Kandinsky.

In fact, their group placement was randomized. It was a trick, and kind of an unfair one. After all, the brain is wired to

Upward by *Wassily Kandinsky, 1929.*

embrace the group, once we're told that groups exist. It's not really optional.

When the boys were asked to allocate monetary rewards to each other anonymously, most gave more rewards to boys in their supposed artistic preference group. The Klee boys favored other Klee boys over the Kandinsky boys, and vice versa, even though they received no tangible benefit for doing so.

Our affinity for categories shows up in children from a very young age. Kids group people by race and gender before they know how to read. White American children show a subconscious bias against pictures of Black faces by the time they're in elementary school. This seems to be true even for White kids attending majority Black schools. This doesn't mean these White kids all grew up in overtly racist homes; nor does it mean they would necessarily act on their biases. It means that humans have survived by being aware of status differences, and we learn which categories matter in our society in all kinds of quiet, insidious ways.

This is why it is so dangerous to set up binary choices in our communities, on purpose, as Jefferson and Adams understood when they railed against the idea of political parties. There are much better ways to do politics, as we'll see, but we rarely question our binary traditions. National referendums, for example, seem like the ultimate form of democracy: ask the people what they want! But referendums collapse complicated issues into two categories: Yes or No. Good or Bad. Republicans or Federalists. Old Guard or New. Klee or Kandinsky. This plays right into our hardwired bias against the "other."

In 2016, binary referendums rocked the status quo on three continents. Voters were asked to approve or reject, among other things: in Britain, a scheme to split from the European Union; in Thailand, a new constitution that human rights groups said diminished democratic freedoms; and a 297-page peace deal in Colombia, following half a century of civil war.

In real life, most people have complex, ambivalent feelings about things like immigration, globalization, democracy, corruption, drug trafficking, and reparations for victims. Their knowledge is uneven, and their opinions are manifold. But the referendums forced them to choose a side, to see the world in two dimensions.

After all these referendums finished, splicing Britain from the European Union, adopting a newly restrictive constitution in Thailand, and rejecting a peace deal in Colombia, *The New York Times* asked political scientist Michael Marsh whether referendums were ever a good idea. "The simple answer is almost never," he said. "They really range from the pointless to the dangerous."

Labels get created to serve a purpose for someone at a given point in time. Then the categories take on lives of their own. Which is one reason referendums are so risky. One person's idea of a category is different from another's, and soon the category can be hijacked by others.

In Muir Beach, the Old Guard did not refer to themselves as the "Old Guard." The nickname was Gary's invention. Like other categories, this one required emphasizing one aspect of his opponents and setting aside—or actively ignoring—the rest. For example, the Old Guard didn't necessarily think of themselves as a united bloc. They were not controlled by a party machine, nor were they always in agreement. Two leaned Libertarian. One just didn't like to spend money. Another seemed to like being liked. All of them were trying to give back to their community through volunteer service—just like Gary. All of them loved Muir Beach. Some of the Old Guard might have been tempted to brand *Gary* as the Old Guard; he had lived in Muir Beach longer than anyone else on the board, after all.

So why did Gary use the label? What did the "New Guard" represent for him?

Gary seemed to be trying to prove something, and it was about more than a bus stop.

storytelling

I first met Gary when I was reporting on polarization in politics. More and more people were sorting into partisan camps and demonizing the other side. The categories of good and evil, red and blue, racist and not racist were getting really clear, too clear. People were starting to believe that they could know one another's moral core without actually knowing one another at all. Sometimes I found myself surrendering to the same impulse. It felt very hard to resist.

My own profession of journalism seemed to be making everything worse. No news story changed anyone's mind; it just left people feeling angry, disgusted, or hopeless. Immigration, police brutality, impeachment, the economy, climate change: everything was viewed through the filter of group biases.

I kept thinking about the 2015 viral internet phenomenon known as The Dress: looking at the same image, millions of people had seen two totally different color patterns, and no amount of argument could change their perception. Some people saw a dress that was blue and black; others saw white and gold. The filter—our eyes, in the case of the dress, and our identity, in the case of politics—mattered far more than the facts.

But instead of arguing over a dress, which was harmless, people were deeply divided over big things that actually mattered. Half the country saw Trump as a savior; the other saw him as a monster. Opinions didn't change much, no matter what happened.

So when I heard about Gary's work getting underneath conflict, I was curious. I wanted to know if there was another way to do journalism, one that made conflict interesting again.

The first time I interviewed Gary, I asked him if he had seen any political coverage lately that interested him. I suppose I was hoping he had some alternative news source, one I didn't know about. He said no. "Journalists are completely trapped in this," he said matter-of-factly. "There is no room for the story to take a different turn."

What was that "different turn" that the story could take? "You need to know what the conflict is really about," he said.

Here was someone who had seen thousands of conflicts up close, not some clueless idealist. And he was telling me that I was missing the real story—because I was in the Tar Pits, just like everyone else.

Then Gary invited me to join his next training. He'd never trained journalists before. But what I was trying to do was not radically different from what good mediators did. We both wanted to help people understand themselves, their problems, and the world a little better.

I arrived at the training in Mexico and immediately wondered if I'd made a mistake. The group consisted of lawyers and therapists and me, alongside Gary and his colleague Catherine Conner. The day began at 7:30 a.m. with a full hour of meditation, led by Norman Fischer, a Zen priest and friend of Gary's. I started sweating. A full hour of meditation! Every day, for a week?

But everybody else went along with it, and so I did, too.

For an hour, we sat in a circle, not moving. Before these sessions,

I'd only been awake and still for that long at the dentist. This was worse. Gary explained that meditation helps train the brain to be more reflective and open, even in the midst of conflict. So it's an important part of his toolkit. And I knew, in theory, that he might be right. I'd read the studies. Meditation can reduce blood pressure, ease the symptoms of anxiety and depression, and help people sleep better. For other people, excercising, gardening, praying, or listening to music can have a similar effect. Anything that helps the mind be a little more still and present.

In my case, being still and present was not a strength. So I used that first hour of stillness to brainstorm excuses I could make to get out of meditating for the rest of the week.

Then we moved on to a lesson on looping, and my confidence returned. I figured I would crush this one because I had spent much of my life listening to people tell me stories. I did it for a living. I always prepared carefully. I nodded and smiled. I furrowed my brow at all the right moments. I was charming, for God's sake!

But that is not listening, Gary said. Proving you've heard someone is very different from acting like it. People instantly sense the distinction, he said.

We got into pairs and tried it out. It did feel different from my normal listening. Looping forced me to really listen, first of all, and not think about my next question, or when I could get another cup of coffee. It meant letting the other person lead, and I had to follow, which was a little scary.

When I checked to see if I'd understood what the person said, I found I'd gotten it slightly wrong more often than I would have expected. Then I'd try again and again until I got it right.

Then, when we switched, I felt what it was like to be heard. And I had to admit that Gary was right. You can tell when someone is really listening to you. It's about more than the nodding and the smiling.

That week changed how I work in fundamental ways, more than anything I'd done in two decades as a reporter. Gary's toolkit included all kinds of ways to make conflict more interesting: from looping to asking deeper questions to investigating the understory.

From then on, I looped people whenever I interviewed them. I started looping my family, my friends, even strangers sitting next to me on an airplane. I didn't always do it well—or at all. But when I did loop, I felt a little more present, a bit more useful.

I sometimes interview people with whom I profoundly disagree. Then, looping turns out to be particularly critical. It helps me listen, even when I don't want to. It takes a lot of practice but it has helped me experience what it's like to understand *and* disagree at the same time. It turns out that is possible. You can do both. You can and you must, if you want to stay out of the Tar Pits.

I also put a Post-it note with some of Gary's questions on my office wall, and I started asking them whenever I interviewed anyone involved in any kind of conflict.

"What would it be like if you got what you wanted here?"

"What do you want your opponent to understand about you? What do you want to understand about them?"

I also started meditating—for a whole ten minutes a day. Which still seemed like a lot.

Gary and I kept in touch. He'd mentioned that he'd recently run for office in his little town, and it wasn't going the way he'd expected.

"no eyeball rolling"

On February 3, 2016, Gary presided over his inaugural meeting as president of the Muir Beach Community Services District Board of Directors.

He introduced a new set of rules, called the "Principles of Unity," which he had drafted with help from Tanya, the community organizer and his closest adviser. He posted the principles on the wall of the community center, where the board met.

"Be respectful of others."

"One person speaks at a time."

"No name calling."

"No eyeball rolling."

During the public comment period, each person would be limited to just three minutes of speaking, according to the principles. This way, the gadflies who had rambled on at past board meetings would not be able to hijack the conversation; there would be space for more voices to be heard. When Gary introduced this time limit, one resident objected, but the board briskly adopted the rules anyway, by a vote of four to one. The dissenting vote was from a member of the Old Guard. Gary didn't worry too much about it.

He and Elizabeth rearranged the chairs for the meeting so that everyone, including the board, sat in a large circle, at the same level. The idea was to make the meeting feel inclusive, to give the power back to the people, just as Gary did in his mediation trainings.

When people spoke, Gary looped them. He distilled what they said into the most elegant language he could muster and then checked to see if his summary was right. He also established a dozen different volunteer subcommittees, open to any and all, in hopes of bringing more residents into governing the town—just the way he'd brought the full ensemble of musicians into the room in his work with the San Francisco Symphony.

There was a subcommittee for community engagement, for audits, for trails, for roads, for everything that might matter to the residents. The public could come to subcommittee meetings, but only the subcommittee members would be allowed to talk—so that the meetings wouldn't get bogged down.

"I really welcome anybody in this community that wants to participate in any of these committees," Gary said. "The more, the merrier."

He was doing what he'd promised—infusing local politics with new energy and civility. His allies loved the new rules. That felt good. But some people made jokes. They called the new rules "Gary's psychobabble" and they rolled their eyes, violating multiple Principles of Unity at once.

There were other changes, too. Under Gary's leadership, there were no more bowls of snacks, no more time set aside for socializing. People could do that on their own time, Gary figured.

The first meeting he presided over lasted exactly two hours, as scheduled. Looking at the clock, he beamed with pride. In the past, the meetings had droned on well past 9 p.m., draining everyone's spirit—or at least Gary's spirit. Ending on time seemed like another victory, this one for basic human decency.

"It was all very exciting," he said. "I felt heroic, righteous." He was bringing politics back to the people, where it belonged. "It's amazing," Gary noticed, "how inflating it can be to have power and feel like you can get something done."

Gary's wife Trish left the meeting after the first hour, claiming Artie the dog was getting restless.

the righteous

Gary wasn't unfamiliar with the adversarial culture endemic to politics. You could say he was born into it, actually. Long before he'd moved to California, Gary had been raised in a family of litigators in Bridgeport, Connecticut. His father was a lawyer. So was his uncle.

It wasn't easy for Gary's father to start a career as a Jewish lawyer in the 1930s and 1940s. In many parts of Connecticut, White Christians followed gentleman's agreements not to sell homes to Blacks, Jews, or other minorities. Many country clubs and law firms were closed to him, explicitly or not.

Gary's father learned to never show weakness, even to himself. "He was an example," Gary said, "of someone who never failed, even when he was failing." At the dinner table, Gary said, every conversation was about who was to blame, and it was never his father. If his father lost a case, it was because a juror was drunk—or a judge was biased. "Any problem with the outside world was, 'We were right and they were wrong,'" Gary said. But from an early age, Gary wondered what was missing from his father's stories. He couldn't say so out loud, but he distrusted his father's righteousness.

Righteousness, it must be said, worked well in court much of the time. And sometimes it led to significant moral victories. There are times when fighting "them," with every tactic available, is the only good choice.

In 1940, a White Greenwich woman accused her Black chauffeur of raping her four times in one night, then kidnapping her, tying her up, and dumping her in a reservoir, before trying to stone her while she was in the water. The chauffeur admitted having sex with his employer, but insisted it had been consensual. The police claimed he'd confessed to rape. Somebody wasn't telling the truth.

The case provoked lurid headlines, spurring some White families to fire their Black employees out of fear that they might meet the same fate. That's when Gary's father and uncle took the chauffeur's case. They worked alongside a Black lawyer at the NAACP named Thurgood Marshall.

Together, the lawyers identified the inconsistencies in the woman's improbable story. They realized how little evidence the prosecutor had against their client. Gary's uncle already believed the prosecutor to be a bigot. "He hated everybody," he said later, "if you were a Polack, if you were a Jew, if you were a wop."

At the trial, the attorneys mercilessly attacked the woman's credibility. They used every trick they could think of to sow doubt in the government's case. Gary's uncle cross-examined the woman, needling her with questions. *Why had she invited the chauffeur into her bedroom when she was only wearing a bathrobe? Why hadn't she dislodged the phone receiver to alert the operator that she was in trouble?* Then he pulled out a handkerchief and had Gary's father gag him exactly as she'd said the chauffeur had done. The jury looked stunned when he showed how easily she could have called out for help when a police officer had stopped their car at one point that night.

The all-White jury deliberated for nearly thirteen hours. Finally, the verdict came in: the chauffeur was found innocent of all charges.

It was a powerful story, one Gary would hear his entire childhood. It encapsulated the essence of being a great lawyer, according to his father: "Heroic, take no prisoners, fight for the underdog." The world *was* divided cleanly into categories: Good and Evil, Right and Wrong. And you fought until your side, the good side, won. The ends always justified the means.

Gary went to law school and joined the family business. For five years, he worked as a trial lawyer at Friedman & Friedman, and he was good at it, too—aggressive, cutting, quick. "I was an attack dog." He loved the adrenaline rush when he made it seem as though a witness was lying on cross-examination, even if the witness was telling the truth. He felt powerful. But he also felt, from the beginning, a deep unease with the entire enterprise. It was not unlike the feeling he'd had at the dinner table as a kid, doubting his father's stories. "I had to divide the complex world into oversimplified camps labeled 'right' and 'wrong.'"

In one case in 1973, Gary represented a woman who had been rear-ended at a traffic light. She was suing the man's insurance company for damages, citing injuries she'd suffered in the crash. But the odds were against her, and Gary was up against a more experienced attorney, an insufferable prep school type who thought highly of himself and not at all about Gary.

Gary came up with a strategy: throughout the trial, and especially during the closing argument, Gary depicted his client as a woman deserving of compassion. She was quiet, a bit overweight, and struggling to pay her bills as a young writer. Who should the jury trust, her or a big insurance company?

The jury awarded $5,500 to Gary's client—nearly $32,000 today. He celebrated, hugging his client, feeling triumphant. Just then he turned and saw the look on the other attorney's face. The prep school man looked crestfallen, humiliated. He'd have to go back to his firm, Gary knew, and explain why he hadn't settled the case for far less weeks before, when he'd had the chance. "I remember being so elated, and then I felt so sad," Gary said. "I didn't like him, but I felt sympathetic to what that must feel like." Gary averted his eyes, unable to make eye contact with the lawyer. This happened after other verdicts in other cases. He felt, with each victory, like he'd lost something, something he couldn't quite put a name to.

At age thirty, the month he was to be named managing partner of his father's firm, he quit. His family was crushed. His father had planned his whole life around Gary taking over. Judges called Gary into their chambers to tell him he was making a terrible mistake. But Gary didn't change his mind.

He and Trish moved to California, where Gary invented a new way to practice law. Starting with Jay and Lorna, his friends who wanted a divorce, he brought both sides of the conflict together to listen and be understood. His father did not approve. Real men practiced law in a courtroom, fighting it out until there was a single victor. Not this. But Gary felt like he was living right for the first time in his life.

private melodies

As labels go, New and Old Guard are very gentle. Gary was not dehumanizing his opponents. But the labels created clarity, like Klee and Kandinsky. They simplified the election in a way that was motivating for Gary. He was the agent of change, along with his allies. The Old Guard? They were the agents of the status quo.

The problem is that the usefulness of labels begins to decay the moment the election results come in—that is, when the governing needs to begin. At that point, people need to cooperate to get things done, especially in democracies. But the primal feelings generated by the competition linger, long after the ballots are counted. In fact, to expect a politician to truly unite a community after winning a contested election is to utterly misunderstand human psychology.

Once Gary had won, the conflict mindset was almost certain to get worse, not better. The feeling of winning can make the victorious side feel more aggressive, not less. Winning at just about anything tends to boost testosterone.

When Gary talked about that election outcome, he always referred to it as an "unprecedented landslide." He hadn't just won; he had done something no one else had ever done. He was using outsized language. The way he saw it, the stakes were very high, much higher than they appeared to me, an outside observer.

By summer, the meetings were starting to become more tense. Gary spent much of his energy enforcing the Principles of Unity.

"I really hope to hold people to our three-minute limit tonight," he told the spectators as he opened up the June meeting.

When one person tried to ask a question about a different subject, Gary cut him off. "Not tonight," he said.

The man raised his voice. "Well, I'm not going to leave here until I get a chance to publicly comment."

"Well, you can stay all night," Gary said, "but we're not going to address it."

The man persisted. But Gary would not yield. "I'm going to stop you right there. You're out of order."

Nine minutes later, Gary officially opened up the public comment period and allowed the man to speak. "You've got three minutes," he reminded him. The process mattered.

Later that night, when Gary came home, he encountered more pushback—this time from his closest confidant, his own wife. He was cutting people off, hurting people's feelings, Trish told him. "You are running these meetings so tightly. It's all about the time limit," she said. "I was sure you would be able to bring the magic to these meetings. And to me, you are doing the opposite."

Gary defended himself. The Old Guard had been sending their minions to the meetings to obstruct change and criticize every initiative, he told her. Trish did not seem to appreciate that he was under attack, no matter how many times he tried to explain, using that specific word, "attack." He'd intended the subcommittees to represent democracy, inclusion, and fresh ideas. The Old Guard saw bureaucracy: wasteful and unnecessary. Everything he did, it seemed, was met with new aggression and derision.

Gary thought his affection for Muir Beach was apparent, and so was his devotion to fairness and inclusivity. He thought it was obvious why he was creating the subcommittees: to get more people involved, as he kept saying. And it was true! Why wouldn't people believe him?

It felt like his opponents were just out to get him, and that may have been true some of the time. It's also true that we all suffer from the illusion of communication. We overestimate how well we have conveyed our intentions and ideas.

We think people can read our minds because we know our own minds so well. Gary thought it was obvious why he enforced the three-minute rule and created the subcommittees. But was it?

the illusion of communication

If you were to tap out the rhythm to "Happy Birthday" on a table right now, how hard do you think it will be for other people to guess what song you're tapping? Maybe try it out. Pick a popular song, any song, and tap it out. See if anyone can guess what it is.

When college students were asked to tap out the rhythm of any of twenty-five well-known songs, they predicted that the people listening would correctly guess about half of them. After all, the person doing the tapping could "hear" the melody, the instruments, and even the lyrics in her head. It was so obvious!

Out of 120 tapped-out songs, the listeners guessed just under 3 percent correctly.

This is the illusion of communication. We consistently overestimate our ability to communicate. We lack empathy for what it is like
to be outside our own heads. The listener occupies a different reality,
hearing only a series of dull, barren taps, one after the other. It sounds
like nothing at all.

"The biggest problem in communication," as the saying goes, "is
the illusion that it has taken place." This illusion comes from two
profoundly human mistakes: First, we think we have conveyed our
intentions and desires clearly when we haven't. And second, we don't
really know what our intentions and desires are. In many conflicts, we
have only the flimsiest grasp of the understory, both our own understory and the one belonging to the other side.

When Gary was doing the tapping, it was extremely difficult to
get outside of his own head—to realize just how differently the world
appeared to everyone else. And the same was true for the Old Guard.
They did not hear what Gary heard. They were listening to their own
private melodies. In experiments, people generally overestimate how
obvious it is to others when they are amused, alarmed, nervous, or
even lying. We think we're an open book, and we're not.

When we behave badly, we naturally take into account all the
details that led us to do what we did, all the circumstantial evidence. I
still remember a red light I accidentally ran in Texas, many years ago.
I was on assignment in a city I didn't know, trying to find an address,
and I just didn't see the light. Someone honked, and I looked up just
in time to see the red light, as I blew past it. I felt shocked, embarrassed, and grateful that no one had gotten hurt. Never did I consider
that maybe I was just a reckless asshole.

When we consider other people's behavior, by contrast, we re-
flexively blame their inherent moral failings. I saw someone run a red
light the other day in my neighborhood in D.C., and I immediately
concluded that the driver was arrogant. The laws didn't apply to him,
apparently! Even as I write this, I remain convinced of my judgment,
despite the glaring hypocrisy it implies.

In reality, some people who run red lights *are* arrogant. Others are distracted. Or depressed. Or angry about other things. Many twenty-something reckless drivers become safer drivers in their forties. It's hard to carry that complexity around in our heads, so we default to the idiot-driver reflex. Particularly if we don't know or trust the other driver. We're easy prey out here in the sunshine, and we need to identify the enemy.

The truth is, people didn't trust Gary, and he didn't trust them. This distrust made the idiot-driver reflex harder to disrupt. His neighbors brought their own feelings and assumptions to the meetings, their own desires to belong. Gary's changes upended traditions that many of them had helped to build. They were the ones who had brought the bowls of snacks to the meeting. They had seen these small rituals as important, a way to show neighborliness and hospitality. What Gary saw as commonsense reforms felt, to some, like a rebuke.

Even when his changes were good, they were coming too fast for some people. He wasn't listening to everyone the way he had as a mediator. He couldn't let other people own the problem and the solution, the way he did at work; he felt, as the president of the board, that he had to co-own those things, because he'd be held responsible for the results. He wasn't as curious about the concerns that lay underneath the Old Guard's complaints. Because he wasn't in the middle anymore. He was part of the conflict. To some extent, he'd created it.

He was looping like crazy, at least he was trying to. But it seemed like the same people needed to be heard, over and over again. He couldn't let them hijack the meetings. There had to be space for other neighbors to talk. But where was everybody?

That was another problem: he was doing everything he could to get more people into the room, beyond the most vocal kvetchers, but they weren't showing up. The most reasonable people in the neighborhood didn't care enough about the board's decisions to spend their evenings on them. The people who had encouraged him to run, who had said they wanted change, were not at the meetings. Anyone who has served in any form of public office will recognize this problem. Extremists have outsized influence because they always show up, when everyone else stays home. They are the ones on Twitter, day and night, when everyone else is out living their lives.

This absence felt like a betrayal on one level; on a deeper level, it felt like a personal failure. Gary's identity as a man who healed conflict and helped people come together was under threat. His tools for negotiating differences—looping, going down the Why trail, giving everyone a voice, respecting the process—those tools weren't working, and the implications were devastating for him personally. Just like the crock pot was not just a crock pot for the couple in his office, Gary had more at stake than it appeared.

Without realizing what was happening, Gary had been drawn into the conflict trap. Everything he did to resolve the conflict—inviting more people, enforcing the rules of civility—seemed to make it worse. That is what happens in the Tar Pits.

"it felt like we were at war"

It was around this time that Gary made a tactical error. Muir Beach needed to raise the water rates. The rates hadn't gone up in seven years, even though water management costs had increased. The town had been covering the difference using money from various other sources, but California law required that water be paid for using water utility payments only. So to comply with the law, Gary supported doubling the water rates, virtually overnight.

The Old Guard erupted in outrage. They reminded everyone that Gary had said he knew *nothing* about water at the debate. How could they allow him to double the water rate? "The rates don't need to be increased by one hundred percent," Hugh said at a public meeting. "That's like off-the-charts high."

No one likes to see their utility bill double. For most families in Muir Beach, the increase would have amounted to about $300 in additional costs a year—a significant amount of money. But remember, this was happening in a relatively wealthy community: the median household income was $112,000, almost double the national average. For most residents, $300 was really not a lot of money. And just in case it was, the proposal would have granted a 50 percent discount in water rates to any household earning less than $90,000 a year.

But the blowback to the proposed increase was not just about money. It was about the idiot-driver reflex. It was easy for Gary's neighbors to assume the worst about the water rate increase. To attribute Gary's proposal to his inherent character flaws, rather than the situation. He must be arrogant, power hungry, or incompetent, they thought. Just like someone who runs a red light. What else could explain his tendency to cut people off in meetings and create unnecessary subcommittees? It all made sense, in a way.

In retrospect, Gary might have been better off proposing a gradual increase, over five years. He'd thought about that option, but then he was persuaded that the Old Guard had been wrong to ignore the shortfalls and it was time to do right by the community. He imagined there would be some grumbling before everyone agreed that the 100 percent increase was a necessity. Instead, the move galvanized his opponents. They started accusing Gary of wasteful spending. They mounted a comeback campaign for the next election, further dividing the town.

By October of 2017, the *Marin Independent Journal* was deploying Gary's labels in its headlines: "Muir Beach Election Pits Old Guard Against New." The categories were now explicit. Only this time, the "insurgents" were not Gary and Elizabeth; they were Jim and Hugh, two members of the Old Guard who had decided to run for election to stop Gary and Elizabeth. Gary's labels had been hijacked.

The tension was palpable. Another local newspaper ran another story about the "two camps," this time quoting a Muir Beach woman: "I do not feel the comfort of passing certain people on the street," she said.

By then, Gary had started to see his own town's politics mirrored in the national news. Just like the politicians on TV, his critics were playing dirty, he believed, using half-truths and fear to turn people against him. It was grandiose of him, he now admits, but at the time everything fit neatly into place. He had a new label for the Old Guard, a new narrative, and it was even more powerful than the old one. He started to identify the Old Guard with Trump.

"I couldn't get it out of my head," he said. "It felt like we were at war." The community disagreements had morphed into high conflict: an all-consuming, larger-than-life, urgent fight. "I no longer saw them," Gary told me later. "I no longer had a sense of proportion about me, and I lost myself."

The board's disagreements were different from Gary's mediation cases. Well, they weren't that different; they just felt different, to Gary. "Instead of hostility being directed between parties at each other, it was directed at me," he explained. That was excruciating. Here he was, a renowned expert in conflict mediation; he could have been lecturing around the world, writing more books, and taking on lucrative cases. Instead, he had chosen to devote a good part of his time to work—for free—to help his tiny town. Where was the gratitude?

This feeling of being unappreciated, even rejected, by his neighbors was powerful. It felt like a kind of toxin. Why, he wondered, did it bother him so much?

cyberball

In the mid-1990s, social psychologists started studying the effects of exclusion, rejection, and ostracism in the laboratory. They found they could easily, and dramatically, induce these feelings in people. For instance, at the University of Toledo, a psychologist named Kipling Williams brought 228 college students into his lab, one by one, ostensibly to do a brainstorming exercise. Before the exercise began, however, two other people in the waiting room (who worked in the lab, unbeknownst to the student) would "discover" a ball in a pile of things and begin tossing it around. At first, they'd throw the ball between all three people in the waiting room. Then, after one minute of jovial ball play, the undercover researchers would start excluding the subject of the experiment and just throw the ball between the two of them, without explanation. They'd continue playing this way for four minutes, until the official researcher returned to the room.

When the ball tossing changed, the excluded student would initially laugh and try to make eye contact with the ball throwers, attempting to reingratiate herself. When that didn't work, she would typically stop smiling, withdraw, and become quiet. She might suddenly search for something in her backpack. Though the ordeal lasted only four minutes, the atmosphere was intensely uncomfortable for everyone involved. The researchers found it difficult to continue throwing the ball. Other researchers even found it difficult to watch from behind a one-way mirror. The exclusion triggered an almost primal sense of distress in anyone who witnessed it.

In later experiments, the psychologists found they could create the same sense of exclusion digitally—through a simple online game they named Cyberball in which two or three other players toss a virtual ball to the participant before stopping. (In fact, the other players are digital avatars controlled by the programmer.) Despite the cartoonish nature of the graphics, the same pattern emerged as in the face-to-face experiment: it only took a couple of minutes for the excluded player to feel intense surges of sadness and anger.

More than five thousand people have now participated in these Cyberball studies, across at least sixty-two countries. Some of these people had their brains scanned while they played. The scans show heightened brain activity in the same areas triggered by physical pain. Williams began referring to the effects of rejection and ostracism as "social pain."

Remarkably, social pain does not seem to vary depending on a person's personality type. How can all of us feel such anguish even from a brief virtual encounter with digital avatars? How can something so impersonal feel extremely personal?

Humans have certain fundamental emotional needs, including the need for a sense of belonging, for self-esteem, for control, and for a meaningful existence. These needs are nearly as important to our survival as food and water. Social rejection threatens these needs.

For Gary, serving on the board jeopardized all four of these fundamental needs. He no longer felt a sense of belonging in his own neighborhood. His self-esteem, which was tightly bound to proving he could bring people together to work through conflict, was fracturing. His carefully honed process, including the subcommittees and time limits, was mocked by the so-called Old Guard. What did it mean for his life's work that his toolkit wasn't working in his own town? Was his whole career some kind of joke?

Rejection is especially debilitating when it blindsides us, as it did for Gary. In experiments, people who expect acceptance and encounter rejection instead tend to react with more hostility. That's because threats that are unexpected and unpredictable feel more dangerous to us. In Gary's case, he had been recruited to run for election as a savior and he was received, at least by some, as a nag, buffoon, or villain. The only rational way to make sense of it, without gutting his own sense of self, was to blame the Old Guard.

In study after study, ostracized people typically respond the same way. First, they try to win back the affection of others. They hasten to conform and comply (or try to). If that doesn't work, they become aggressive. And people who feel disrespected, as Gary did, respond with even more aggression than people who simply feel disliked.

Despite everything he knew, Gary succumbed to blame. "I became defensive," he admitted to me, much later. "I became aggressive. I became strategic."

Aggression usually guarantees more social rejection. But it does succeed in one way: it gives us a renewed sense of control over our environment, thus restoring one of our most fundamental needs, if only temporarily. Likewise, if we demonize people who have excluded us, we can help restore our damaged self-esteem: we are good and they are evil. Demonization can give us a sense of purpose, as well. We are fighting evil. What could be more meaningful?

When politicians muster the courage to defy their party leaders and call out lying and misbehavior, they often end up ostracized from their party and their people. They experience intense social pain, which either forces them to return to the fold, becoming overly compliant to the party line—or to lash out to protect themselves.

This is why shaming politicians typically backfires. It can feel good. It can restore that sense of agency, temporarily. But shaming is an extreme form of social rejection. It is different from applying pressure on someone who cares what you think or who needs your support for some reason. That can work. But shame has the opposite effect. It almost always makes the opponent stronger. Especially if someone from another group does the shaming. It cements the division, bringing the other side closer together in fear or anger, emboldening them.

It affirms the belief that they are on the side of good and their critics are on the side of evil. In June of 2018, the owner of an upscale, rural Virginia restaurant called the Red Hen asked Trump spokesperson Sarah Huckabee Sanders and her family to leave, citing her support for Trump's policies toward gay people. Then a waiter wrote about the incident on social media, and reporters started calling Sanders for comment. She responded from, as she saw it, the moral high ground: "Last night I was told by the owner of Red Hen to leave . . . and I politely left. Her actions say far more about her than about me," Sanders wrote to her 4.2 million followers on Twitter. "I always do my best to treat people, including those I disagree with, respectfully and will continue to do so."

President Trump weighed in, calling the restaurant "filthy" to his 71.4 million followers. Threats poured in, against the restaurant's owner, the town's mayor, the police, and the farmers who supplied the restaurant. Seventy-five people showed up to protest and yell at each other outside the restaurant, which closed for ten days. Sanders ended up getting Secret Service protection. Ku Klux Klan flyers appeared in the neighborhood surrounding the restaurant. The Tar Pits got a little more crowded each day.

"I feel like we have lost you"

By the summer of 2017, Gary's son, Cassidy, was starting to hear little passive-aggressive comments from people he knew in Muir Beach. "How's 'the president' doing?" people would say, referring to his dad by his title, with an eye roll. He didn't know what to say, so he'd smile and change the subject.

Gary's wife, Trish, noticed that certain people would no longer make eye contact with her. "It made me really sad. It was painful," she told me. "I became 'Gary's wife,' and people didn't like Gary." One day, she told Gary she didn't feel like she had friends in Muir Beach anymore. She came to dread the monthly board meetings.

The conflict stalked Gary, too. He'd wake up at two in the morning, his mind spinning with plotlines. He'd imagine ways in which he could force the Old Guard to finally and publicly admit that he was right and they were wrong. He'd replay the meetings in his head, over and over. He tried meditating more, in his lean-to by the sea; it didn't work. "If you think meditation is the solution to everything, think again," he told friends.

For the first time in his career, Gary could not take a forty-two-minute bicycle ride home to escape this conflict. The conflict inhabited his own neighborhood. "This is where I live. This is where my children and grandchildren come to visit." When he took Artie for a walk, he'd feel the hostility emanating from certain neighbors. Someone told him that Hugh, a member of the Old Guard, had said Gary was "Napoleonic" and didn't listen. It was incredible, Gary thought. The man who taught listening to thousands didn't know how to listen? He confronted Hugh about it, but Hugh denied ever saying such a thing.

Gary felt trapped. "The feeling of hatred coming at me is a nasty feeling. Especially when you're walking the dog, and you know people have said things about you that are not true, and you can't counter them, because if you counter them, you're giving life to them."

Hearing Gary talk this way was alternately reassuring and alarming. On the one hand, if even the godfather of conflict mediation can't help getting pulled into conflict traps, then we can all be forgiven for some of our pettiest moments. On the other hand, it felt ominous. If Gary could not resist the traps, what hope is there for the rest of us?

That summer, Gary found himself obsessing over small things, building them up into huge issues. At family gatherings, he couldn't stop talking about the details of neighborhood disputes. There was the fight over Airbnbs and other vacation rental schemes, which seemed to be popping up everywhere in Muir Beach, stoking controversy. Then there was the continuing tension with the U.S. Park Service, which lingered long after the bus stop squabble. Gary would go on and on about every debate coming up at the board meetings. He wasn't seeing these conflicts the way he did at work: as a system to be investigated by listening to people's deeper concerns and nudging them out of an adversarial dynamic into one of mutual problem-solving.

"He was taking things to heart," Cassidy said. "He was getting defensive. There was a 'good' team, and a 'bad' team, people who are for him and against him. You no longer felt like there was a real back-and-forth; he was sort of talking to himself."

One by one, Gary's family members tried to intervene. At lunch one day Cassidy confronted him. "There is this kind of poison seeping into the house, causing you to lose sleep, and you just can't see it," he told his father. "Honestly, it's bizarre to be the son of the godfather of mediation and see you have such insight into 99 percent of things—and then 1 percent of things, you have no awareness."

Gary's daughter, Sydney, had her first child around this time. But her dad was always thinking about the board, and his tone was often short. It hurt her to feel this distance. Like her brother, she felt as though she had to say something. "I feel like we have lost you," she told him.

Trish complained that she didn't know who Gary was anymore. This is something the loved ones of people trapped in conflict often say, that they don't recognize their spouse or sibling or friend. One day, Trish said she wanted to move out of Muir Beach. That comment left him reeling. He replayed it over and over in his head. How could it be that his attempt to preserve the magic of Muir Beach had killed it instead?

the letter

"In very few conflicts is one side totally right and the other side completely wrong."

—Gary Friedman, *Inside Out*

Gary had five years in his term, but his ally Elizabeth was up for reelection sooner, in November of 2017. By then, the town meetings had become taut with tension. When government officials mandated that the local well water be treated with higher levels of chlorine to protect residents from a bacterial pathogen, the Old Guard began claiming that Gary had allowed dangerous amounts of chlorine to enter the water supply. They assumed the worst. Gary was appalled by the accusation. It was reckless—and hateful.

This is one way we get caught in a conflict trap: if we think someone is hateful, we are not going to try to understand them. We may not even talk to them again at all. "Contempt is the sulphuric acid of love," said John Gottman, a psychologist who studies marriage. The presence of contempt is the strongest predictor of divorce that he has found. And contempt doesn't even have to be present for it to *feel* like it is present.

Gary and the members of the New Guard believed they were more moral and correct in how they were governing Muir Beach, but so did the members of the Old Guard. They thought of themselves as the ones who understood the water system, as the ones who had dedicated years of their lives to the town, but were being discarded and dismissed by cocky, clueless, political novices, one of whom had won by a measly four votes.

In the days leading up to the 2017 election, Gary realized that his side was losing. The Old Guard might win enough seats to retake control of the board. Tanya, the labor organizer and Gary's closest political adviser, suggested he do something dramatic, to speak truth to power. Together, they drafted a letter criticizing the Old Guard. Gary signed it and posted it on the town's website. "What I did is, I fought back," Gary said. Point by point, he eviscerated his opposition—well, that's what he thought, anyway.

"You failed all of Muir Beach in your most basic fiduciary duties," Gary wrote in the letter, accusing the town's previous leaders of not conducting financial audits in the past. "Reckless would be a kind word for the manner in which you, and the previous board leadership, handled our community's precious taxpayer supported resources."

It felt urgently necessary to defend himself and Elizabeth. And Tanya agreed. "You need to do a letter that's going to expose these lies. That's how you deal with right-wing thugs." Some of the people attacking the water rate increase were the very ones who had failed to conduct the audits before he took office. This hypocrisy was too extreme to ignore.

"The fact that you are now criticizing details of recent audits, documents which you completely ignored in the past, strikes me as a remarkable testament to your lack of humility and almost shocking absence of any shame, contrition or sense of responsibility."

Six times in the letter, Gary cited the failure to conduct audits "for eight (8) consecutive years." Six times he wrote out the number eight and then put the numeral in parentheses. It read like a legal brief he might have written at Friedman & Friedman, so many decades before. He wasn't Gary the mediator anymore; he was Gary the trial lawyer.

Surely, he thought, now that he'd laid out the facts, people would have to acknowledge that he was right. "In my opinion," he wrote, "you are lucky to have so far avoided administrative, civil or perhaps even criminal inquiries based on your intentional and repeated violations of the law."

As he got ready to post the letter, he felt troubled. Something was not quite right about it, something about the tone. He didn't feel entirely good about it.

He posted it anyway.

those guys are the *worst!*

It is easy to believe that other people are vulnerable to high conflict, but not us. Even hearing Gary's story, we can convince ourselves that this was about *Gary*—his ego, his blind spots. Poor man. Surely we are different. We would not lose our minds, not like that.

Some people are better than others at managing stress and conflict, it's true. They can control their emotions and collaborate even

An American and a Swedish astronaut participate in a spacewalk on December 12, 2006.
NASA

under extreme duress. These are the kinds of people NASA looks for when picking astronauts. The most recent class of eleven astronauts was chosen from a pool of 18,353 applicants. That's an acceptance rate of 0.06 percent. Which means it is seventy-five times easier to get into Harvard than to get into NASA's astronaut program.

With so many people to choose from, NASA goes to great lengths to select exceptionally resilient individuals. "You depend on each other for your life, really," said Jay Buckey Jr., a former astronaut who helps astronauts manage interpersonal stressors in space. "There is a high premium on being able to avoid really toxic conflicts."

Candidates undergo extensive psychological interviews, among other tests. Anyone who makes it through tends to be highly adaptable, socially agreeable, mentally stable, physically fit, and exceptionally good at working with other people under stress.

Then, after they get accepted, astronauts get training on conflict management and communicating under duress. Their training, which includes simulations for managing conflict with other crewmembers, can give them an actual chemical advantage. They are less likely than the rest of us to experience dramatic spikes in stress hormones, the kind that degrade our ability to think clearly when we are frightened or angry.

In fact, there may be no one better equipped to resist the magnetism of conflict than an astronaut. And yet, what happens on just about every mission? Even on every *simulated* mission?

Conflict. It's inevitable. "You can't pick a crew without conflict," said Kim Binsted, the principal investigator for NASA-funded long-duration space exploration simulations in Hawaii. "You can pick a low-drama crew. But not a no-drama crew."

Astronauts take longer to get ensnared in conflict—much longer than I would take, for sure—but it does eventually happen. And this matters now more than ever, because NASA hopes to send astronauts to Mars in the next decade. A Mars mission will take about 520 days, which is longer than anyone can resist significant conflict, even an astronaut.

In the longest simulation of a deep-space mission to date, conducted in Moscow starting in June of 2010, six men from four countries spent seventeen months living in a small concrete building, pretending to go to Mars. They lived without sunrises or sunsets, without real-time contact with friends or family. Each week, they answered a survey about interpersonal conflicts.

There were forty-nine conflicts that they bothered to report. Presumably, there were more piddly, irritating ones that didn't make the survey. There are, it's safe to say, unlimited sources of conflict in outer space, as on earth. Crewmembers get distressed by bad news from home and take it out on one another. They have trouble sleeping and get on each other's nerves.

But there is one particular kind of conflict that's virtually guaranteed to happen: conflict between the crew and Ground Control, down on earth. It's the power of the binary all over again. There are two groups: this one here in space, *my group*, and that one down there on earth, *the other*. So a lot of the astronauts' frustration gets redirected onto Ground Control.

In that Mars simulation, the crew reported five times as many conflicts with Ground Control as with each other. It was the New Guard and the Old Guard all over again. In space, they call it the "Ground-crew disconnect."

"The crew thinks Ground is asking too much, being unreasonable, being unresponsive, asking the impossible without knowing what it's really like to be there," Binsted said, rattling off all the ways this "Ground-crew disconnect" manifests itself. Meanwhile, "Ground thinks, 'Why are they being such prima donnas? I'm just asking them to do this one thing!'"

Of course, Ground Control is easy to hate. They aren't there. They can't empathize with what you're going through. And on a Mars mission (or simulation) it takes forty minutes to send them a text message and hear back. There's no way to have a phone or video call with earth from deep space, so all the conversations are by text. Which means the interactions are stilted and unsatisfying. Stripped of the nuance that comes from voice tones and body language, text communication is almost guaranteed to lead to misunderstandings.

Binsted is the Gary Friedman of space travel. She understands conflict unusually well. But when she spent four months sealed into a simulated space habitat herself, she, too, experienced conflict between her group and Ground Control. Even knowing everything she knew, she found herself in this very predictable conflict trap. Just like Gary. When she talked about it to me over lunch, a full thirteen years later, she still sounded peeved. "I'd say to this day that Ground was making a mistake."

These days, before participants enter new simulations, Binsted warns them that this ground-crew conflict will happen. They listen and nod and, often, imagine that it won't happen to them, now that they know. "It always happens," Binsted said. Then she added, laughing, "It's great to have an out group!"

Even on much shorter space missions, you can hear a note of tension in the stoic interactions archived at NASA. Consider this back-and-forth recorded in 1965, as astronaut Ed White relays his spacecraft's coordinates to Ground Control, a routine communication.

> White: "Zero one. Three four. Zero. Zero. Niner."
> Ground: "OK, Ed, let me correct you on that. It's zero one three. Four zero. Zero nine."
> White: "That's what I said, flight."
> Ground: "Ah, negative, I believe you read, 'Zero one. Three four . . .'"
> White: "OK . . . I read it right the first time."
> Ground: "OK, you read the right numbers. You didn't read it with the right, uh, beat."
> White: "The right *what*?"
> Ground: "You didn't read it with the right beat."

Astronaut White was not easily rattled. On that same mission, he became the first human to walk in outer space. But you can hear his disdain for Ground Control, bristling just under the surface.

Josh Ehrlich is a systems engineer for Lockheed Martin Space Systems Company and an aspiring astronaut. He spent almost eight months locked away with five strangers in a Mars simulation in 2017. When we met for coffee in Washington, D.C., I got the sense that he is a generally pleasant, positive person. But he, too, had experienced tension with Ground Control. What surprised him the most, he said, was how this tension actually strengthened his bond with his crewmates.

"There are times when you'd get an email from mission support, and you'd be like, 'What is this person thinking? They're nuts!' And then you'd say, 'Hey, look at this!' And in those moments, it was like a bonding experience."

We want to feel like we belong in our group, like we are understood. One way to instantly build that connection is at the expense of the other group, whether it's Ground Control or the Democrats or the company headquarters in San Francisco. Those guys are the *worst!*

"this is a personal attack"

"When conflict takes over, it creates its own reality."
—*Gary Friedman and Jack Himmelstein*, Challenging Conflict

Gary had barely called the meeting to order when Joel interrupted him. It was the last meeting before the election.

"I'm really disappointed, Gary, that there are three items that I asked you specifically to put on the agenda and that you very carefully decided you were not going to put on the agenda," Joel said, his voice tight. "I think these are important matters, subjects that the board needs to discuss."

Joel was a fellow board member, the same one Gary had persuaded not to run for board president, two years earlier. Back then,

Gary had liked Joel, enjoyed seeing him at neighborhood get-togeth-
ers. But now he found Joel difficult. He talked too much, lost his
temper too easily, and slowed things down, in Gary's opinion.

One of the three items, Joel said, was the letter Gary had posted
on the board's website. The letter was "totally out of order," Joel said,
"and I am extremely disappointed, that well in advance of this meeting, I made the request to you, and you absolutely refused to put
[these items] on the agenda."

Gary responded with forced collegiality. "I did, and thank you for
your comments, and we can't talk about them because they're not on
the agenda."

It sounded like a theater of the absurd. Gary had refused to put
the items on the agenda, and so the board couldn't talk about them—
because they weren't on the agenda.

"If we were going to talk about them, we'd have to give advance
notice to the community by putting them on the agenda," Gary continued, "so they're not going to be on this agenda for tonight, which
isn't to say that they're not important and legitimate to be discussed,
and we'll have the opportunity to put them on a future agenda."

Another board member complained about her own issue being
left off the agenda. Gary persisted: "It's not on the agenda."

A spectator yelled out, "Make an exception!"

"Yeah!" another man shouted. Gary was losing control of the
meeting, and it had only just begun. They hadn't even adopted the
infamous agenda yet.

"Wait a minute, hold it! Hold it!" Gary shouted over the audience. "Please. Please. No, no, no, no. Hey, wait a minute, wait a minute. I'm running this meeting, I'm doing the best I can, please hold
your comments."

Joel brought up the letter again. "I would really like to know, and
it should be discussed here, how a very inappropriate letter got on the
website."

This time, Gary shut him down immediately, without even referencing the agenda. "All right, I'm not interested in responding to personal attacks."

"That wasn't a personal attack," Joel replied.

"That was," Gary said. "To me."

Somewhere deep down, Gary knew he'd made a mistake by posting the letter on the town's website. It was exactly the kind of thing he would have criticized his father for doing, long ago. He'd felt queasy about it when he'd posted it, and now Joel was forcing him to reckon, publicly, with his failure to live up to his own ideals.

Then Joel did something shocking, something Gary had never expected. "I have completely lost confidence in your ability to serve as president of this board," he said. And he called for Gary's immediate removal. "And I am making a motion—"

Gary interrupted him, sounding desperate: "You can't make that motion. It's not on the agenda."

"It does not have to be on the agenda, Gary."

Gary felt cornered. Just two years ago, in this very same space, Gary had talked about bringing the magic back to Muir Beach. His family had beamed back at him from the audience. He and Joel had been friendly. He'd even mediated a conflict for Joel's son once, years before. Yet here he was, presiding over a parody of a town council meeting, on the verge of being thrown out of *volunteer* office in a tiny town no one had ever heard of. How had it come to this?

Gary's letter had triggered all the tripwires of conflict. Defending himself was fine; doing it by attacking others out of hurt and anger wasn't. Not because it was wrong, but because it doesn't work. Blame, like shame, makes our opponents dig in. It's very predictable, like a law of physics, as Gary should have known, better than almost anyone.

"By that time, I was pretty much convinced I was doing God's work, that I was standing up to Trump." In reality, Gary and his opponents were fighting over a $300 water rate increase. The future of American democracy was not on the line. No one's life was at risk. These were very fortunate people living in a literal paradise by the sea, arguing over small matters in the grand scheme of things. But that was irrelevant. The conflict defined everything.

In response to Joel's attempted coup, Gary pointed to the board's bylaws, which did not allow for such a maneuver. Like a drowning man, Gary was holding on to the procedures and protocols for dear life. The meeting lurched onward until finally, two hours later, Gary opened up the floor for public comments. A neighbor named William approached the microphone.

"That letter," William said, "was full of inaccuracies, falsehoods, libelous statements, and was just plain mean."

Gary could not take it any longer. He jumped up to defend himself, his chair grating against the floor of the community center.

Gary: "Okay, I just want to say, I stand by the letter!"
William: "No, let me finish. Let me finish."
Gary: "No, your three minutes are up!"
William: "No, it is not."
Gary: "Yes, it is! I've had you on the clock. William, William, no, no."

In fact, William had only used ninety seconds of his allowed time. But Gary felt he had no choice. He had to put a stop to these attacks. He had to protect himself.

William: "The fact is, that you were out of line—"
Gary: "William, this is a personal attack, and I am not going to accept this. Three minutes is up. No, stop! Stop! Your three minutes is up, and thank you. Look, personal attacks are not part of it. We have Principles of Unity."

It was impossible, from inside the conflict, for Gary to see the irony. The spectators began talking over him. Two minutes later, Gary made a motion to adjourn the meeting. It would be his last regular meeting as president.

"I was in awe of him"

Hugh, of the Old Guard, had been Gary's neighbor for twenty-three years when Gary ran for office. He'd actually turned to Gary to mediate a property dispute with a Muir Beach neighbor, years before. So he had thought, initially, that Gary would be the ideal person to serve on the board.

"There's nobody I would've trusted more than Gary with this job," Hugh told me. "I was in awe of him."

When Hugh heard that Gary was running for office, he'd been thrilled. In fact, he'd asked Jim, the board president at the time, if Gary could be president if he won.

"I thought it would help heal the tone," Hugh told me, dryly.

So what had happened, from Hugh's point of view? Talking about it, even two years after the letter incident, Hugh sounded sad and a little mystified.

Hugh had spent sixteen years serving Muir Beach, first as an elected board member and then as the district manager. He knew a lot about the roads and the water system, and he thought he was good at what he did.

Before Gary took office, Hugh had tried to be efficient. He admits he didn't always communicate everything to everyone. There were no committees. But he did try to create a sense of community. Each month, he brought coffee and snacks for everyone who showed up to the board meetings, and there were no time limits on talking.

Then Gary took over. Within a year, Gary had created twenty-three committees. Hugh still remembers the number.

A major roads project that Hugh had helped launched two years earlier ground to a halt. Gary very intentionally undid everything Hugh had done, at least in Hugh's view.

At first, Hugh tried to go along with the new system, despite his doubts. But when he tried to join the new personnel committee, he was told that Gary did not want him on it. "Gary felt that Muir

Beach was too dependent on me." He hadn't even known there was a new water committee until after it had been formed. "I felt a little put off," Hugh said. "I'd put in roads, sidewalks, pipes. I was certified in municipal drinking-water treatment. I felt like I had useful skills."

Gary had intended to be *more* inclusive, but he was excluding Hugh. It was as if Gary and Elizabeth had suddenly stopped tossing Hugh the ball, for no reason he could understand.

Until I spoke to Hugh, he had no idea that Gary had, for years, been referring to him as part of the "Old Guard." That's not how he thought of himself. At all. In Muir Beach, Hugh was an expert on infrastructure. Hugh got things done. That's how *he* understood his role in the community. Under Gary's regime, these things no longer mattered. He considered moving. He told his grown children that he just didn't like the feeling of Muir Beach anymore. Just like Gary's wife, he wasn't sure he belonged there anymore.

Finally Hugh decided, with Jim, to run against Elizabeth, Gary's ally, in the next election. Really, he was running against Gary, even though Gary's term was not yet up. He had his own group, urging him to run, to get things done again. "There were a lot of people in the community who wanted things back the way they were."

Then came the letter from Gary, accusing him and Jim of all manner of mismanagement. "I was floored," Hugh said. "I went into defensive mode." The campaign got ugly. Hugh couldn't wait for it to be over. What really stung is that he had actually supported Gary's initial campaign. Like Gary, he'd expected to be appreciated for what he'd done; instead, he'd been ostracized.

Social pain can be contagious. And the more painful it got for Hugh, the worse it got for Gary.

paralyzed

The run-up to the election, Gary said, felt like a "cesspool." The town voted against the water rate increase, killing the whole thing. He was miserable. But he felt paralyzed, unable to do anything but watch the nightmare play out. He couldn't wait for it to be over. Just like Hugh.

The conflict trap makes it incredibly hard for us to dig ourselves out once we get stuck. We know we want peace. We figure out what we're willing to compromise to get there. The other side does, too. We're so close—but then we find we can't budge. The invisible forces that pulled us into the Tar Pits, including binary choices, social pain, the illusion of communication, and the idiot-driver reflex, all become stronger.

We don't want to be the first to make a peace offering, even one we're willing to make, because we worry this will be seen as a sign of weakness and then we'll be asked to give up more. We don't trust that the other side really wants to make peace. Every objection to making peace speaks directly to our biases and stereotypes. We can't stop thinking of *our* side and the *other* side.

This happens even in much bigger, more intractable, and more consequential conflicts. For instance, two thirds of Palestinians and two thirds of Israelis support the basic elements of various peace plans that have been proposed in the past. And people want to live peacefully, without the gauntlet of checkpoints or the fear of bombings. Yet, the conflict continues.

Eran Halperin is an Israeli psychologist who researches conflict. Whenever he gives a lecture in Israel, he likes to ask how many audience members have heard of something called the Arab Peace Initiative. This was a peace plan unveiled in March 2002 by Saudi Crown Prince Abdullah. Under the proposal, Arab countries would offer Israel "normal relationships and security," in return for its full withdrawal from territories occupied since the 1967 war. The plan represented a remarkable concession compared to previous Arab positions, earning qualified praise from leaders around the world. The initiative was endorsed by all the member states of the Arab League that same year. And re-endorsed again in 2007. And again in 2017.

Halperin does not ask audiences if they support the Arab Peace

Initiative. He just asks if they've *heard* of it. The initiative has been covered routinely in the news media for nineteen years now.

"I've never encountered a situation in which more than 5 percent of people raise their hands," Halperin told me. "It is in the media, but people don't want to hear it. It contradicts everything they have in their minds about this conflict." The Arab Initiative is practical and substantive, and yet it doesn't even register. People have lost their peripheral vision to the conflict. They have blinders on, the psychological kind. "If you believe that the other side will never change, that they will always try to trick us, that we are the ultimate victims, there is no reason for you to even bother looking for this opportunity," Halperin said.

Americans, too, have become blinded by conflict. Democrats think Republicans are richer, older, crueler, and more unreasonable than they are in real life. Republicans, meanwhile, think Democrats are more godless, gay, and radical than they actually are. The most politically engaged people are the most mistaken about one another.

Americans on each side imagine that almost twice as many people on the other side hold extreme views than actually do. Both Democrats and Republicans also dramatically overestimate how much the other side dislikes them.

These mistakes sound trifling but they can be catastrophic. If you feel threatened, you cannot feel curious. If you think the other side is more extreme and hateful than it actually is, you will vote for anyone, no matter how unhinged or divisive, to keep the other side out of office. About half of American voters in 2016 said their votes were defensive, based more on who they were voting *against* versus who they were voting for.

Meanwhile, the institutions meant to help us become better informed seem to be having the opposite effect. The more time Americans spend consuming news from a range of sources, the more inaccurate their views of the other side. And the more education that Democrats, in particular, acquire, the more ignorant they seem to be about Republicans. Democrats with a postgraduate degree are *three times* as inaccurate in their perceptions of Republicans as Democrats who dropped out of high school.

On election day, Elizabeth, Gary's closest ally, was voted out of office. It was Gary's worst nightmare. She and Joel were replaced by Hugh and Jim, Gary's fiercest Old Guard rivals, the ones to whom he'd addressed his infamous letter. Gary's term didn't end until 2021, but he had no clear allies left on the board.

"This was a beatdown. That's what they did to Elizabeth," Tanya said, "It was self-interested, misogynistic, hateful." Gary's letter, Tanya thought, was not the problem. The problem was the lack of follow-up. "The letter was great. But you know they're going to hit you back after that." Gary should have kept going, Tanya told me. He should have created a petition calling for an end to the hostile language and the lies. He should have knocked on more doors.

The new board got rid of almost all of Gary's subcommittees. "I got Obama'd," Gary said. The Old Guard was rapidly undoing everything he'd accomplished, just as Trump was doing at the same time to Obama's legacy, three thousand miles away in Washington. "They emasculated or reversed just about everything."

"I felt a deep sense of humiliation, pain, and sadness," Gary said. He spoke about the election in dramatic terms: "We were thrashed. It couldn't have been worse."

Listening to Gary talk this way was disorienting. It was like he was under a spell. I wanted to shake him, to remind him of everything he had taught me and thousands of others. Couldn't he see that he was trapped in a conflict, that the conflict itself was in control?

factions

Now, we assume political parties are a necessary evil for a functioning democracy. But as we've seen, America's founding fathers would strenuously object. Alexander Hamilton called political parties the "most fatal disease" of popular governments. In his farewell address, George Washington warned that "they are likely in the course of time and things, to become potent engines, by which cunning, ambitious, and unprincipled men will be enabled to subvert the power of the people and to usurp for themselves the reins of government."

Hamilton, Washington, Jefferson, and Adams recognized the power of adversarial systems to bring out our worst tendencies. Washington's family had come to the New World to avoid the violence caused by feuding groups, which had torn England apart in a civil war in the seventeenth century. When people get sorted into oppositional categories, high conflict becomes more likely—by design.

In the legal world, Gary had created an entirely new design, with a new set of rules, for handling conflict. And it had worked! People flock to mediation all over the world, proof that adversarial systems are not the only—nor the best—way to manage conflict.

But when Gary tried to change politics, just like he'd changed the law, he used the old, adversarial design. He relied on advice from Tanya, who saw the world in binary terms. There was an *us* and a *them*. He was trying to play a new game under the old rules. It was as if he'd walked into a courtroom and tried to investigate the crock pot before a judge and jury, facing a prosecutor. That could never work.

But it feels like this kind of us-versus-them division is inevitable. What would another game look like, when it comes to politics?

Right now, some five to seven million people currently do politics in a way that explicitly rejects adversarialism. They have done for democracy what Gary and his colleagues did for the legal system: created a new, nonadversarial game, one designed to exploit our instincts for cooperation, rather than competition.

It's not a country or a city. It's a religion. One I knew nothing about before writing this book. But bear with me, because this is a real-life experiment that has been going on for over a century, all over the world.

The main idea of the Bahá'í faith is that we are all connected. There is no *us* or *them*. Bahá'í teachings revere Jesus Christ and the Prophet Muhammad, believing that all major religions come from one spiritual source. The community started in the mid-1800s in Iran, and it has spread just about everywhere. There are 150,000 adherents in the United States. The largest community is in India. But there are no ministers, no clerical leaders to run things. So how do they make decisions?

Each spring, everyone in each of the seventeen thousand Bahá'í locations gathers together to elect leaders. It's very close to a pure democracy, operating in 233 countries and territories.

Here's the twist: everything about these elections is designed to reduce the odds of high conflict. There are no parties in Bahá'í elections. No binary categories are allowed. People are not allowed to campaign for a position—or even discuss who might be the best person to serve. They can only discuss which qualities are most needed.

After a prayer, every Bahá'í writes down the names of nine people who they think have the experience and character to lead the community. Once the secret ballots are counted and the nine "winners" are announced, there is no celebrating.

When she was first elected to her local spiritual assembly in Atlanta, Georgia, Nwandi Lawson was working as a senior political correspondent for Georgia Public Broadcasting and anchoring a political show called *Lawmakers*. She had too much to manage already. In fact, she'd left the meeting early that evening to put her toddler daughter to bed.

Then came a knock at her door, later that night. It was a fellow Bahá'í. The woman handed her a gift bag containing some scented lotion and said, "You were elected."

"Oh," Lawson said. "Okay."

She was expected to serve for one year, whether she wanted to or not. This is part of the deal when you become a Bahá'í, Lawson knew. Still, she felt surprised by the choice.

"I had voted for other people. I hadn't thought of myself as some-one who would be elected," Lawson told me. "I was a relatively new Bahá'í, and I was quite satisfied to let other, more experienced people run the community."

That reaction is exactly what made Lawson right for the job. The Bahá'ís try to select people who do not *crave* attention and power. "Being elected is not a status symbol," said James Samimi Farr, a Bahá'í spokesperson. "It's a call to further humility."

This is the opposite of traditional elections, of course, which self-select for people who yearn for recognition. Who else is willing to shamelessly boast about themselves in stump speeches and cam-paign literature, for months on end? Who else has the drive to ask people for money, over and over again? This is especially true at the national level in the U.S. Who else but a narcissist would have the motivation to endure the expense, the exhaustion, and the scrutiny of a long, contentious election?

Once elected, Lawson began attending weekly meetings of her local assembly. They were charged with overseeing Bahá'í weddings, managing the educational programs, and handling the budget for her community of roughly eighty Bahá'ís.

Here, too, Bahá'ís try to constrain the ego and induce unity. In every meeting, they follow a protocol called "consultation," and it's designed to allow people to speak their mind without getting too attached to their own brilliance. If, for example, Lawson suggested that the group expand their educational programs by partnering with a local nonprofit, that idea would become the property of the group the moment she uttered it. It would not be Nwandi Lawson's Idea. As a result, she might feel less of a need to defend the idea, should other people offer up alternatives or criticisms. It wasn't about her anymore.

None of this was easy, Lawson told me. "Because we do have ego. And when someone knocks your idea down, it's hard." It helps to keep in mind the principles that are supposed to govern these con-sultations, including humility and patience. And Lawson does not always measure up. It's a constant work in progress. To remind herself, she keeps a list of these ideals on her refrigerator door. "Every time I get some milk, eggs, or butter, I need to look at it again."

If, after some deliberation, her Bahá'í group votes to pursue an idea, everyone commits to trying it wholeheartedly, even those who originally disagreed. If it fails, the group holds another consultation and reevaluates. "'I told you so' is never permitted," Lawson said laughing.

Over the years, she's gotten better at learning to relax her grip on her own ideas. Not just among her fellow Bahá'ís but all the time. She uses the consultation model at work and at home with her family. It tends to lead to better, faster meetings that yield more creative solutions.

Meanwhile, at the same time that Lawson was learning how to serve in elected office as a Bahá'í, she was watching traditional politics come undone at work. When she'd first started working at CNN in the early 1990s, she'd been energized by the statesmanship of some of the politicians she covered, even the ones she'd disagreed with. But by the early 2000s, there was much less to admire. "As the years went by, I was like, 'Uh, no, this is just people yelling at each other.'"

Her experience in the Bahá'í community has changed her understanding of what a political system could achieve, if it were designed differently. There is a better way to figure things out, she has concluded, and it is actually kind of liberating to experience.

"The aim is not to get kudos for yourself or show off as the one who yells the most. The aim is to solve the problem." In those early days, she was surprised at how much her elected assembly could get done in one meeting, despite the need for consensus. Once people were actively trying to set their egos aside and work together, things got a lot easier.

If social scientists designed a religion, it would look like this. The key insight from decades of research into group behavior is *not* that groups will always demonize one another. Humans are not inherently violent or evil. Warfare, in fact, is a fairly recent phenomenon in the arc of human history, first appearing roughly ten thousand years ago, when simple hunter-gatherer groups began to settle down and became more socially complex and compete for resources. For 180,000 years before that, humans did not participate in collective violence in groups, as far as archaeologists can tell.

No, the big lesson is that humans can be nudged to demonize—*or to cooperate.* The traditions and systems matter far more than we think. "If we took the same population of people and assigned them to one social world, we could make them really generous to one another," sociologist Nicholas Christakis wrote in *Blueprint: The Evolutionary Origins of a Good Society,* "and if we put them in another sort of world, we could make them really mean or indifferent to one another." This insight hints at how to fix social media and the Internet generally. Platforms like YouTube and Facebook were designed to drain our attention and divide us, but they could be redesigned to reward cooperation and decency. It is not that hard.

Since her first term, Lawson has gotten elected many times, serving pretty much continuously in some form or another for eighteen years. Each locality also elects delegates who then elect a nine-person national assembly, which in turn votes for an international body, based in Haifa, Israel. The same principles apply, restraining the ego at every level of governance.

All of these traditions are designed to help people understand each other and solve problems, without dehumanizing one another. In this way, Bahá'í elections are to politics what mediation is to the legal system: a different game altogether. One designed to exploit the human capacity for cooperation, rather than competition. It's not perfect, but it is an example of what humans can do, in a different kind of game altogether.

blurred lines

We are used to looking at every political story through the lens of us and them, winners and losers. The Bahá'í model feels like a long way off. But there are incremental ways to reduce the binary in politics. It's not a mystery, nor is it a religion.

First, give people more than two choices. It doesn't fix everything, but it reduces the power of the binary. Complexity doesn't collapse into *us* and *them* quite so easily. Ranked-choice voting is one way to do this. Voters choose not just their No. 1 choice but their No. 2 and No. 3 choices, in case their No. 1 does not get enough votes. That way, our loyalties get distributed. And more people feel heard, even if their first choice loses. It's not an all-or-nothing proposition.

Another way to reduce the binary is to shift to proportional representation, where seats in Congress get allocated in proportion to the votes won by each party. This way, smaller parties can still win seats, even if they don't win a plurality of votes. People still have a voice, even in the minority.

Globally, we can see the difference. People living in countries with proportional representation tend to have more trust in one another, researchers have found. They suffer from less polarization and see their political system as more fair. Which makes sense, since it *is* fairer. Even if their preferred party does not get the most votes, they still have a voice. They can still be heard, which we know by now is half the battle.

Most democracies use proportional representation and have more than two parties. The United States is the exception. Its reliance on winner-take-all systems and binary parties is, from a psychological perspective, designed to create high conflict. Which may help explain why the United States is more polarized than most countries in the world today.

Of course, voting schemes are only part of the solution. Many multiparty democracies, including France and Brazil, are very polarized. But generally speaking, less binary systems make conflict a little less magnetic. To take the smallest possible example, imagine if, in addition to the Old Guard and the New Guard, Gary had invented a third group label in Muir Beach. Let's just imagine he'd called this group the "Safe Guard," referring to the people who just didn't like to take risks. There were those people, after all. It would have made the labels more accurate and less caricatured. There would be *us, them,* and that other *them.*

Binary thinking washes out all the details and contradictions so we can draw a crystalline partition between good and evil, right and wrong. It takes more cognitive work to keep that illusion going in other systems. In one experiment, a thousand American adults were randomly assigned to participate in fictional elections. The Americans assigned to the traditional, winner-take-all process perceived the elections as less fair than the ones assigned to proportional systems, where seats were distributed according to the ratio of votes. The winner-take-all participants also behaved less generously toward others after losing. They held a little bit of a grudge. That's how binary systems work. They cultivate grudges.

Under proportional representation, the dominant parties still need to work with the less powerful parties to get anything done. They have to create coalitions. So there is my group, your group, and *our* group, the one we need to get a consensus. More people are "in the room," so to speak. It's not exactly like Gary's mediation model, but it's closer. It's less adversarial because the categories are tangled up with one another.

There are different ways to get to less binary politics, but the larger lesson is clear. "We need a politics that scrambles our innate tendency to see the world in binary terms," Lee Drutman wrote in *Breaking the Two-Party Doom Loop,* "by keeping political coalitions fluid and flexible, allowing enemies and allies to change."

It works outside of politics, too. In any situation where cooperation matters, keep the groups flexible. Avoid schemes that designate one winner and one loser, one group that's on the inside and one that's on the outs. Mix up the identities as often as possible.

Want to decide if your church should allow interfaith marriages? Don't put it up for a yes-no vote, whatever you do. Want to open a branch office in Brussels or Detroit? Rotate your employees in and out on a regular basis. Don't let the groups stagnate and take on their own meaning. Avoid referendums. And for God's sake, don't communicate by Slack, Twitter, Facebook, email, chat, or text if you have something remotely sensitive to say. Unless you're on a Mars mission, there is always a better way.

Just as we are wired to group people into categories and discriminate accordingly, we are wired to cooperate. The difference is in the design. "Good institutions elevate our inner angels; bad institutions feed our inner devils," Drutman wrote.

Sometimes, the binary works out okay. For example, team sports can operate with clear winners and losers, most of the time. (Until violence breaks out, or until people start cheating in order to win at any cost.) But much of the time, in businesses, neighborhoods, families, and countries, blurring the lines between *us* and *them* is like buying insurance for your own sanity. It generates healthier conflict.

Sometimes this blurring happens by accident. When I worked at *Time* magazine, I identified with the writer group. We bonded by complaining about the editor group. The editors deleted our artful turns of phrase. They made our stories shorter and more boring, or so we told ourselves. Then one day, the editors went on a retreat together, leaving us writers in charge. This had never happened before. Journalists are not, as a rule, big on retreats. But for whatever reason, we writers were each given a section to edit, and we had to put out the magazine by Friday night.

This started out as a thrill. Finally, we were in charge! All was right with the world! As the week wore on, though, the exuberance waned. We didn't want to hurt one writer's feelings by reassigning his story to another person, who we knew was a better writer. So we didn't. We were forced to make compromises. We had to be practical. Deadlines had to be met. For one week, we got to see what it was like to be the "them," which made it harder to caricature the editors in the future. The job swap confused the categories. It would have been a brilliant management intervention if it had been on purpose. You can't easily default to the idiot-driver reflex if you are the idiot.

Knowing what I now know about human behavior in groups, I try to be more aware of the power of the binary. I avoid casually using the word *them* about other people. I notice when my friends or family talk about *us*, referring to their fellow Republicans or Democrats (something that did not happen ten years ago but now happens often). I ask them who they mean, a small attempt to slow down the binary. Are they now working for the Democratic National Committee? When they talk about "them," do they really mean to generalize about a hundred million people they don't know? At work, I try not to bond with other journalists by casually badmouthing the editors or the younger generation of reporters. If my protégé gets elected president one day, I don't want to end up on a stagecoach, peeling out of town.

But I'll be honest. I fail all the time. The temptation to feel righteous, to claw back a sense of agency, to deflect blame, and seize the moral high ground, is hard to resist. It's critical to try, but if Gary couldn't resist the magnetism of conflict, well then, we're all vulnerable.

So the next natural question is, how do we get out of the trap, once we've fallen in?

The Hatfield family. West Virginia State Archives

chapter 3

the fire starters

Along the Tug Fork of the Big Sandy River, on the border between Kentucky and West Virginia, the Hatfield and the McCoy families lived peacefully for generations. Both families built log cabins, farmed the land, and hunted for meat. They fought for the Confederacy in the Civil War. They intermarried. There is no known evidence of animosity between the families for over half a century.

Then one day in 1878, Randolph McCoy visited Floyd Hatfield's farm and thought he recognized one of the pigs as his own. Hatfield must have stolen his pig, he concluded, and no one could convince him to let it go. So McCoy complained to the authorities, who organized a trial.

The judge appointed a jury made up of equal parts Hatfield and McCoy—six from each family. Then something surprising happened. One of McCoy's own relatives decided against him, causing him to lose the case and the pig.

For McCoy, the loss must have stung. But he accepted the result.

He did not take revenge against the turncoat relative. He did not grab his rifle and capture the pig by force, in the night. The dispute seemed to have been handled. Done and dusted.

A full year and a half after the trial, however, two of his nephews got in a fight with a witness who had testified against McCoy in the trial. They beat the man to death. This was the moment the feud between the Hatfields and McCoys combusted, when a small dispute morphed into an intractable conflict.

Over the course of the next decade, there was a vicious stabbing, a string of vigilante shootings, posse raids, and a Supreme Court case. A house was burned to the ground. A man was hanged. Women were beaten. All told, about eighty different people got drawn into the feud across the region.

Each loss compounded the next. At least a dozen people were killed. The dispute between the Hatfields and the McCoys became notorious, the quintessential blood feud.

"the war spirit in me has abated"

The first mystery of this book was the story of Gary Friedman. How do we get drawn into destructive conflict, the kind that makes us lose sleep and ignore our grandbabies? Why can't we stop the spiral, even when it is making our lives worse? Even those of us who should know better?

We've identified some of the invisible forces at work: the way that binary categories (like the Old and New Guard or Democrats and Republicans) nudge us into an us-versus-them mindset, collapsing complexity. How social pain, caused by rejection or exclusion (perceived or real), provokes aggression, which causes more social pain, most of the time—even in a simple ball-tossing game. And we've seen how cognitive biases keep the conflict going, blinding us to important details.

In this maelstrom of emotion, it becomes harder and harder to access the understory, the real reason we are fighting. So we get locked into a tug-of-war over the crock pot (or the pig), while the deeper conflict burns on, underground.

Conflicts, like wildfires, do not all spread the same way. Some fizzle out. Some go dormant for decades. What makes the difference? Confirmation bias is powerful, but it doesn't, by itself, lead to war. Why do some conflicts erupt, spreading like a contagion, holding entire communities hostage for years? While others simmer? The Hatfield and McCoy conflict started as an interpersonal one between a small number of people—not unlike the conflict between Gary and the Old Guard. In both cases, the neighbors involved had various allies in their corners and ways of categorizing one another, binary stories they told themselves.

Like Gary and his neighbors, the Hatfields and McCoys had options other than violence. They were free White men, with plenty of space to roam. They had a functioning legal system. Blood feuds were rare in the Tug Valley at the time. So what happened?

We'll return to Gary, to see what he did next and how he navigated the Tar Pits of local politics. Suffice to say, he did not resign. He did something much more surprising.

But for now, our next story is about how conflicts explode, when they do. We'll discover four conditions that can act as fire starters. These are the accelerants to watch out for, in any conflict:

- Group identities
- Conflict entrepreneurs
- Humiliation
- Corruption

These four fire starters speed conflict up and spread it around. They make conflict far more meaningful and essential than it was before—which makes any conflict much harder to interrupt.

But not impossible.

In 1891, "Cap" Hatfield, the second cousin once removed of the man originally accused of stealing that pig, sent a letter to the editor of his local newspaper in West Virginia. The battle, he declared, was over. "I do not wish to keep the old feud alive, and I suppose everybody, like myself, is tired of the names 'Hatfield and McCoy,'" he wrote. "The war spirit in me has abated, and I sincerely rejoice at the prospects of peace." And that was the end.

Twelve years of war were followed by over a century of peace.

Even violent conflicts can downshift, becoming tolerable and sometimes even useful. Most conflict, after all, is a force for good. It allows *us* to defend ourselves, to speak our mind, and pushes *them* to be better. And vice versa.

For that to happen, the fire starters usually need to lose power—or be undermined or replaced, quite intentionally. There is an unwinding that has to happen. To understand how people get out of violent conflicts, we need to understand how they got in.

"it's always deeper than it seems"

I've known Curtis Toler for four years, and I've never seen him without a baseball hat. Usually it looks new, like it's never been worn before. He is muscular, taut, like a man carefully held together.

Each time we meet, he starts out guarded, arms crossed across his chest. He does not smile. Each time, I worry that he is finally sick of talking to me. Which

Curtis Toler in Chicago. Sean Patrick Forrest

would be understandable. I've taken a lot of his time, interviewing him about conflict. But then he starts telling stories, stories that are vivid, funny, unforgettable. And we stay there, talking like that, for three or four hours.

Curtis spent two decades leading a large gang in Chicago, pursuing a vendetta that was as old as he was. He has been shot six times, and he's done two bids in prison. And yet there is nothing inevitable about his story, he knows. There is mystery in every conflict, including his own. He's spent a lot of time investigating the understory of his own life.

"I didn't believe I was just born violent," he told me. "So I wanted to know, Why did I end up being so violent?"

These days, Curtis prevents high conflict as a full-time job. To do that, he has to understand it. He has to study it like a treasure map. And this is something he loves to do. "I've always been really inquisitive about my own behavior and other people's behavior."

The second half of Curtis's life is a mirror image of the first. He's the same person, but everything is reversed. He works at a Chicago organization that targets young men most at risk of getting shot or shooting someone else. He listens to these young men and counsels them and shows up, even when no one else will.

Curtis also works as an actor. He plays a version of his old self in *The Chi*, a Showtime TV drama about life on the South Side of Chicago. It is a quality show, but for Curtis it can feel like a vacation. "I'm always telling the writers, 'It's not violent enough!'" he said, laughing. "'This is Chicago! Make it realistic.'"

In every gang conflict he encounters, Curtis tries to get to the understory, or what he calls "the root cause." For example, there was one bloody gang rivalry that had lasted for years—and was still going on. All the guys involved had been friends at one point. They'd grown up in the same neighborhood, gone to the same elementary and high schools.

Curtis started asking how the conflict started. He talked to a lot of people, including the principal of the high school, and he eventually learned the origin story: "It was over a watch," Curtis told me, and then he laughed, a deep belly laugh, shaking his head. He laughed like this whenever he said something unsettling, I noticed. As if to say, *Can you believe this? Aren't people incredible?* Someone had left his watch on the sidelines during a basketball game, and after the game, it was gone. This watch was the crock pot, the proximate cause of years of violence.

When Curtis stopped laughing, his voice was controlled and low again. The watch was not just a watch, he said. "It's always deeper than it seems."

The origin story of a conflict often gets forgotten altogether, he's found. Sometimes the rivalry is handed down through generations, and no one alive today even knows how it started. "A majority start with really small things in Chicago."

a hat to the left

When Curtis was growing up on the South Side of Chicago, he loved to dance. Not just any kind of dancing but popping and locking, a kind of hip hop dancing where he made it look like he was dancing under a strobe light—but there was no strobe light. He would move and freeze and pulse and freeze.

Curtis made people stop and smile when he danced. In this way, he was a lot like his mother, Rita, the life of a party. A model and dancer, she was Curtis's original dance partner.

By age eleven, Curtis could do all the moves, from animations to slow motion to gliding. With practice, he learned to control every muscle in his body. Watching him was like watching a video that was glitching, on and off, to the beat of the music. He loved the way he could make other people gasp, doing things they thought could not be done. As he got bigger, he got stronger and collected more tricks he could make his body do. He and his best friend, Jesse, would hang out in the park and practice doing back flips off a low wall. Over and over again, they'd launch themselves off that wall, to the rhythm of a bass line from a boom box in the distance. Two unstoppable boys, spinning in space.

That spring, Curtis watched on live TV as Michael Jackson did the moonwalk for the first time on *Motown 25*. He'd always loved Michael, but this was something else, something amazing. There he was, all sequined silk, gliding backwards onstage to "Billie Jean." Curtis stared at the screen, unblinking, tears running down his face.

That very night, Curtis got to work practicing the moonwalk. He put on his grandmother's white church gloves, pushed off the full-length mirror in the hallway, and grooved his way backwards, over and over. He was so excited that his mom let him stay up to watch the late news, which promised to replay the footage of Michael moonwalking.

Curtis played basketball, too. He wasn't especially good at it, but basketball was religion in Chicago, and everyone had to practice. And Foster Park, located less than a block from his house, was the Mecca of that religion in 1983.

One day, Curtis saw something unusual at Foster Park. One player was dominating all the others. This guy was 6'8", the tallest person Curtis had ever seen in person. But the thing that mesmerized Curtis was the guy's grace: he ran the court with a kind of liquid ease. He moved like a cat burglar, scaling walls of players, defying gravity. "You could just see that this guy was different, you know. The smoothness of it."

He was actually a little like Michael Jackson that way. He made you gasp. Then, just at the right moment, he'd pounce, taking and making a heroic jump shot, the kind where you knew in your gut that a miracle had happened.

Curtis had heard that NBA players sometimes played pickup ball at Foster Park. This guy must be a professional, he figured.

"Who is that?" Curtis asked the girl standing next to him.

"That's Benji," she said.

All the girls seemed to know Benji Wilson's name. But Benji

was not a pro ball player, not yet, anyway. He was in high school, a good-looking young man with dancing eyes and a slow smile.

And there was one other thing. Benji had his baseball hat turned to the left on the court that day. A hat to the left, Curtis knew, meant someone was a member of the People Nation, an alliance of gangs that included the Black P Stone Nation, named after Chicago's South Blackstone Avenue.

This mattered. Because, not long before, Curtis had become a Stone, too. So he and Benji were connected, Curtis thought, a smile spreading across his face. The feeling of awe he'd had while watching Benji play began to turn into something else. It felt like pride, the kind that fills your chest up. They were like family, he and this shimmering young man.

living vicariously

Each of us has an infinite number of identities, arranged in a hierarchy that changes all the time. We belong to groups we consciously recognize as well as ones we don't. Think for a moment: Which of your own groups would you defend, if they were attacked today? Whose pain would you feel as though it were your own?

Your family might come to mind first. What about your neighbors? Some of them yes, some of them no, I'm guessing. People who look like you? Who vote like you? What about your countrymen?

Loyalties are surprisingly dynamic. You might defend your fellow citizens if they were being attacked by outsiders. But the rest of the time, you might not. You might feel like some of your fellow citizens are to be defended against.

Strangely, I feel most American when I leave America. In other countries, where I am seen as different, where I feel different, my nationality rises to the top. I find myself trying to explain America to others. Suddenly I think I can generalize about 329 million people. It's absurd but somehow very natural to do. In these moments, I can be very quick to acknowledge my country's failings, but it bothers me when foreigners make the exact same arguments. How dare they? I immediately think of several devastating accusations that I could level against their own countries, and then I stop myself from doing so.

This is mostly an illusion, if you step back from it. I will never meet, know, or even hear about the vast majority of my fellow Americans. But it's a powerful feeling all the same, one that can be turned on and off.

Most of human history, there were no nation-states, no country identities at all. Humans did not assume they had anything in common with other humans whom they would never lay eyes on, hundreds or thousands of miles away. But since humans invented national identities, we've gotten quite convinced of their realness, willing even to kill and to die for them.

As soon as I am back in my own country, my identities reshuffle subconsciously. I become Writer or Neighbor or Parent, depending on the moment. Other Americans become, in my eyes, loose groups of individuals again, more different than alike.

Group identities are complicated, shifting, and powerful forces. They represent the first fire starter in Curtis's story. Powerful group identities like gang affiliations can make conflict far more volatile than it would otherwise be. They exert a force that is larger than the conflict itself. Whether clans or gangs or army battalions, groups generate vicarious experiences, spreading suffering and pride around like aftershocks. Groups can supersize conflict, turning a regular conflict trap into a prison.

In a way, groups are like conflict itself: most of the time, they are a force for good. Groups give us structure, safety, and purpose, making humanity's greatest accomplishments possible. Without groups, there would be no cathedrals, no Pyramids, no World Cup, no symphonies, no eradication of smallpox.

So what makes group conflict, so central to the human story, spiral into endemic violence, trapping entire communities—sometimes entire countries—for generations?

In the late 1800s, the Hatfield and McCoy dispute started out as a modest dispute over a farm animal. There was nothing all that unusual about it at the time. But when the judge in the case chose a jury that was half Hatfields and half McCoys, he made it something else. Now it was a full-blown group conflict, one that pressed much deeper loyalties into service.

The jurors must have had various group identities, some of which overlapped with the parties in the dispute (Men, Farmers, War Veterans). The plaintiff McCoy and the defendant Hatfield shared many identities as well. They were not all that different on paper.

The most obvious difference was their family identity. This name separated the jurors, as well. And so this identity must have become salient, rising to the surface during the trial. It's interesting to think about what might have happened if the case had been slightly different. If, for example, it had been a male Hatfield accused of beating up a female McCoy. Then which identity would have been salient?

As it was, the judge must have activated powerful family loyalties when choosing the jury. There were two sides, dangerously meaningful. Then, when one of McCoy's own relatives turned against him during the deliberations, the verdict became that much more loaded. The ruling against McCoy wasn't just a loss. It was a betrayal, a very public one. That kind of betrayal incites social pain, not unlike the sting of rejection experienced by Gary in his neighborhood.

Still, McCoy accepted the verdict, nevertheless. Remember that a full year and a half went by without major incident. But groups are hard to control. They contain multitudes. That is why group identities are such potent fire starters: it only takes one or two rogue cousins to create mayhem.

After the cousins beat the witness to death, the conflict grew geometrically. Every time another family member or ally was hurt or humiliated, everyone else in the group experienced that pain, too.

In laboratory studies, when people watch a loved one receive a mild electric shock, the part of their own brain that assesses the meaning of pain gets activated. Their brain responds as if the shock were happening to them, in other words. For those neurons, there is *no apparent difference* between literal, first-person pain and collective, group pain.

We viscerally feel each other's pain. And each other's pride and joy. Basketball fans act differently after they watch their team win. They feel better about themselves, compared to fans who have just watched their team lose. They even predict they will perform better on puzzles and games. This is, in this context, a charming quirk of the human condition. We live by proxy. We overestimate our own abilities, riding high on a victory we had nothing to do with.

When Curtis saw Benji sink a perfect shot from behind the arc, he felt it physically, like a jolt of triumph, almost like he'd done it himself. In a similar way, each new loss or triumph in the Hatfield and McCoy feud was felt by not one or two but *eighty* people. With every act of retaliation, eighty brains lit up in a similar way. This is how group conflict becomes a contagion.

"you're not latino, man!"

The first time Curtis joined a gang, he joined the wrong one by mistake. He was nine years old. He was getting picked on because he was light-skinned and because his grandmother could afford to buy him an Atari. He was the oldest of three siblings, born to a sixteen-year-old single mom, and he had no big brother or father around to protect him or give him advice. Kids kept saying he looked Latino because of his light skin, and he wasn't totally sure what Latino meant. But he knew Latinos joined the Latin Kings, and so he went where he thought he belonged.

The gang initiation happened one day after school. The other Latin Kings handcuffed Curtis to a small tree and beat him up.

Mostly, they took body shots, but one punch hit him in the mouth. After that, Curtis was told he had to fight his friend Steve, who was also trying to join the gang. Then both boys had to fight some other guys. They got accepted, and Curtis felt proud, like he was someone.

The feeling didn't last long. "What the hell is that? You, a Latin King? You crazy!" his cousins said. They laughed and laughed. "You're not Latino, man!"

That was embarrassing. He'd wanted to belong—and instead, he felt humiliated. This group was not his group after all. He looked for another option, and he found, not too long afterward, the Vice Lords. He had relatives in that gang, he'd been told. That much he knew. Maybe this was his group.

One day, after Curtis became a Vice Lord, he got on his bike and headed to a play rehearsal at the YMCA on the West Side. He was about ten years old, playing the role of a pirate, and so he biked through the city wearing a pirate hat in black and gold—the colors of the Vice Lords. He was loud and proud and hard to miss. A group of Stones saw him, beat him up, and took his bike, one of the nicest bikes he'd ever had. It was the first time he ever got jumped on the streets of Chicago.

It was a lesson. Curtis understood then that he was being watched. Signals were being sent out and received. That was just the way it worked. It wasn't personal.

A year later, when his family moved to Foster Park, Curtis did not hesitate to join the Stones himself. He wanted to match the other kids in the neighborhood. He wanted to belong, so he needed a new group. It didn't matter that they'd beaten him up the year before.

Here's the tricky thing about groups: they can ignite conflict, but they can also extinguish it. This is the second paradox of conflict. Groups bring obligations, including the duty to do harm—or, in other groups at other times, the obligation to do *no* harm, to make peace. When people find a way in and *out* of violent conflicts, there is almost always a group at work, in the background.

Everything depends on the group's norms and traditions. What is the right way to deal with conflict? What constitutes an affront? When is it time to turn the other cheek? The way the brain evaluates the meaning of pain or threats depends, in part, on the group's leaders.

conflict entrepreneurs

As sisters go, Tricia and Julie Nixon were inseparable. They were maids of honor in each other's weddings. They remained close when their father became the first U.S. president to resign from office, after the Watergate scandal. "They smile or wave or cry together in a thousand pictures," journalist Margaret Carlson wrote, "standing by their father and each other."

Then in 1997, three years after their father's death, twenty-five years after Watergate, the sisters fell into high conflict. They could not

Newlyweds Julie Nixon and David Eisenhower pose with Tricia Nixon, the bride's sister and the maid of honor, at the Plaza Hotel in New York City on December 22, 1968. Bettmann/ Bettmann via Getty Images

agree on how their father's library should be run. Whether it should be managed primarily by the family or by outsiders.

We all know stories about estranged siblings. After their mother's funeral, actress sisters Joan Fontaine and Olivia de Havilland stopped speaking to one another. They were still estranged thirty-eight years later, when Fontaine passed away. In Germany, brothers Adolf and Rudolf Dassler founded a sportswear company together, but then split up over a perceived slight. Adidas and Puma, the resulting companies, remain competitors today.

In fact, the loving ideal that we think of when we talk about brothers and sisters turns out to be relatively rare. Only about a third of American adults report having a close, supportive relationship with a sibling. Another third have either a hostile or a competitive relationship. The rest are generally apathetic about their sibling—or have fond feelings but rarely speak.

Siblings represent the longest relationships most of us will ever have. Our parents exist in our lives for about fifty years, if we are lucky. But our siblings can be with us seventy to eighty years. That's a lot of time for misunderstandings, mistreatment, and resentment to build. All sibling relationships start in conflict, as children competing for our parents' attention, and the crock pots accumulate. It's like a political campaign that lasts a lifetime.

Meanwhile, parents and other friends and family can sway the conflict dynamics. They can make sibling conflicts less toxic. But sometimes, they do the opposite. They add to the paranoia and hostility, seeding doubts and whispering rumors. These people are what we'll call conflict entrepreneurs, our second fire starter after group identities.

In the Nixon sister feud, family members and library employees took sides. Lawyers got involved. The library's director was accused of fanning the fire. "He's done what all the Nixon haters couldn't do— drive a wedge in the family," a library board member said.

Angry letters got leaked. Two lawsuits were filed. A $20 million dollar bequest to the library sat unused, because the sisters could not agree. "There is complete estrangement between the sisters," a library employee said.

It was a classic high conflict. Everyone was worse off, except for the lawyers. "I think it is very sad," Julie said, five years after the dispute had begun. "It's very heartbreaking because I love my sister very much." No matter how much she wanted to end the conflict, it kept grinding on. And it might have continued until one of them died. Many sibling conflicts do.

Then one person interrupted the spiral. A judge ordered the sisters to resolve the conflict. "There is going to be a party," the judge said, "and everybody's going to come."

On a warm summer day in 2002, the sisters met behind closed doors at the InterContinental, a luxury hotel on Biscayne Bay in downtown Miami. Two off-duty police officers kept guard outside the conference room. A mediator appointed by the court was there, sworn to silence, along with a gaggle of lawyers. At one point, the sisters broke away from the group and went off by themselves to talk. Just before two in the morning, they reached an agreement.

A conflict that had lasted five years was resolved in less than twenty-four hours. The final agreement was only two pages long. Once the conflict entrepreneurs got sidelined, it appeared, the sisters were free, at last. The conflict became healthy. The women shared an emotional hug outside of the conference room. "Julie and I have always loved each other for more than fifty years," Tricia said, "and we always will."

One way to prevent high conflict is to learn to recognize the conflict entrepreneurs in your orbit. Notice who delights in each new plot twist of a feud. Who is quick to validate every lament and to articulate wrongs no one else has even thought of? We all know people like this, and it's important to keep them at a safe distance.

In practice, this can be hard to do, especially for people trapped in the conflict themselves. Because conflict entrepreneurs are often very important in people's lives. They can be loving, persuasive, and charismatic. The best ones make themselves essential. They become central to a group's identity, and without them, it's harder to feel like there's an *us*.

stone love

The Stones were an especially powerful group because of their leader. The group had been cofounded in the 1960s by a larger-than-life young man named Jeff Fort, who called out racial injustice across the country. Fort wielded his charisma in unusual ways. He advised local politicians on how to combat poverty, and he got invited to President Nixon's inauguration.

When Curtis was growing up, Fort's reputation in the community was legendary. When he and his entourage walked by elementary school playgrounds, kids would swarm the fence to get a look at him. Fort preached the virtues of Islam and Black Power and gave young Black men a space—a literal space—to come together, in a building the Stones bought on South Drexel Avenue. (By the 1980s, Fort had created a new gang called the El Rukns, which Curtis would also join. To avoid confusion, I'll keep referring to the organization as the Stones, as Curtis generally does today.)

The Temple, as it was called, had a steel door with three bolted locks. It served as a disco, a weapons arsenal, and, on Fridays, a mosque. Fort moved around the city in a chauffeured Cadillac limousine, escorted by bodyguards. He wore dark sunglasses, even in the courtroom. He had a throne—an actual throne—inside the Temple, or so it was said. He handed out new shoes to kids who needed them. To a boy like Curtis, Fort was power.

From the beginning, Fort understood how much boys and men in Chicago wanted to belong to something bigger than themselves. That's what made him such a good fire starter; he intuitively understood the psychology of conflict. He made T-shirts for all the Stones to wear, and came up with a list of sacred Stones values: Love, Truth,

Peace, Freedom, and Justice. There was a special Stones handshake, a special Stones way of wearing your hat and your belt buckle, a Stones way of being.

When younger boys wanted to join the gang, they had to get parental permission. Fort pushed gang members to finish high school and shun drugs and alcohol. But the Stones were simultaneously operating one of the more successful dope rings in Chicago. By the early 1980s, you couldn't sell uppers and downers or even weed on the South Side without getting the okay from the Stones and sharing your profits. The Stones were rumored to have branches in Milwaukee, Minneapolis, and Columbus, Ohio.

Curtis wanted to be part of it all. So in middle school, he forged a letter from his mother and joined the Stones. His friend Jesse became a Stone, too, and because of all the gymnastics he'd done, Jesse was strong. He became known for his ability to handle himself with his hands. If Curtis got in trouble with a rival gang, Jesse would appear and start throwing people off of him. And Curtis would do the same for Jesse and other fellow Stones. For Curtis, it felt like he'd found his people, finally. Each day, he turned his hat to the left, and he knew he was not alone.

part real, part lies

In the beginning, groups get created in order to solve a problem for someone. That means they can be based on ethnicity, religion, shared kin, or whatever works as a glue to bring people together. The nature of the group can change as the nature of the problem changes. Decades can go by in relative peace, and then something happens, usually a dispute over land, money, or politics, and new life is injected into old grievances.

Groups are part real, part lies. And the worse the conflict gets, the bigger the lies get.

In Syria, about half a million people have been killed in the recent civil war, which is viewed as a devastating ethnic and sectarian conflict. But it was not, when it began, about group divisions at all. It was about graffiti.

In March 2011, in a quiet border town named Dara'a, a group of teenage boys spray-painted the words "Freedom" and "It's your turn, Doctor" on the wall of a high school, implying that Syrian president Bashar al-Assad, a dictator who was trained as an ophthalmologist, would be the next ruler to fall during the Arab Spring upheavals that had spread across Tunisia, Egypt, and Libya.

In response, Assad's security forces arrested the boys and refused to tell their parents where they were. The teenagers were beaten and tortured for weeks. When the locals protested, security forces fired at the crowds, killing several people. The protests spread to other cities. The regime brutally suppressed the uprisings with tanks and air power.

In this spasm of violence, people began to retreat to groups for safety, awakening old, latent identities. It was a way to survive, physically and mentally. People needed a compass with which to navigate the carnage, and many grabbed the one most readily available to them.

Syria is run largely by Alawites, a sect of Islam whose members include Assad. But they represent only 12 percent of the population. Meanwhile, Sunnis make up the majority of Syria but have little political power. As word of the regime's brutality spread, some Sunnis began to consider the ruling Alawites to be their enemy and attacked them. The Alawites, in turn, feared that they'd be massacred in Sunni revenge killings if Assad were overthrown. They were outnumbered, and so some started forming militias to protect themselves, which then confirmed the Sunnis' worst fears.

"As people, we don't want anything to happen between us," a Sunni man named Mohammed told a reporter in 2011, just three months into the conflict, before anyone was calling it a civil war. "But the people in this regime are forcing us to hate Alawites."

Mohammed could feel the group conflict taking over, manipulated by Assad and other opportunistic leaders. Even as he felt pulled into it, he could see it for what it was. An old and dear Alawite friend of his texted him to ask if his family was okay. He told his friend of twenty-five years the truth: that two of his sisters had just been killed in a government crackdown in his town.

Very quickly, latent identities came back to life in Syria, and the divisions deepened. It was a feedback loop of the most diabolical kind. The old religious and ethnic cinders, quiet for many generations, roared to life, fueled by conflict entrepreneurs. "Ethnic wars do not just happen," political scientist Gary Bass wrote, "they are made."

Fire starter leaders seize the opportunities embedded in conflict and turn them to their advantage. Assad's regime needed Syrians and other global leaders to feel even more terrified of his opposition than of him, and so the regime intentionally helped the more radical elements among his opponents. They released extremist prisoners and even funneled weapons to protesters.

It sounds crazy. Why would a dictator like Assad help the people trying to overthrow him? Because he understood fear. He knew that fear hardens group identities. He needed to make the conflict about fighting terrorists, rather than about his own crimes against his own people.

Syria may feel far away to many people reading this book. But the more I learned about conflict, the more familiar these patterns started to feel. All over the world, fire starter leaders intentionally play on our identities.

Narendra Modi in India, Jarosław Kaczyński in Poland, Donald Trump in the United States, and Recep Tayyip Erdoğan in Turkey. They were all master fire starters. They intentionally stoked rival identities to boost their popularity and power, just like gang leaders, inciting contempt and turning neighbors on neighbors.

Identity manipulation is very hard to resist, given our basic wiring as humans. But not impossible. To begin, it is important to be vigilant. To notice when one of our identities feels newly electrified, and to ask the question: *Who does this serve?*

Just as leaders can exploit our worst instincts, they can call us to our best selves. We each contain many versions of ourselves, which can be summoned or suppressed, depending on the moment.

proof of hope

After that first sighting on the basketball courts of Foster Park, Curtis got the chance to see Benji play several more times. "That's Big Ben!" he'd say when he spotted the teenager's lanky frame prowling the courts. Sometimes he'd stand on the sidelines and just watch Benji shoot free throws, tracking the ball from Benji's hands to the net, like the two were connected by a magnetic force. It was mesmerizing.

When Curtis stared like this, Benji didn't run the younger boy off. He just took shot after shot after shot, like a man at work, his deep-set eyes locked on the task.

In 1984, Benji led his team at Simeon Vocational High School to the state championship. Chicago's first Black mayor, Harold Washington, came to the school on Vincennes Avenue to congratulate them. That March, Benji's name appeared in the *Chicago Tribune* no fewer than twenty times. He was a local celebrity on the cusp of going national. The paper even ran a front-page story about Simeon high school, calling it a "school of winners" in the headline.

This mattered to Curtis because his neighborhood was changing all around him. Redlining, the practice whereby banks refused loans to people in certain disproportionately Black neighborhoods, had been officially outlawed, but it continued in less obvious ways. Curtis's neighbors were largely Black and middle-class, earning incomes at or above the citywide average, but they had a hard time getting loans to fix up their homes or buy new ones. Of the neighborhood's 121 buildings, over half were vacant.

Crack hadn't made it to Chicago yet, but most kids knew an aunt or an uncle hooked on heroin or pills. The once bustling 79th Street commercial strip was becoming a marketplace for drugs, prostitution, and liquor stores.

But then, undeniably, there was Benji Wilson. When he was on the court, Benji lit the place up, proof of hope in Foster Park. By the transitive property of the hood, Benji belonged to all the kids on the South Side. And especially to his fellow Stones. At recess, when twelve-year-old Curtis charged up the court and took wild, impossible shots, in his mind he was Benji Wilson, too.

The next school year, *Sporting News* magazine ranked Benji as the No. 1 high school basketball player in the country. Benji's team at Simeon High School was on track to win the state title once again. The more fame Benji got, the harder he seemed to work. If he'd put up three hundred shots a day last year in Foster Park, he would do four hundred a day this year.

By November, he had narrowed down his top three college choices to the University of Illinois, DePaul University, and Indiana University. When he visited DePaul, Benji stood eighteen feet from the basket and made twenty shots. He only missed three. DePaul was ranked second in the country, but no one on their team could match him.

Michael Jordan came to Chicago that fall to play for the Bulls. It was obvious right away that he was the best person on that team, and Curtis was excited for his hometown team. He hoped that Benji would play for the Bulls, too, one day. Because Jordan was from North Carolina, which was all well and good. But Benji was a Stone from the South Side.

One day in November, right before Thanksgiving, Curtis was lying on the couch, watching the nightly news with his grandfather, like he always did. Then a story came on that made him sit up and listen. Earlier that day, in broad daylight, high school basketball star Benji Wilson had been shot twice, the announcer said. It had happened on Vincennes Avenue, near Benji's high school, while he was walking with his girlfriend on his lunch break.

"They done shot that boy?" his grandfather said quietly.

Curtis didn't answer. He was struggling to understand what he was hearing. The bullet had pierced Benji's liver and his aorta, whatever that was. Doctors were operating on him at that very moment. Kids were holding a vigil at the hospital. His condition was serious, they said. But Benji was seventeen, and he was strong. God willing, Curtis prayed, Benji would still be able to play ball. His first game of the season was scheduled for the next night.

When the newscast ended, he and his grandfather watched the game that came on next. But Curtis couldn't stop thinking about the news. Imagine Benji Wilson getting shot. Right on Vincennes Avenue, a place he'd walked by so many times. *Benji Wilson.* It seemed impossible. Benji had no enemies. Why would anyone want to hurt him?

Benji died at 6 a.m.

Curtis heard the news at Foster Park the next day. The air left his chest.

Pain took its place, the kind of pain that spreads through the body, like acid, eating away from the inside.

Plenty of people died, Curtis knew, even at twelve years old. Not just old people, but young people, caught up in the violence of the drug trade. But heroes didn't die. Not like this. In his head, thoughts began spiraling.

Why did it have to be Benji?

He was short of breath.

Who else is there? We have nobody else.

"Guess what?" a kid said. "Billy and Omar killed him."

Another punch in the chest.

Billy and Omar? Curtis *knew* Billy and Omar. They lived around the corner. They were just regular kids, nobodies.

The newspapers said that Billy Moore, sixteen, had fired a .22 caliber pistol at close range, with his friend Omar Dixon at his side. "This was a random, senseless shooting," a police detective told the *Chicago Tribune.* "It was just one of those things that happens in the streets."

But Curtis did not accept random and senseless. On some level, below his awareness, he could not live with random and senseless.

No, Billy had to have recognized Benji. He was the tallest kid in the neighborhood. Famous. Unmissable. Billy must have been jealous of Benji, that's what it was.

Now what?

Rumors snaked their way through Foster Park. Billy had gone after Benji, some folks said, because Benji's hat was to the left.

Because Benji's hat was to the left.

"Where are they?" Curtis begged. He knew the way to Billy's and Omar's houses, and he wanted to make someone feel the pain he was feeling. They'd taken a member of his family—snatched away a whole city's hope, and for what? Now he felt rage, the kind that pushes pain to the side.

The funeral was held two days after Thanksgiving. In his casket, Benji was dressed in his blue and gold Simeon basketball uniform. Beside the casket was a flower arrangement in the shape of a basketball, adorned with Benji's number, 25. Ten thousand people came, spilling onto the street. The speeches at the three-hour ceremony were piped out to the mourners through speakers mounted on trucks. Mayor Washington spoke, his voice cracking as he promised a new push to end gang violence. The Reverend Jesse Jackson lamented the senselessness: "A superstar is dead—shot down, unarmed, in cold blood."

But Curtis wasn't at the funeral. He was busy trying to make things right. That weekend, Curtis stole his grandfather's .357 Magnum revolver and began a pursuit that would occupy him for years to come.

"the nuclear bomb of emotions"

Conflict can explode when social pain becomes unbearable. When it becomes something worse than exclusion, when it becomes humiliation.

Humiliation is "the nuclear bomb of the emotions," the psychologist and physician Evelin Lindner wrote. That's why it's the third fire starter, following group identity and conflict entrepreneurs. Humiliation poses an existential threat that jeopardizes the deepest part of ourselves, our sense that we matter, that we are worth something. It is "the enforced lowering of a person or group," Lindner writes, "a process of subjugation that damages or strips away their pride, honor and dignity."

People need to matter. It's a fundamental requirement for life, like oxygen. Our need to matter lies underneath all kinds of group conflict. When, like Curtis, we find ourselves in situations where revered members of our group can be snuffed out randomly, the obvious conclusion is that we don't matter either. That is crushing, like a loss of oxygen.

Notice that Curtis's first thoughts on hearing about Benji's death were about his own place in the world. "Who else is there? We have nobody else." Humiliation creates desperation. As Nelson Mandela once said: "There is nobody more dangerous than one who has been humiliated, even when you humiliate him rightly."

In interviews with more than two hundred people involved in conflicts in Somalia and Rwanda, Lindner found that humiliation permeated their stories of victimization—*and* persecution. Often these stories were told by the same people. Feelings of humiliation drive acts of humiliation, and on and on the cycle goes. Humiliation can become an obsession, she found, "as significant and consuming as any form of addiction or dependence."

Which is why it is so surprising that humiliation gets ignored so much of the time. You rarely read about humiliation in history books or in news coverage of political conflict. In his travels around the world, *New York Times* columnist Thomas Friedman noticed this omission. "If I've learned one thing covering world affairs, it's this: The single most underappreciated force in international relations is humiliation," he wrote. Most journalists pay far more attention to battle strategy or the pursuit of land, oil, or power. But to ignore humiliation is to miss a powerful understory, driving all manner of conflict. It afflicts prime ministers and generals just as much as it does guerrilla fighters and gang members.

As a prison psychiatrist, James Gilligan conducted many interviews with men who had been convicted of serious crimes. He started to notice that humiliation was connected to violence like smoke to fire. "I have yet to see a serious act of violence that was not provoked by the experience of feeling shamed and humiliated, disrespected and ridiculed," he wrote, "and that did not represent the attempt to prevent or undo this 'loss of face.'"

This cycle never ends for some people. "There are people who thrive on humiliation," Lindner wrote. "They are addicted to feelings of humiliation, provoke them systematically and perpetrate acts of humiliation to 'avenge' the humiliation they feel they have suffered." Watch out for these people, Lindner warned. If someone like this gets into a position of great power and taps into a reservoir of humiliation in a country, war and genocide can follow.

But what constitutes humiliation? This is a slippery question. During World War II, guards in concentration camps would order prisoners to make and remake their beds until they were perfect, Holocaust survivors told psychologist Nico Frijda. Male Holocaust survivors said they felt humiliated by this experience. But the female survivors did not feel humiliated. They interpreted it differently, another indignity among many. Either way, the guards were harassing the inmates. But whether it felt *humiliating* depended on a person's identity and concept of the world. What it means to be a man. To matter and not matter.

Humiliation is not an objective matter, as it turns out. It is an emotion, our culture and values shape how we interpret our emotions. This is not to say that humiliation is imaginary; the pain is real and excruciating. But one of the most startling revelations of modern science is that emotions and thoughts cannot be separated. They are intertwined.

When we feel humiliated, it's because our brains have conducted a rapid-fire evaluation of events and fit it into our understanding of the world. To be brought low, we have to first see ourselves as belonging up high. To take a trivial example, I've only been golfing once in my life. I don't care about golfing. At all. If I swing the club with all my might and utterly miss the ball (as I did at least once), I feel a little foolish. I laugh at myself. But I don't feel humiliated. Because being good at golf is not part of my identity. If Tiger Woods did the same thing, it might feel humiliating. Particularly if it were caught on camera.

The greatest humiliations are the ones that feel public. During peace talks in 2004 in Northern Ireland, the IRA agreed to destroy its weapons. The opposition asked that the IRA take photographs, proving they had done so. It was a matter of transparency, they said, that's all. The IRA's leaders refused. It was one step too far, this demand for photographs. The peace talks stalled. "One man's transparency is another's humiliation," said Gerry Adams, president of the political wing of the IRA.

If humiliation is the nuclear bomb of conflict, and humiliation is subjective, then it can be manipulated. It can be incited on purpose. This is a radical idea. Today, more than ever perhaps, many people think about emotions as being reflexes, triggered by events. That's where the concept of safe spaces comes from on many college campuses: the idea that people need to be protected from triggers that can set off emotions.

And yet, a century of research has not been able to identify a universal physical pathway for emotion. There is no identifiable, consistent, and objective measure of anger, for example. Emotional experiences vary wildly from culture to culture—in how and when they are understood and expressed. Emotions, in other words, are socially informed. We help create them.

In this way, crushing humiliation is *not* like a loss of oxygen. It is partly a product of our mind and our experiences. Emotions are real in the same way that national identities are real. But they are not objective facts.

No matter what, Curtis was going to experience pain on the day that Benji died. But consider the different ways, in a parallel universe, that Curtis might have interpreted that loss.

Benji did not know Curtis's name, keep in mind. They were not friends. Curtis's day-to-day life did not need to change when Benji died. It's possible to imagine a scenario in which Curtis would have experienced deep sadness and even fear when Benji was killed. But not humiliation.

At the time, in his only available reality, Curtis instantly felt Benji's death as a threat to the deepest part of himself, to his sense that he mattered. He felt a flood of emotion on Benji's behalf, and he wasn't alone. It was the flip side of collective pride he and his friends felt when they saw Benji play basketball. This was collective humiliation, experienced by proxy when a hero gets stripped of his humanity. It was the forcible lowering of someone who was up high, and it was done right out in the open, for everyone to see.

Many forces and experiences shaped Curtis's interpretation of Benji's death. But one important part of his history was his experience with sudden violence. Ever since age seven or so, Curtis had been witnessing brutality up close. Not just against fellow gang members but against his most intimate group, his family. Again and again, he'd seen his mom get beaten up by her boyfriends, a whole series of them. He himself had been fondled by one of these men.

One thing Curtis decided early on was that he wasn't going to let what happened to his mom happen to him. He wasn't going to be "prey," as he put it. So he needed to be on constant alert to protect himself from such threats, which were hard to predict. His brain had to look for cues, warnings in the tiniest things. A cue could be the way someone looked at him. Or the way a hat was tipped. The world was full of threats, and he had to be hypervigilant.

This is what chronic stress and trauma can do to people. Anything that reminds our brain of previous trauma is interpreted as a threat, even when it is not a threat. Conflict becomes extremely hard to avoid.

Other things shaped Curtis's interpretation of Benji's death, too. Groups develop ways of looking at the world, default frames to help them understand what is happening. Leaders prioritize certain emotions over others.

This is why certain languages have words for emotions that do not exist in other languages. For example, in Finland, the word *sisu* (pronounced SEE-su) means a sort of inner fire, ferocity in the face of great odds. It's an important word, one that is cited for all kinds of Finnish accomplishments, from growing potatoes in frozen soil to building the best education system in the world today. But English has no word for *sisu*.

In the 1960s, when the anthropologist Jean Briggs lived among the Utku, an Inuit group in the Arctic Circle, she noticed that they tended to reject anger. It just wasn't allowed, culturally speaking. Small children were allowed to get angry and throw tantrums, but after about age six, people were expected to exhibit *ihuma*, a kind of deep self-control that produced outer calm or laughter, instead of rage. People still got visibly angry, but not very often.

In many gangs, the culture is the opposite of the Utku. To be angry is to be strong. Any slight, being stared at or called a bitch or shoved, is seen as a potential threat. Not just to a gang member's physical safety. But also to his masculinity, his sense of mattering in the world. Other emotions get suppressed, just like anger does among the Utku. There is no tolerance for fear, for example, especially in the face of disrespect. To do nothing in response is to be humiliated. So in gangs, humiliation can become a default frame, a way to instantly interpret any chaos and injustice in the world.

From a young age, then, Curtis was literally surrounded by threats, perceived and real. He saw too much evidence that he did not matter. So Curtis found backup in the gang, and he learned to respond to anything that made him feel small or frightened with overwhelming force.

Billy and Omar were arrested and held in jail almost immediately after the shooting. In response, Jesse Jackson and other leaders called for swifter prosecution of juveniles. "If Benjamin Wilson spent Thanksgiving in the morgue," Jackson said, "at Christmas the killer should be in the penitentiary."

But prison did not feel like anything close to justice, not to Curtis. He had to find a way to stop this pain. Billy and Omar were members of a rival gang, the Gangster Disciples, Curtis knew. Benji's death was personal, not random. They killed Benji because his hat was to the left, Curtis had heard people say. It made a kind of sense. And so it also made sense what he had to do next.

A beloved brother Stone had been killed by a Gangster Disciple. If he couldn't get to Billy and Omar, other Gangster Disciples would suffice. Groups contain multitudes.

"I really didn't know anything about the Disciples except that they wore opposite colors and wore their hats different," Curtis said. "And then people start telling you stories about things that Disciples have done to Stones."

In this way, the Stones cultivated their hatred of the Disciples. The Disciples were ignorant and low-class, the Stones said. "Dirty Folks" is how Stones referred to them. They were low, and the Stones were up high.

"It was embedded in our minds that we were better than the Folks," Curtis said. "There was always this thought of supremacy, that we're better than. And I think that whenever that's in there—a better-than, a less-than—there's always room for war."

If the Disciples were using guns, he needed a gun, too. He had to protect himself, and he had to seek revenge. Soon he was shooting at Disciples on Billy's block, boys he'd been moonwalking with just weeks before.

He doesn't remember feeling any doubt. There was no space for doubt.

What if Benji had been killed by a *Stone*, not a Disciple? That scenario was not hard to imagine. These things happened in the chaos of the streets. But it *was* difficult to imagine how he would have reacted.

"It would have hurt, but I think, in my mind, it would have probably been easier, right?" he said, looking off into the distance. "I think it would have been more introverted. It would've hurt inside. Probably something I would've held to myself, sat in a corner and cried. But I wonder."

Back then, Curtis's friend Jesse reacted to Benji's death a little differently than Curtis. He joined the fight against the Disciples some of the time, but not always. He had mixed feelings.

"Man, this gang shit is okay, but I'm trying to do something different," he'd say. Jesse was a go-getter. He started selling hot dogs in the parking lot of a drugstore not far from Foster Park. It was a profitable business.

Not long after Benji was killed, Jesse was found dead in that parking lot. He'd been beaten to death with a piece of wood with nails sticking out of it.

Something in Curtis shifted when he saw Jesse in that open casket, wearing a wig, looking like a stranger, because his head had been so damaged. It was hard to avoid the conclusion that Jesse's life did not matter. Which meant that Curtis's life did not matter.

Once again, Curtis suffered a sudden, devastating loss. And once again, he had an explanation, one that made a sick kind of sense. The drugstore was Disciples territory. And everyone knew Jesse was a Stone. They'd killed him for being a Stone, just like they'd killed Benji.

Curtis was at war. That's how it felt. Nothing less. Boys could be butchered at any moment, for no good reason, without remorse, because of the group to which they belonged.

And so, as the wrongs accumulated, the gang conflict became more and more necessary to Curtis. The group rivalry provided purpose and order, a coherence where there was none. Things didn't happen for no reason, even when they did.

We all have this tendency, to look for a narrative that makes sense of the world. This is why conspiracy theories take hold. This is why many people were convinced that 9/11 must have been a government conspiracy. That the mass shooting of twenty schoolchildren in Newtown, Connecticut, must have been a hoax. Just like Covid-19. There is a perverse comfort in these falsehoods. Conspiracy theories reassure us that life is not, after all, fragile and chaotic. No, in fact, powerful people are pulling the strings, on purpose. And they must be stopped.

After Jesse's death, Curtis evolved from being an ordinary gang member to a full-fledged gangbanger. He went from being a guy who carried the weapons to a guy who used the weapons. The wrongs piled up, and the lines of causality all seemed to lead back to the Disciples. It felt like the only way, even when it wasn't.

"the telling"

> "The enduring attraction of war is this: Even with its destruction and carnage it can give us what we long for in life. It can give us purpose, meaning, a reason for living."
>
> —Chris Hedges, *War Is a Force That Gives Us Meaning*

Group conflicts are about more than what people say they are about. They are fueled by emotions and biases that make things simple, too simple. In these ways, group conflicts resemble interpersonal conflicts, like Gary's. But group conflicts can last much longer, for two reasons.

First, groups distribute the conflict, spreading it around. In Mark Twain's *Adventures of Huckleberry Finn*, a character named Buck describes a feud that has gripped his family for three decades. "'Well,' says Buck, 'a feud is this way. A man has a quarrel with another man, and kills him; then that other man's brother kills *him*; then the other brothers, on both sides, goes for one another; then the *cousins* chip in—and by-and-by everybody's killed off and there ain't no more feud. But it's kind of slow, and takes a long time.'"

Emotions are more contagious than any virus. You can catch them through stories, without any human contact. And of all the emotions

Children near a protest of a British Army patrol in Derry, Northern Ireland, in August 1972.
© Eamon Melaugh (cain.ulster.ac.uk/melaugh)

people experience in conflict, hatred is one of the hardest to work with. If humiliation is the nuclear bomb of emotions, hatred is the radioactive fallout. That's because hatred assumes the enemy is immutable. If the enemy will always be evil, there is no reason to ever consider any creative solutions to the conflict. The enemy will never change. In that sense, hatred is different from anger: anger holds out the possibility of a better future. The underlying goal of anger is to correct the other person's behavior. The logical outcome of hate is to annihilate.

Hatred prolongs and escalates conflict, and it can motivate people to commit massacres. Here's what one participant told Israeli researcher Eran Halperin when describing her hatred toward Palestinians: "They will never change. They were born unfaithful, and they will die this way. Even after 40 years in the grave, you shouldn't trust an Arab."

Over time, humiliation and hatred accumulate, making it feel impossible to abandon the conflict. The more people invest in a conflict, the harder it is to withdraw, even if it's in their interest. Anyone who defects from the turmoil would also have to betray the group. So group conflicts go on and on because of all the cheerleaders and reinforcements.

This is part of what makes group conflicts so resilient. If you can't find the offender, you can find his child or his friend—or just someone who lives on the same block. The targets are limitless.

The second thing groups do is to speed everything up. Groups let us skip steps, causing conflict to escalate much faster. To identify friend or foe, group members find shortcuts, even if they have to invent them. In Chicago in the 1980s, the Disciples wore Chuck Taylors and scratched out the five-point star on the shoe, since it looked like the pyramid symbol for the Stones. They wore blue and black, while the Stones wore black and red. The Disciples wore their hats and their belt buckles to the *right*, while the Stones, everyone knew, wore their hats and their belt buckles to the *left*. Gang members could even identify each other from their posture. Stones crossed their arms right over left, while the Disciples went left over right.

The Stones wore Polos and penny loafers. They were the preppies, the ones whose grandparents had jobs and owned homes, with grass yards. The Disciples tended to come from low-income housing—or at least that's how Curtis saw it. There was a class divide, albeit a small one: some Disciples were poor, and some Stones were, too, but they didn't think they were. Like most group conflicts, there were real differences and imaginary ones. Both kinds of differences kept the conflict going.

The truth is, these distinctions were totally arbitrary. Had Curtis lived five blocks over, he would have joined the Disciples and tipped his hat to the right. This was impossible for him to imagine, so deeply did he feel his allegiance to the Stones and his hatred for the Disciples. But like most people entangled in group conflicts, whether religious or political or criminal, his fate was swayed by those twin whims, family and geography.

In Northern Ireland, there were 3,600 deaths attributed to the Troubles, as that conflict was known. There, the two sides had to invent ways to tell each other apart, just like the Stones and the Disciples. Protestants largely wanted the union with Great Britain to continue, so they supported the Unionists. Meanwhile, most Catholics supported a united Ireland, separate from Great Britain. They endorsed the Nationalists.

But Unionists and Nationalists looked superficially identical. They celebrated the same holidays and prayed to the same God. But they were easy prey out in the sunshine, just like our ancestors. So, to tell each other apart, people guessed one another's identity based on their names or their sports jerseys. Protestants were more likely to watch typically English sports like soccer and rugby. Catholics tended to follow Gaelic Irish sports like hurling. Someone named William or Victoria was presumed Protestant. Someone named Seamus or Siobhan was assumed to be Catholic.

People also paid obsessive attention to geography. Catholics lived on this block, everyone knew, while Protestants lived on another. The line between real and imaginary differences was fluid. Many said they could tell Catholics or Protestants apart based on the spacing of their eyes, the color of their hair, even how much jewelry they wore. This sorting process came to be known as "telling."

In Foster Park in the early 1980s, there were two blocks where a lot of families affiliated with the Gangster Disciples lived. That is where Curtis channeled his rage after Benji and Jesse were killed. Those two blocks became a battlefield.

Even in less violent group conflicts, people engage in "telling." Most Democrats are White, middle-class, and heterosexual. Most Republicans are White, middle-class, and heterosexual, too. So what then? Americans now guess each other's partisan leanings based on what they eat, drive, and drink. People who go to Starbucks or Chipotle are assumed to be Democrats; people who frequent Dunkin' Donuts or Chick-fil-A are presumed Republicans. And based on these unreliable cues, surveyed Americans say they'd be more or less likely to want to live, work, or hang out with one another.

As with gang conflicts and most other feuds, political preferences are more arbitrary than we think. The vast majority of Americans did not "choose" their political persuasion. They followed the political persuasion of their parents. They are not making rational choices about politics based on years of study of all their options—no more than they've studied all religions before choosing one (or none). It's often a matter of chance, but it doesn't feel that way.

It may seem silly to compare Northern Ireland with the United States, or gang warfare with political polarization. But something significant happens when groups assign meaning to superficial cues. The enemy is caricatured. It is easier to dismiss and demean a cartoon villain. In conflict, you feel some contempt for a caricature, and, in peacetime, you might just avoid discussing politics with them. All of which perpetuates the conflict by preventing us from knowing one another for who we actually are. And if violence were to break out tomorrow between Democrats and Republicans in an American town, cues like coffee cups and sandwich wrappers could become a matter of life or death. Like a hat turned to the left.

revenge works

After Benji and Jesse died, Curtis didn't dance much. His identities got reshuffled, leaving less and less space for him to maneuver. He was a Stone, most of all, and that blocked out other parts of his personality: "It was hard being a tough guy and dancing. They're like opposites."

Besides, by the mid-1980s, house music was the new big thing, not popping and locking. This new electronic dance music was created in the underground clubs of Chicago. And the city's most famous house DJs and nightclubs were gay, and Curtis couldn't have anything to do with that.

The gang taught Curtis that real men were supposed to be aggressive, with a hair-trigger temper. The gang set the bar for what counted as humiliating, and it was breathtakingly low. Never allow disrespect, or else it will never stop. When kids made fun of him for dancing, he stopped popping and locking at Foster Park. Then he stopped dancing anywhere. He got a tattoo of a pyramid, the gang's symbol, on his chest. He let go of whatever didn't fit the gang's definition of a man.

In eighth grade, a girl called Curtis "gay." When he heard about it, he went looking for her. He found her in her classroom and slapped her across the face hard, in front of everyone. He got suspended for that, but he hadn't felt like he had a choice. His friends said Curtis had an Incredible Hulk switch. He'd be friendly and calm and then, *Bam*, he'd just start inflicting harm on people.

Revenge is a way to escape the pain of humiliation. It is rational, at least in the short term. It may lead to more loss eventually, but for a brief period, revenge works. It can rebalance the equation.

Rather than marinating in the pointlessness of it all—the slow-motion tragedy of life in a neighborhood with 40 percent unemployment, corrupt politicians, untrustworthy police, and broken schools—Curtis became part of something bigger than himself. He was a Stone.

Violent conflict gives people a sense of meaning that they don't want to lose. The hotter it gets, the more essential it feels. Fire starters accelerate this process. Conflict entrepreneurs encourage people to find the meaning in conflict, and it's not hard to do. By framing events as "humiliating," they detonate the nuclear bomb of emotion.

After the 9/11 terrorist attacks in the United States, Osama bin Laden released this statement: "What America is tasting now is something insignificant compared to what we have tasted for scores of years. Our nation [the Islamic world] has been tasting this humiliation and this degradation for more than 80 years. Its sons are killed, its blood is shed, its sanctuaries are attacked, and no one hears and no one heeds."

After the fall of communism in Eastern Europe and the bloody suppression of protests in Tiananmen Square, the Chinese government needed to find ways to regain public support, particularly among young people. In 1991, the government launched an education campaign designed to highlight China's collective victimhood at the hands of Japanese and Western imperialists, going back to the mid-1800s. The campaign funded memorial sites and required all teachers, soldiers, and state employees to take regular classes in patriotic education. In 2004, it recommended three hundred films, books, and songs designed to boost patriotism, including one book titled *Never Forget Our National Humiliation.*

Conflict entrepreneurs draw on absolutist rhetoric, sweeping language that tends to make people more attached to conflict and less flexible. In a smaller way, this is what Gary's adviser, Tanya, did in Muir Beach. She described his battle against the Old Guard in the same grandiose language she uses in her labor organizing work. "In my world," Tanya told me over dinner near Muir Beach, "there are two sides, and it's a war."

She compared the Old Guard to Trump and the New Guard to Obama three times in our conversation. She talked about the "good people" and the "bad people" in the neighborhood. And she sounded ready to go to war all over again, a full two years after Gary had lost power on the board. "Part of me feels like we should just run a team and kick them out," she said, "just to prove we can."

This language sounds like satire, as I write it here. Who would talk this way about a neighborhood election? But in person, Tanya was very compelling. Her conviction was so powerful, so competent, like a force that lit her up from the inside. It was hard to resist.

It reminded me of another time someone pulled me close and insisted we were at war. I was a reporter at *Time* covering homeland security, talking to Michael Chertoff, the then-secretary of homeland security. We were speeding through D.C. in his chauffeur-driven black car, and he was uninterested in answering the questions I wanted to ask him. It was more than five years after 9/11, and he seemed worried. He had something he wanted me to know about terrorism. "This is a war," he kept telling me, even though I hadn't asked.

I had covered 9/11 in Manhattan, where my husband and I were living at the time. I remember the sound of fighter jets arcing across the sky, the sight of thousands of dust-covered Americans walking uptown, away from the rubble, the bitter stench that hung in the air for weeks afterward. I spent years covering those attacks and others, listening to the stories of victims and survivors. I wrote a book about what they told me. So terrorism was not abstract to me. I understood the stakes.

But that day in the black car, when I mentioned that a lot of terrorism experts advised treating terrorists like a criminal network, given how they operate (compared to nation-states in times of war), he rejected that language out of hand. Terrorism was nothing like crime, he said. Terrorism was an "existential threat." It seemed very important to him, to his department, and maybe to his budget to frame it this way.

This language made a lot more sense coming from Chertoff than from Tanya, admittedly. But I've learned to pause when someone uses the language of war (absent an actual, honest-to-God war, of course) and ask myself that question again: *Who does this serve?* Grandiose language is one way conflict entrepreneurs manipulate our emotions. It clarifies everything, washing away important details, energizing us to fight, to sacrifice, to ignore the costs.

In Paris in 2015, three weeks after a series of ISIS attacks had killed more than a hundred people, psychologist Daniel Rovenpor and his colleagues asked a large group of Parisians to read an article about the French government's plans to prevent future attacks. One version framed these actions as "calculated" and "measured," while the other described the same countermeasures in loftier language, such as "more powerful than expected" and "total war." The Parisians who read the more dramatic language were more likely to say they found meaning in the conflict compared to the ones who read the more restrained content. They were also more likely to agree to statements like, "Because of the recent acts of terror, I now have a greater sense of purpose in life."

The pursuit of revenge can bond us together, in our own groups, delivering a sense of exhilaration and mission. Conflict entrepreneurs understand this, and so they talk about conflict like it is a religion unto itself, a way to make sense of the world and our place in it, a sacred flame that must never be extinguished.

Revenge can stanch the pain of humiliation, but it exacts a punishing cost. It requires total devotion, the kind that eventually becomes a sort of prison. Wherever he went, Curtis learned to scan the street, up and down, to see who was coming, which cars were slowing down for no reason. He tried to be the last person to leave a room, so his back was never turned on anyone. He took different routes home from school.

Eventually, families with Disciple members had to move away from Foster Park. The neighborhood became less forgiving. There were whole blocks where Curtis couldn't go. When he was about twelve years old, he got shot twice—once in the foot and once in the side. And who do you think shot him? It was those Disciples, of course.

murder city

Since the Cold War ended, wars of all kind have declined dramatically. And the wars that do happen tend to kill fewer people than in the past.

Why is this? Partly, humans have gotten better at preventing wars and keeping the peace. We've come to rely more on third parties like the United Nations and other groups to help facilitate peace deals and monitor compliance afterward. These institutions are designed, however imperfectly, to activate our cooperative instincts, not our adversarial ones. Like the Bahá'í elections, where no one is allowed to campaign, they have a lot of built-in guardrails to prevent high conflict.

These institutions often fail. As a species, humans are in our infancy when it comes to creating mutualistic cooperatives like this, and we have a long way to go. But there's no denying that wars and violent death generally have become rarer over time, thankfully.

Today, about eight of every ten violent deaths happen *outside* of recognized conflict zones, in places like Chicago. In 2015, more people were killed in Brazil, which was not "at war," than in Syria, which was. This kind of grinding violence looks, in many places, like the kind of gang clashes and everyday brutality Curtis encountered growing up in Chicago. In other places, it features paramilitary killings and organized crime.

If we've gotten better at preventing wars in some places, we've got a long way to go to contain this kind of chronic nonwar violence all around the world. For example, why was Chicago so much more violent in 2018 than, say, Los Angeles or New York City? Why was St. Louis, Missouri, located just three hundred miles from Chicago, almost *three times* deadlier than Chicago? In 2018, St. Louis had a higher murder rate than Cali, Colombia; Chihuahua, Mexico; or Guatemala City.

For centuries, scholars have tried to figure out what predicts endemic violence. Is it a function of poverty or culture? Is it about the competition for resources? Or the number of rival groups?

The existence of groups, ethnic or religious, does not seem to make a country more prone to civil war. There are some very diverse places that are also extraordinarily peaceful. Amsterdam, for example, is home to some 180 different nationalities. One in every two residents is a first- or second-generation immigrant. But in 2018, only fourteen people were killed in Amsterdam. *Fourteen people.* More than ten times as many people were murdered that year in my home base of Washington, D.C., a slightly smaller city.

What about access to guns? Yes, to a degree. It's harder to kill large numbers of people without high-powered weaponry. Americans possess almost half of the world's civilian-owned guns, despite representing less than 5 percent of the world's population. As you might expect, the United States also has a homicide rate 50 percent above the average for developed countries.

If groups can make it easier for conflict to escalate, guns can make it easier for conflicts to end in murder. But like other complex social problems, violent conflict depends on the interaction of many different things, like a chemical equation. Guns matter, and so do other things. It's the combination that's poisonous.

What about a weak police force or government? When governments falter or fail, violence fills the void. And that makes sense. But what causes a state to be weak? It's not simply a matter of a failing economy; for the most part, violent crime does not rise or fall in lockstep with GDP.

The most vexing problem, particularly for democracies, seems to be a *complicit* state, as foreign policy scholar Rachel Kleinfeld found. In Pakistan, for example, the intelligence service has given money, and sometimes weaponry, to radical Islamist groups to use against various political opponents. The government does this while simultaneously pointing to the threat of radical Islamists to justify its own budget. The corruption metastasizes.

Regular people learn that they cannot rely on the government, and so they seek justice in other ways. Violence becomes normalized. Societies become decivilized. "Ordinary people become impulsive, quicker to anger, more ready to see violence as normal," Kleinfeld wrote. At that point, it becomes much harder for governments to restore order. The state creates a monster, and it takes over.

In Chicago, the first gangs were White gangs, run out of volunteer fire departments. When professionals took over the firefighting in Chicago, the gangs shifted into neighborhood taverns, where politicians started sponsoring them. In the late nineteenth century, these politicians created "athletic clubs," groups of largely Irish immigrants who intimidated voters and stuffed ballot boxes to ensure their bosses' reelection. Over the next fifty years, the gangs enforced racial segregation, too. Chicago politicians enacted restrictive racial covenants that prohibited Black people from buying or renting properties in White areas, and whatever the laws could not accomplish, the gangs did. They attacked African Americans who voted against the Democratic machine that dominated Chicago politics, and they deployed violence and fear to make sure Black families stayed out of White neighborhoods.

Politicians outsourced the dirty work they wanted done, in order to preserve their power. The state was complicit in the violence in Chicago back then, just as it is in Pakistan today. It's not a coincidence that mob boss Al Capone made his career in Chicago, running a multimillion-dollar bootlegging, prostitution, and gambling operation there in the 1920s. Around this time, Chicago earned the nickname "Murder City," with a homicide rate twenty-four times the national urban average.

Well after political machines had lost their hold over other American cities, Mayor Richard J. Daley continued to rule Chicago like a feudal lord. From 1955 to 1976, Daley controlled some 35,000 patronage jobs, which he used to demand loyalty from Democrats and render Republicans irrelevant.

Since Curtis's birth, three dozen aldermen have been convicted on corruption charges in Chicago. That's nearly one in every five members of the City Council over that period. More people have been convicted on federal political corruption charges in Chicago than in any other sizable U.S. city. The stories of kickbacks and bribery schemes follow a sickening rhythm. One of the only American judges ever convicted of fixing murder cases was from Chicago—convicted of fixing three murder cases involving gang conflicts.

Today, Chicago is not comparable to Pakistan. But the history of government-sponsored violence and the continuing tradition of corruption at the state and city level perpetuate the spirals of violence. Much has changed, but not nearly enough. It is impossible to understand the bloodshed in the streets of Chicago today without understanding this understory.

Each homicide costs the city of Chicago about $1.5 million. But most killings go unsolved. If you murder a White person in Chicago, you have about a 50 percent chance of getting away with it. If you murder a Black person, you have a 78 percent chance of getting away with it, Chicago public radio station WBEZ found in 2019. The police are not trusted, and neither is the city or state government. (Illinois ranks last in the nation when it comes to trust in state government.) So violent groups step in and exact a kind of justice where there is none.

The worst violence in Chicago today is clustered in just a handful of neighborhoods. In these places, groups speed up confrontations and perpetuate blood feuds, making them as dangerous as the most unstable countries in the world. Most of this violence has nothing to do with drug markets. It starts instead with personal beefs that escalate into vendettas, flaring up on social media and exploding in real-life gun battles.

One of these neighborhoods is the neighborhood surrounding Foster Park, where Curtis grew up.

"a lovely surging"

"Violence helps the individual to escape the irrelevance of his existence, fills the emptiness of his life and provides him with the heady experience of power over himself and over others."

—Alison Jamieson, *The Heart Attacked: Terrorism and Conflict in the Italian State*

Curtis had been close to his mom his whole life. Around the time he became a Stone, though, his mother married a new man, a huge man who had a cocaine and heroin habit.

So Curtis took up a new hobby, one that fit into his new identity in a way that dancing did not. He got a weight set and put it in the kitchen, getting bigger and stronger day by day. He needed to defend himself and his mom from the monster in her bedroom.

Curtis also started playing football, and he was good. His family talked about college and pro ball and who knows what might happen. Football kept him steady, kept him going to practice each day, leaving fewer hours for gangbanging. Curtis was chosen to be salutatorian for his eighth-grade graduation, and he tested into a magnet high school for science and technology. There was still more to his life than the gang.

But right before the graduation ceremony, a Disciple caught him out of his neighborhood with his hat to the left. The Disciple beat Curtis with a baseball bat. He woke up in an ambulance. He didn't do the graduation speech, because of his concussion. He had trouble getting his graduation cap to fit on his head, over the swelling.

Then, in high school, Curtis was in the backseat of a friend's car when they drove into a light pole. Curtis tore his ACL, and that was the end of his football career.

What hurt Curtis the most was the look in his mother's eyes. It was more than just disappointment; it looked, to him at least, like disgust. Her son the dancer was no longer dancing; her son the football player was no longer playing football. He had been their ticket, and he'd thrown it away. His football coach came to the house to give him his highlight reel, for a keepsake.

If there was a way out for him and his family, he didn't know what it might be. This narrowing is how conflict becomes intractable, leaving less and less space to maneuver. Some days, it seemed like all he had left was the conflict with the Disciples. That never ended.

In March 1989, when he was seventeen, Curtis found his mother's body in an alley. She'd been stabbed in the heart by his stepdad. After killing her, his stepdad had taken her wallet and used the money to buy drugs.

Curtis had not been able to save her. Even though he'd lifted weights. Even though he'd found a backup army in his gang. Even though he'd warned his mother to take a gun with her that night. He'd failed to prevent the thing he'd feared most. Never mind that he was on crutches at the time, still healing from the car accident. He'd cast himself as her protector, and now he'd lost his closest confidant, his dance partner. He was broken and alone.

What Curtis wanted then was to kill the man who did this. He wanted to do it slowly, painfully. He had to find a way to ease the pain he felt. Revenge was the only way to equalize the injustice, according to everything he'd learned as a boy in Chicago and as a Stone. A man could not rely on the authorities to do what must be done. So he called on his brother Stones to help him.

Together, they went to the home of his stepdad's family. Still on crutches, his gang members at his side, Curtis banged on the door. No one answered. He kicked the door with his one good leg. Finally, someone answered and insisted his stepdad wasn't there. He didn't believe it.

Curtis had brought a Molotov cocktail to throw through the window, to light the place up. That would send everyone running. He went to the car to get it. He'd used a Wild Irish Rose wine bottle. But before he could throw it, one of the Stones stopped him. "We came for him, not for the family," his friend said, and Curtis backed down. It was a fleeting example of the second paradox of high conflict. Just as groups can incite violence, they can suppress it.

Four days later, Curtis's stepdad was arrested. He was charged with first degree murder and sentenced to thirty-nine years in prison.

But no counselor showed up at Curtis's door. He had his grandmother, but she was overwhelmed with raising his little siblings, and with her own grief. Most of these days, his family was just the Stones.

Violence came more easily after that. Each time Curtis pulled the trigger, he literally saw his stepdad's face. It made hurting people satisfying. The conflict with the Disciples became a war by proxy, or what psychologists call displacement. He couldn't take a gun to the broken institutions of Chicago. He couldn't kill his stepdad nor the boy who shot Benji, his basketball hero. None of the actual causes of his suffering were in his sight. This did not stop him from fighting, however. Instead, it propelled him.

"There is a sense of being in anger," Toni Morrison wrote in *The Bluest Eye*, "A reality and presence. An awareness of worth. It is a lovely surging." Having power over someone, even the wrong someone, still feels like something.

That October, the feds raided the gang's Temple in the middle of Friday prayers. Over fifty federal agents surrounded the place, breaking down the doors with sledgehammers and blowtorches. They rounded up much of the gang's upper hierarchy, indicting sixty-five of the members on racketeering, murder, kidnapping, firearm, drug, and other charges. By then, Jeff Fort, the founder of the Stones, was himself locked up, having been convicted on elaborate domestic terrorism charges.

All these arrests created a leadership vacuum, and so Curtis rose through the ranks, skipping entire rungs of the ladder, becoming a leader at a time when he himself desperately needed to be led.

Curtis became the muscle for his family, too. He wasn't going to let his younger siblings or any of his relatives die the way his mother had died. His family members learned to call him whenever they had a problem, and he'd send a battalion.

"What was crazy was being young and starting to have adults being afraid of you," Curtis said. "Being able to have some power when you are feeling powerless."

One day, he went to visit his girlfriend at her job at McDonald's. He walked in and scanned the place, like he always did, looking for threats. The guy working the fryer had his hat to the right. Curtis took one look at him and went to the manager. That guy had to go, he told him. He couldn't have a Disciple working there, right next to his girl. No way.

When he came back later, the Disciple was still there, with his hat to the right. Curtis couldn't believe it. That hat felt like a taunt, right in his face. So what else could he do? Curtis and his friend vaulted over the counter and started beating on the manager. It was a rush, seeing a grown man cowering before them.

One day, his grandmother came home from a community policing meeting and started crying. "The whole meeting was about you," she told Curtis, "you and your friends are destroying the community." He would never forget that moment, watching his grandmother, one of the strongest people he knew, weeping. "You're my grandson, but they're talking about you like you're an animal."

There were days when it felt like the Hulk was taking over, and he could barely remember that back-flipping boy he used to be. It was scary sometimes, what came over him. That's why Curtis didn't drink or do drugs. He didn't want to feel more out of control than he already did.

One month after his mother's death, Curtis and other gang members beat a man with a broken bottle. They hurt him so badly that the guy ended up paralyzed.

Not long afterward, Curtis was shot again. This time in the head. He'd been in a dispute with a Vice Lord, but he and the guy settled it with a conversation on the street. Seconds later, another Vice Lord shot Curtis, not knowing the conflict had ended. Groups contain multitudes.

Curtis lay on his porch, unable to speak, and heard a police officer say they could write him off. It was a miracle he didn't die right then.

He graduated, somehow, but three months after he turned nineteen, he was arrested four blocks from Foster Park carrying a loaded Smith & Wesson .357 caliber revolver. A woman had called the police, claiming Curtis had come to her house and threatened to kill her relative. Curtis pleaded guilty and was sentenced to two and a half years in prison. Because of his gang influence, he was sent to Stateville Correctional Center, a maximum security prison.

Maybe, he thought, he'd find Benji's killer in prison. Or his stepdad. That was something to hope for.

hypnotized

You might be reading this and thinking, I'm not part of a gang or a blood feud. Not yet anyway. What does this have to do with political polarization? Or the fight I had with my brother last year at Christmas?

Curtis's story is an extreme case. But it's through the extremes that we can see the contours of the commonplace more easily. We don't all live in a world in which violence is normalized and encouraged, luckily for us. But many of us know what it feels like to be stuck in some kind of Tar Pit, in a dispute that takes more than it gives. It might be a conflict with a spouse or a coworker or someone you don't even know. But the feeling is similar. You might have imaginary conversations with this person. Whenever your anger fades, you catch yourself actively reviving the feeling, inexplicably stoking the fire, reminding yourself of all the reasons you have to feel wronged—and maybe even discovering new ones.

Groups do this *for* you. As soon as you get distracted by some other part of your life, groups remind you of the conflict. Other group members continuously catalogue all the wrongs you've experienced, never letting the fire go out. It happens on talk radio and on Twitter. The group immortalizes the conflict, like an eternal flame, never untended.

It also happens in prison, of course. When he got there, Curtis did not find Benji's killer or his stepdad. But he did find the ideology that kept his group going. In prison, he learned what the Stones were really about. One of Jeff Fort's brothers was in the same facility, along with other high-ranking gang leaders. There was a command structure, a way of doing things right. "It was a kind of respect I'd never seen before." Everyone prayed at a certain time. Islam was a way of life, not just talk. If you got an order to do something, you did it, no questions asked. It was like *The Godfather* in there, and Curtis was impressed.

He read and memorized the Stones' constitution, bylaws, and pledge. He spent hours talking to the older Stone generals, listening to their stories. He was capable of great discipline and dedication, and so were these Stones. "Anything I've ever been part of," he said, "I always go deep." A big laugh.

The Stones were outnumbered by the Disciples in prison, but it seemed like they never lost a fight. Whatever they lacked in manpower they made up for in organization and devotion. It was something to see. So now Curtis found a spiritual scaffolding to go with his gang identity, a way to manage his pain that was bigger than petty feuds at McDonald's. He was like a soldier discovering an elite unit of the Special Forces. There was something more out there, and he became part of it.

To this day, Curtis can recite the Stones' Creed from memory, without pausing to think:

> *Out of the darkness into the light,*
> *Blackstone give us courage,*
> *Blackstone give us sight,*
> *Blackstone give us something that no man should be deprived of,*
> *A happiness called Stone Love . . .*

Ideology is not as important to group conflict as emotion. But ideology matters. It can justify violence, just like grandiose language, providing a deeper sense of purpose than the conflict might have without it. Ideology can make people feel they are part of something bigger.

In 1993, Curtis left prison with more responsibility and conviction than he'd had going in. By then, Chicago had changed, too. Crack had finally made its way into the neighborhoods, and there were huge sums of money to be made. The city's homicide rate peaked soon afterward, due in part to the spike in violence between the Stones and the Disciples.

"It was bodies dropping all over the place," Curtis said. He started traveling around Chicago with security, armed men who formed a perimeter around him wherever he went. Just like Jeff Fort, the Stones' founder, who was by then in prison for life.

Curtis made money, more money than he'd ever seen. He bought cars. He started a strip club. He knew these things were in direct conflict with Islam and the values the Stones had claimed to endorse, but he did it anyway. He still went to Friday prayers, didn't he? It's easy to ignore hypocrisy when you have an enemy.

A year later, at age twenty-two, Curtis was again charged with possessing a gun. He was sentenced to prison for three and a half years.

After he got out, he got arrested again—this time for possessing cocaine. He ended up getting lucky, and the charge got dropped. But in jail, he had enough time and space to ask himself, *How did the police know where I would be on that day?* Only his brother Stones could have known. He wondered, not for the last time, if their loyalties were to the Stones or to the dollar. It was getting hard to tell.

part II

out of conflict

Airplane flying over Chicago's South Side in 1999. Chicago History Museum, ICHi-174009; Ron Gordon, photographer

chapter 4

buying time

As he got older, Curtis got better at staying out of prison. He studied the law and the minefields of the so-called "War on Drugs." The law punished crack possession much more harshly than cocaine. So Curtis never carried crack. If he got caught with five kilos of raw cocaine, he knew he was facing about ten years, far less than he'd get for the same amount of crack. He resigned himself to doing the ten years, if need be.

Curtis got accustomed to a feeling of heaviness that came over him every so often, especially on Mother's Day and his mom's birthday. He still fantasized about finding his stepdad and Billy, the boy who had killed his basketball hero, but he got better at controlling the Hulk switch in his head. He got married to his lifelong girlfriend, the one who had worked at the McDonald's, all those years ago. He had four kids. He withdrew from some of the more violent obligations of gang life. Other people took those risks, younger people. Years went by, and it seemed to Curtis, in his early thirties by then, like he would spend the rest of his life watching over his shoulder—or in prison.

Then something unexpected happened at his son's fourth-grade graduation. Curtis was, at the time, expecting to go back to prison any day. The feds were targeting gang leaders in Chicago, and people all around him were getting locked up. He knew it was just a matter of time.

On that day, though, his son stood up with his classmates and sang that old *Chicago* song, "You're the Inspiration." It was a cliché, and Curtis knew it. But for some reason, as he stood there, watching his son sing, the song felt like a knife to his heart.

Curtis's son was autistic, and Curtis felt sure he knew the reason: he'd been violent toward the boy's mother when she was pregnant. Then, after the baby was born, Curtis had driven around with his son in the back of the car when he'd gone out shooting rivals—or getting shot at by them. No wonder the boy was terrified of loud noises. The fault lines were not hard to find, Curtis thought, and they all led back to him, the father and the gang leader.

> *You're the meaning in my life*
> *You're the inspiration*

As he listened, he did the math. If the feds nabbed him today, his son would be eighteen when Curtis got out of prison. And right then, it was as if the lies he had told himself about Benji Wilson's murder, his life with the Stones, the need to meet every affront with violence, just collapsed in on themselves.

The biggest lie was that he was doing what he did for his family. To provide and protect. He just couldn't buy that line anymore. If he was selling drugs for his family, why did he have four cars? Was it helpful to his family if he disappeared into a cage for a decade?

Oh fuck, he thought. Sitting there, tears streaming down his face, he offered up a foxhole prayer he'd said many times before. *God, just give me one more chance*...His wife looked over at him and did a double take. Was he *crying*? Curtis was not a man who cried in public. Or in private. He was the guy who had beaten up her boss at McDonald's because of some dude's hat. Who was this guy?

He didn't explain himself to her, though. That was not something he knew how to do back then.

Afterward, Curtis tried to return to normal. He picked up a shipment of drugs to sell, like usual. But this time, driving away with the drugs in the car, it felt different. There was no thrill, no sense of power and purpose. It was just depressing. He knew he had to bag the drugs and distribute them, just like he'd always done, but it seemed pointless. "Why am I doing this?" he kept asking himself. He had no good answers anymore.

When he got home, he did nothing. He just left the stash there, untouched, for a week. Something he'd never done before. His cousin called and called, but Curtis didn't answer. It was like his mind knew what to do but his body wouldn't comply. Finally, his cousin showed up and demanded he hand over the drugs, which he did. He also gave his cousin one of his cars, a Chrysler, so he could sell it and use the money to hire someone to do the tasks Curtis was supposed to do.

This is what's known as a saturation point—the point where the losses of a conflict finally seem heavier than the gains. Curtis had hit bottom, a critical moment for anyone who shifts out of high conflict. Sitting there, surrounded by drugs he didn't have the energy to bag, his mindset was not so different from that of so many other people who finally have had enough. Divorcing spouses who call up their lawyers and tell them to make a deal. Senators who announce they will not run for reelection. Guerrilla fighters who quietly walk away from their unit and never come back.

About six months later, Curtis called his cousin.

"I'm done. You can have everything."

Silence. His cousin was waiting, Curtis realized, for the code word. The one they'd agreed to use should he ever get caught, so his cousin knew to get rid of everything—the drugs, the money, the guns. But Curtis didn't say the code word. Not that day and not ever. He didn't say anything.

The silence stretched out uncomfortably.

Finally, his cousin broke it. "What's up, cuz? They got you?"

"No."

More silence.

There was only one other explanation. "Muthafucker, you tryin' to set me up!" his cousin yelled.

"No, come on," Curtis said, irritated now. "I'm just done."

He gave his cousin a large sum of cash and some narcotics. He also gave away the strip club he owned. He felt lighter, at first. Like he could breathe. He had taken this nest of lies off his back, and now he could stand up straight, be his own man. "Even if I get locked up, I'm okay," he told himself. "And I can face my son, even if I'm incarcerated."

"I stopped."

saturation point

High conflicts happen everywhere, often under different names. On the Philippine island of Mindanao, they are known as *rido*. Usually, rido start with a misunderstanding, just like gang conflicts. A cow is found wandering on a man's land, damaging his crops. So the man sells the cow. The animal's owner, thinking the man had stolen his cow, seeks revenge. Clan loyalties turn a dispute into a full-on feud. Soon two men are shot.

Rumors can kill. A slight becomes an affront to the dignity of the whole group. Often, rido intensify around election cycles. Like in Chicago, these feuds guarantee a baseline level of misery for everyone involved.

That misery is the great weakness of high conflict, a vulnerability that can be exploited. "Life with rido is being a prisoner in your house," as one former combatant puts it, sounding exactly like a gang member in Chicago today. "You cannot work, you cannot go out of your house, you cannot help anybody, because you are afraid your enemy may kill you."

Misery creates a saturation point. And a saturation point is a golden hour of opportunity. With gang members, it might happen in the hospital, after you've been shot—especially if none of your fellow gang members come to visit you. Or it might happen if your son sings a song on a day you're expecting to get arrested. But the saturation point must be recognized and seized, or it will pass. This is how other people can be so catalytic, by helping combatants identify a saturation point.

In the Philippines, rido do not get resolved in the formal justice system, generally speaking. Usually, other group members help people see a saturation point. Women play a key role. They are often spared from retaliatory attacks, so they can act as "shields" and try to initiate talks. Then elders and other clan leaders work through their networks to repair the damage, often through payments of blood money as compensation. In this way, women and elders can slow down the conflict and create an opening where there was none.

People who act as shields are all around us. They have enormous power. In 1809, a friend of both John Adams and Thomas Jefferson began to quietly scheme to get them to start speaking again. Ever so gently, over the course of years, Benjamin Rush, a fellow signer of the Declaration of Independence, conjured a saturation point for both men. He told them each that the other was keen to reconnect.

He even told Adams that he'd had a dream in which the two men were reunited after Adams had written to Jefferson. Was Rush telling the truth? We don't know. But when he told Adams about his dream, he even shared the precise words Adams had used in the so-called letter he'd sent Jefferson in the dream, giving Adams a script to use in real life. He created a path out of high conflict with this dream story. And because he knew his friend so well, Rush made sure to compliment him when he did it. Only a man like Adams, who possessed "a magnanimity known only to great minds," would be capable of such a gracious gesture.

It seems too obvious by half. But it worked.

On New Year's Day in 1812, Adams wrote a note to Jefferson. It was just as Rush had prophesied in his dream. Jefferson wrote back. Over the next fourteen years, the two men exchanged 158 letters. "You and I ought not to die," Adams wrote, "before we have explained ourselves to each other." They didn't always agree, but they remained in good conflict, and out of high conflict, until they both died—on the same day—on July 4, 1826, the fiftieth anniversary of America's independence.

"people had grown to love my impostor"

One problem with withdrawing from a high conflict is that nothing else changes. Your enemies still think of you as an enemy. Your friends still think of you as who you were, not who you want to be.

For the first six months or so, Curtis tried to leave "the job" but hold on to his identity as a Stone. Most especially, he tried to maintain his lifestyle, which cost $9,426 a month. Soon, reality set in. The cars started getting repossessed. He couldn't be a gang leader and not participate in the drug market, and he couldn't participate in the drug market without doing violence.

So he let the cars go. He moved to an apartment across town, one of the best decisions he made. If people couldn't find him, they couldn't ask him for money—or for backup, when they needed the Hulk to appear. In this way, he created space for himself, literal space in which to build a new identity. This turns out to be essential.

But he still hung out in Foster Park, still socialized with the family and friends he loved. The temptations were constant. He missed the feeling of his pager going off, the sense that he was part of something important.

Finding a respectable job, meanwhile, was like trying to win the lottery. Curtis had a long arrest record and was known to the police for his gang activity. He had no work experience outside of his gang leadership, no story to tell that employers might want to hear.

Other people missed the old Curtis, too. They did not know this new Curtis, and it seemed like they did not particularly want to know him. "People had grown to love my impostor," Curtis said.

He and his wife had been together since they were teenagers. They knew one version of each other deeply. But when Curtis began what he calls his "transformation," his wife didn't recognize him anymore. Who was this man, crying when Oprah gave away cars on TV? Talking about "peace" all the time? What happened to the brawler she'd fallen in love with?

Just when he started doing right in his life, his wife was talking about leaving him. He was terrified. He'd lost so many people, either to death or prison. But no one he'd loved had left him by choice, like this. Her reaction confirmed his greatest fear, the fear of most people who try to exit high conflict: that his only value was his old self, his conflict self, and that without it, he was worthless.

One day, at his lowest point, his cousin drove up in a new Mercedes-Benz S550, a sumptuous vehicle that cost close to a hundred thousand dollars. His cousin opened up the trunk, which was full of narcotics.

"Man, you know it ain't the same without you, cuz. I need you, man."

Curtis stood there, staring in the trunk. It was like his cousin had just tossed him the Cyberball. He was back in the game. It felt good to feel needed. If he did just a ninety-day comeback, he calculated, he could pay off his bills, get his life back in order, fix his marriage. He could stop letting everyone down, for a little while.

vacillation

Most people who try to leave high conflict vacillate between their old lives and their still-in-progress future selves, sometimes for years. The path out of high conflict is not linear, even in politics.

Radio and TV personality Glenn Beck was a quintessential conflict entrepreneur in U.S. politics. He spent a decade aggressively promoting partisan conflict on Fox News, CNN, and his own subscription TV network. Like other conflict entrepreneurs, he trafficked in grandiose analogies and conspiracy theories that gave his audience a sense of righteous moral clarity. In his first fourteen months on Fox News, Beck and his guests alluded to Hitler 115 times, Nazis 134 times, fascism 172 times, the Holocaust 58 times, and Joseph Goebbels 8 times. Beck knew how to exploit the fear of his mostly White audience, telling them that then-President Barack Obama was a racist with a "deep-seated hatred for White people." Through his unique brand of paranoia, outrage, and hysteria, he drew millions of viewers to a bonfire of rage.

Then Beck started acting strangely, beginning in about 2014. In interviews, he began voicing regret, revealing an ambiguity and nuance that he'd rarely shown before. "I wish I could go back and be more uniting in my language," Beck said on national TV. "I think I played a role, unfortunately, in helping tear the country apart, and it's not who we are."

It's hard to believe anything Beck says, given his history of exploiting conflict for his own ends. And yet, Beck's behavior didn't make sense if it was disingenuous. It was against his interests in so many ways. In the run-up to the 2016 election, Beck broke with his fellow Republicans and most of his audience members to oppose the candidacy of Donald Trump, whom he called "dangerously unhinged." Countering Trump's incendiary rhetoric on immigration, Beck went to the U.S. border with Mexico and handed out $2 million in toys and food, enraging many of his longtime followers. He invited several Black Lives Matter activists to his studio for a conversation. "There are things unique to the African-American experience that I cannot relate to," he told *The New Yorker*. "I had to listen to them."

As the country became more and more polarized, Beck warned left-wing media personalities like comedian and commentator Samantha Bee not to fall into the same conflict trap that had held him in thrall. "As a guy who has done damage, I don't want to do any more damage," he said in a surreal appearance on Bee's show. "I know what I did. I helped divide. I'm willing to take that. My message to you is, please don't make the mistakes that I made. And I think all of us are doing it. We're doing it on Facebook, we're doing it on Twitter."

These were uncomfortable statements for Beck to make. He was a founding father of America's modern conflict-industrial complex. His media empire was built on demonization and fear, which made it extremely hard for him to pivot. He actually admitted as much in a podcast interview with Krista Tippett: "And it's not reasonable to ask people just—'Well, then throw away your career and just stop doing that.' But that's not reasonable. I have three hundred employees that count on me getting up every single day," he said. "Now, how do I change? How do I make this work so I don't flush the jobs of three hundred people?"

Three months after making that comment, Beck had to lay off about 20 percent of his employees at Mercury Radio Arts and The-Blaze. His opposition to Trump had cost him many viewers, he knew. "Loyalty is very important to the conservative mindset."

The old fire starter kept coming back to life. Just three months after saying he wished he could be more "uniting" in his language, Beck called Obama a "full-fledged dictator" and a "sociopath."

Whatever else was going on in Beck's mind, it was pretty clear that he was wrestling with his identity, his group, and his business model. He wanted to get his audience passionate about new causes, other than hating Obama. He was interested in fighting human trafficking and the exploitation of children, for example. But he could not figure out how. "My audience—I can't find a way to make that palpable or not even—safe enough for people to watch it." Like Gary in his community board meetings, Beck was trying to play a new game—while trapped in the old one.

In 2018, he donned a Make America Great Again hat on TV to

announce he'd changed his mind and would vote for Trump in 2020. "I will tell you—the things that you have done as the president are remarkable! Remarkable!" But it was too late for the new Beck to go back to being the old Beck. In November 2019, Beck's cable TV channel went off the air. His radio show continued on, and so did he, stuck in a kind of limbo.

Leaving behind a deeply meaningful conflict identity is never linear. For some people, this vacillation never ends.

distance

When his cousin pulled up in the new Mercedes-Benz that day, Curtis had one precious resource. He had just enough distance, physically and mentally, to pause. As he stared into the trunk, considering his cousin's proposal, he reminded himself of what he knew. There was no end to this conflict. There was no such thing as a ninety-day comeback. This conflict was a perpetual motion machine; you sought revenge for one affront and then there was always another one after that. On and on it went. Kind of like politics.

Curtis also had a pragmatic concern: he wanted to live. He wanted to be around for his kids. He knew that his heart wasn't in the game anymore, and that made him vulnerable. He couldn't survive if he made mistakes, if he lowered his guard out there on the streets.

"Nah, man, I'm good," he said finally, turning his cousin down.

"You're a better man than me," his cousin answered, closing the trunk.

"No, I'm not. I'm just ready, and you're not. But once you're ready, then we're going to get together and talk."

As he watched his cousin drive away, he did not feel good. He did not feel righteous. He felt alone.

A week later, Curtis drove into his garage and saw his neighbor. "Man, that was messed up what happened to your cousin," the man said.

Curtis had no idea what he was talking about. He pulled the car back out and drove to his cousin's house, where he heard the news: his cousin had been kidnapped and killed.

The first thought that ran through Curtis's mind was from his old self: "Shit, if I was with him, that never woulda happened." It was a feeling of guilt and regret, a familiar sensation.

The second thought was from his new self: if he'd been with his cousin, he realized, he'd probably be dead, too. It would be his family weeping, his body in the morgue. It wasn't hard to imagine. But this thought was surprising all the same.

Why wasn't this second thought the same as it had always been, to seek revenge? To make someone pay for the pain he was feeling?

Age changes people, and it is one of the most predictable ways that people abandon crime and violence. People get older and wiser. But Curtis knew it was more than that. It was also because he had created some distance between himself and the conflict. Having reached his saturation point and tagged himself out, he was removed from the day-to-day, tit-for-tat cycle of the streets, and what a difference this made. It gave him space to think other thoughts, to cultivate competing identities. Revenge was no longer the only idea that captured his attention; his Stone identity was not the only identity to which he owed allegiance.

Time and space turn out to be key to shifting out of high conflict, for all kinds of people in all manner of disputes. There are different ways to "buy time," as Curtis puts it, but it must be done. In the Philippines, women and other shields buy time by investigating and snuffing out false rumors, before they can escalate to violence. With Gary's feuding clients, looping for understanding helps him buy time, slowing down the conversation and making sure people feel heard.

One of the greatest dangers of social media is that it speeds conflict up. It holds us captive in the reactive mode of thinking, by design, robbing us of time and space. In that sense, it's like an automatic weapon. If you never have to stop to reload, there's no way your loved ones can tackle you and bring you to your senses.

In Gary's own political conflict, it was only because of the election loss that he had the time and space to realize what had happened to him. How far he'd fallen from his own ideals. For some people, this happens after they get fired. Or divorced or sick. Sometimes a crisis creates a sudden, unexpected opening.

Countries can buy time, too. In the country of Georgia in the 1990s, the government bought loyalty from various groups, literally giving away properties and state agencies to business leaders and mafia bosses. It was a huge risk, layering corruption on top of corruption, but it led to a dramatic drop in violence, as the country's old conflict entrepreneurs began to have a stake in the government's success. The Georgian government filled the space it had created, rebuilding its institutions and the trust of the public.

After his cousin's death, Curtis knew he'd made the right decision. He still had problems, but doubt wasn't one. That experience dissolved any illusions he'd had about going back. Life did not get easier, but the pull to return to the conflict receded.

What he needed, he realized, was a new identity. "You have to replace something with something else," he said. For years, he'd filled any emptiness in his life with his vendetta against the Disciples. But that satisfaction was always replaced by a new loss, a new quest for revenge. Now, he had more stories to tell beyond just that one. Father. Husband. Muslim. And those identities competed for attention.

This, too, is a common story among people who leave high conflict. It's not enough just to reach a saturation point; they must also find new purpose, in a new role, to fill the void left by the conflict. Otherwise, they return to the Tar Pits, eventually.

"damn, I wanted to kill you"

In the mid-1970s, the Palestinian Liberation Organization had a problem. It had created a covert commando unit called Black Sep-

A member of the Palestinian group Black September appears on a balcony in the Munich Olym-pic Village, where Israeli athletes were being held hostage in 1972. Courtesy of Everett Collection

tember, designed to seek revenge for humiliations suffered by the Palestinian people. Very quickly, the ruthless unit had become one of the most feared terrorist organizations in the world. In 1971, Black September had assassinated Jordan's prime minister, gunning him down in the lobby of the Sheraton Hotel in Cairo. The next year, the group had infiltrated the Olympic Village in Munich, kidnapping and eventually massacring eleven Israeli athletes.

But times were changing. New diplomatic options were opening up, and terrorism was damaging the Palestinians' reputation. Yasser Arafat, the chairman of the PLO, needed to disband Black September. How could he convince these trained assassins, who'd devoted their lives to this high conflict, to move on?

After months of debate, Arafat's deputies came up with an un-usual solution, as described by counterterrorism expert Bruce Hoff-man. They introduced the members of Black September to a group of about a hundred Palestinian women, whom they'd recruited from all over the Middle East. They encouraged the commandos to get to know the women. If any of the men and women decided to get married, they were told, they'd get $3,000 and an apartment with appliances and a TV, along with a new, nonviolent job. If these married couples had a baby, they'd get another $5,000. It was like a giant singles cruise, with very high stakes. The scheme was designed to create new identities for the commandos, ones that crowded out their old ideas of themselves.

To the surprise of everyone involved, the matchmaking worked. All the members of Black September got married, one of Arafat's generals later told Hoffman. Whenever these men were asked to travel to another country on nonviolent business on behalf of the Palestinian government, they declined. They did not want to risk being arrested or killed. Like Curtis, they had new roles, as fathers and husbands. Their conflict identity lost much of its grip in the process.

After Curtis left his old identity as a Stone, a bizarre thing happened. It was a coincidence, really, but a timely one. Another man, also named Curtis, was killed in a motorcycle accident. This other Curtis had grown up in the same neighborhood; he'd attended the same high school. Many people, hearing the news, thought that Curtis Toler was the one who had died.

For a few days after that, people came up to Curtis with arms outstretched, embracing him with a warmth he had not expected. Old friends and family members called him up, and sounded so relieved when he'd answered. They'd thought he'd died, and he hadn't.

But what stunned Curtis was how much they cared. He'd thought that his value was his role in the conflict, and now that he'd left the Hulk behind, he was surprised to see that people still loved him. Their sense of Curtis was bigger than his own, and this gave him hope.

Slowly, Curtis began to fill the space the conflict had left behind. He had always been curious, since he was a moonwalking little kid in Foster Park. He'd never lost that desire to understand how things worked. Now he started reading more, studying the history of race and violence in America.

He read *The Mis-Education of the Negro* by Carter G. Woodson, a book that had come out in 1933 but felt timely to Curtis. A teacher, Woodson chronicled the ways that Black Americans had been utterly failed by schools, taught that their race was unclean and unworthy. He revealed the indoctrination that kept Black people oppressed with or without force.

"If you can control a man's thinking, you do not have to worry about his action," Woodson wrote. "If you make a man feel that he is inferior, you do not have to compel him to accept an inferior status, for he will seek it himself."

Reading this, Curtis started to see bigger problems he had not noticed before, circumstances that did not justify his past but helped explain it. "It took me out of the existing world that I was in." He read J. A. Rogers's *From "Superman" to Man*, a 1917 novel about the ignorance of racism. Curtis started to see the ways in which the Stones and the Disciples were participating in their own subjugation. He wondered who all this violence had really served, after all.

After he'd stopped dancing and playing football, his identity had narrowed to a sliver—gang member and almost nothing else. Now, two decades later, he felt it expanding again. There was more to life, and to him. He read *Explosion of Chicago's Black Street Gangs*, by Useni Eugene Perkins, a history going back to 1900.

"I started to understand that this whole thing is so much bigger than the limits I had put on it. This is not a *Blackstone* thing; it's a Black *people* thing!" Recognizing systemic racism in Chicago and America did not demoralize Curtis. It seemed to energize him. He was, as he put it, "getting to the root cause."

There's a word for this in psychology. It's called "recategorization," and it means swapping out a narrow identity for a broader one. This recategorization widened the lens on Curtis's enemy—and on Curtis himself. He started to question the voice in his head that had been telling him, for years, that he was fundamentally flawed. Maybe he wasn't, and maybe those Disciples weren't either. There were bigger problems, underneath the crock pots of gang rivalries and stolen watches. The story he'd been telling himself about his failures as a son and a father was a subplot, he realized, not untrue but not the whole truth, either. He started replacing something small and suffocating with something bigger.

"The root cause is bigger than the pull of conflict," Curtis said. "Everything my people have gone through to get to this point, and now we're killing each other? I owe more to my ancestors than I do to this organization."

He built a new vantage point, above the fray; a way to see himself, his old conflict, and his new purpose, in alignment. This expansion is a running theme in every story I've encountered of people shifting out of high conflict. Something happens to slow time and create space— maybe the birth of a child, maybe the death of a loved one, maybe even a stint in prison or the signing of a peace treaty—and in that precious space, under the right conditions, something new begins to grow.

Around this time, the Reverend Michael Pfleger, a local priest and longtime peace activist in Foster Park, noticed something. Curtis was acting differently. He was no longer part of the problem. He was still hanging out near Foster Park, but he seemed different, removed, like a man in some kind of transition. So Pfleger started talking to Curtis, every time he saw him.

"I was extremely impressed with him, with his intelligence, with his wisdom," Pfleger said. "He was able to bridge the younger guys and the older. When I find people like that, I wanna learn from them."

One day, Pfleger told Curtis he wanted to start a "peace league" for gang members to play basketball. And he wanted Curtis to coach a Stones team, to play against a Disciples team, naturally, in a "peace tournament" featuring four of the most active gangs at the time. It was a way to help neighborhood kids. But Pfleger was also helping Curtis. He was welcoming Curtis home, recognizing his new role in the neighborhood. It was a philosophy that Pfleger preached about in his sermons and on street corners. "We cannot wait for law enforcement or for government," he said at peace marches. "We must reach out to our brothers in the community. Stop demonizing them! Stop telling them they are nothing but gang bangers. Let them know you're our sons, you're our daughters, we love you and respect you."

Curtis was skeptical. These guys were out there killing each other. Now you want them to play basketball in a tournament? Be serious. But basketball legend and Chicago native Isiah Thomas was on board to help. And Curtis knew Pfleger wasn't one to quit. So he agreed, and he started to talk to younger guys he knew were in need of some time and space. With Pfleger and also with CeaseFire, a violence interruption program in Chicago (now known as Cure Violence), Curtis walked up to groups of young men on corners that most people avoided. If he'd been willing to risk his life for the conflict, he could risk it for the peace.

On the days leading up to the tournament, Curtis had trouble sleeping. "My mind was everywhere. I was getting beside myself," he said. There had been near misses during the practices, guys wanting to fight, waiting outside with guns. The situation felt volatile.

The games would be played at Father Pfleger's church, which was in Disciples territory. That was a risky place for the Stones team to be. To reduce the uncontrolled variables, they rented buses to get the players there safely, even though it was close enough to walk.

On September 22, 2012, the buses pulled into the church parking lot. Forty-eight young men came out to play. Chicago Bulls stars Derrick Rose, Joakim Noah, and Taj Gibson came to help coach the teams. Two NBA referees officiated. Thousands of people turned out to watch, more than the church gym could comfortably hold. Hundreds of spectators had to be turned away. There were camera crews from CNN, ABC, and ESPN. The Nation of Islam provided security.

The competition was intense. There were some hard fouls, without a doubt. But not a single act of violence. Men who had been shooting at each other the week before found themselves on the same court. Gang identities temporarily faded, and other identities lit up that day, identities as players, as fans, as Chicagoans.

Afterward, Curtis could breathe again. He marveled at how well it had gone. "It's crazy how, in that moment, everybody could put everything else aside." It was proof of what people could do, under the right conditions, just around the corner from Foster Park.

Maybe it was possible, one day, to expand the identities of these young men for more than a day, to show them how much bigger the sky was than it seemed. Maybe this was something he could do, something that made his past make sense.

In 2014, Curtis and his wife separated. Seeing her go was almost more than he could survive. After all the losses he'd suffered, this one felt like treason. As he followed her social media posts about her new life, it took all his strength not to revert to his old one, spreading the pain around one more time.

These were lonely times. But with each passing month, Curtis's new identity got stronger, clearer around the edges. He got introduced to filmmaker Spike Lee, who gave Curtis a small role in *Chi-*

Spectators at the first Peace League basketball tournament in Chicago. Courtesy of Saint Sabina Church

Raq, a movie about gang violence on the South Side of Chicago. Curtis started speaking publicly about gang violence, appearing on *The Steve Harvey Show* and *The Daily Show*.

The Peace League became a permanent institution, expanding to six and then eight teams, meeting every Monday night for twelve weeks for food and mentoring sessions, followed by basketball. The league offered GED classes for young men looking to finish high school, as well as internships and business suits for job interviews. A Bulls player donated 250 tickets to home games, so that the young men could come to games together.

Two and a half years after they split up, Curtis and his wife got back together. They were both different people from who they'd been. And after their separation, they were able to meet each other as such. It was like Curtis's old life and his new life were starting to function together, intertwined like two strands of DNA.

Not long afterward, Curtis finally found Billy, the man who had shot high school basketball star Benji Wilson decades before, the Disciple he'd been hunting for most of his life. It was on a Friday, and Curtis was attending prayers at a South Side Muslim organization that does violence prevention work. Billy had just started working there, as it happened. Incredibly, they were doing the same work, he and his lifelong enemy.

Now they were middle-aged men. Billy's goatee was flecked with white. But still, when Curtis saw him, he felt twelve years old all over again. Anger and pain coursed through his chest, like the scar of an old war wound had been ripped open. He felt his pulse quicken.

But this was the new Curtis, not the old one. So he walked over to Billy and introduced himself.

"Damn, I wanted to kill you," he said, shaking his head. Then he laughed that deep belly laugh of his. But he kept staring at Billy like he was seeing a ghost, like he was afraid to blink, lest he disappear.

Billy did not remember Curtis from the neighborhood. But he'd had similar encounters before, many times. He'd broken hearts all over Chicago the day he'd killed Benji Wilson, and he knew nothing had been forgiven.

"Did you think I was just going to let you kill me?" Billy said, smiling back at Curtis. Then he said what he usually said in these situations. "Man, I want to tell you what happened."

Curtis paused. Was he really going to let the Gangster Disciple who murdered Benji Wilson explain himself? He inhaled a long, deep breath.

"Shit, okay," he said, and so they began to talk together.

a different story

That morning back in 1984, Billy had left his house early, in pursuit of some form of justice. His cousin Cindy had gotten robbed the day before. She was playing arcade games at a corner store near her high school when some kid had grabbed ten bucks out of her purse. When she'd demanded it back, he'd said, "Bitch, if you want your money, come get it!" Then he'd put the money down the front of his pants and walked out.

That story infuriated Billy. It was about more than the money, see, it was about respect. He didn't go to Cindy's school, but he figured he'd better try to fix this. It felt like his duty. He was sixteen, grieving his father, who had died of lung cancer a year before, and looking to spread some pain around and put things right.

Like Curtis, Billy lived a block away from Foster Park. He'd spent half his childhood there playing baseball, his favorite sport. But he was in high school now, and things had changed. He was a Gangster Disciple, and Foster Park was dominated by Stones. Billy's father had been a Stone once, but that was a long time ago. These days, it was too dangerous for Billy to go to Foster Park.

To help his cousin get her money back, Billy decided to go to her high school the next day. Just in case, he'd better bring the .22 caliber revolver he'd found hidden under his aunt's mattress. If he was going to confront this guy, it felt safer to have a gun. It was, in his mind, like a security blanket, backup he could count on. He tucked it in his waistband and headed out with his friend Omar.

Outside of Cindy's school, Billy and Omar ran into a guy Billy knew, someone who knew everyone. The guy said he knew who had stolen the money, and he would deal with it. This guy was a peacemaker of sorts, just the right person to run into at just the right time. So he gave Billy the money for his cousin from his own pocket. Problem solved.

Satisfied, Billy and Omar walked away, down Vincennes Avenue. They started talking to a girl they knew. Then they waited on the corner, while she went into a store to buy some food.

It was winter in Chicago, and the wind whipped Billy's face that morning, making tears roll down his cheeks. He shuffled back and forth on the sidewalk, trying to stay warm. He started to wonder what he was still doing there. He'd gotten the money. He should be getting back to school.

That's when a tall guy, the tallest person he'd ever seen, shoved Billy out of the way as he went by. Billy almost fell down from the force of the push. At first he thought the guy must be running from somebody. Why else would he shove him like that? But the guy kept walking away down the sidewalk. The guy was angry, talking in heated tones to a girl walking with him. It must have been his girlfriend. Maybe they were having some sort of fight. Billy waited for a beat, expecting the tall boy to turn and say, *Hey man, I'm sorry*. He was hoping the guy would turn. But he kept walking, just like nothing had happened.

Every step away that guy took felt like an insult, like Billy was nothing, nobody.

"Man, ain't you going to say excuse me!" Billy yelled.

The guy turned. In his trench coat, he looked huge. And he looked furious, as if Billy had disrespected *him*, not the other way around.

"Nigga, fuck you! I don't owe you an excuse!"

Billy couldn't believe what he was hearing. "Fuck you, nigga, you pushed me! You need to say excuse me." People were watching. He couldn't let this go.

Benji stepped away from his girlfriend and toward Billy. He wasn't backing down. But Billy knew he did not want to fight someone so big. It was all happening so fast, and it didn't make any sense. Then Billy remembered he'd brought back-up. He unzipped his jacket to show the guy his gun. That would end this.

But it didn't work. Benji did not back down. He had learned to meet disrespect with force, just like Billy. A man did not show weakness; a man did not walk away. Weak men got killed.

Benji's girlfriend started screaming. "He's got a gun! He's got a gun, Ben!"

But Benji didn't seem to care. "What you going to do, shoot me now?"

Billy felt his options falling away. "Man, don't walk up on me!"

Then Benji lunged toward Billy, or maybe away from his girlfriend, who was trying to pull him back. It was hard to tell because it happened so fast.

That's when Billy pulled out the gun. All of a sudden, he could hear his grandfather's advice in his head: *Don't pull a gun on somebody unless you plan to use it.* If he didn't use it, this guy could use it on him.

Billy fired twice, hitting Benji both times. Benji staggered backwards. He was bleeding heavily. He looked, most of all, shocked. What had just happened?

How could it come to this? Two boys are posturing on a sidewalk, and then this?

In that frozen moment, everything changed. Billy had done something he could never undo, and he knew it at once. Just like that, he went from being enraged at Benji to being worried about him. He wanted, more than anything, for Benji to survive. He did not know this boy's gang affiliation; it never entered his mind.

As Benji's girlfriend screamed, Billy ran the other way. He

sprinted past the row houses and the chain link fences, thinking all the time about the boy he'd shot. "He became the most important person to me," Billy wrote later. "This unknown tall stranger I'd left struggling for his life."

When he got to his cousin's house, the TV was on. The programming was interrupted for a breaking news flash. "Benji Wilson, star basketball player, was shot by two gang members in an apparent attempted robbery."

The face that flashed across the screen was familiar. It was the guy he'd shot. The TV was talking about *him*. This was the first time Billy understood he'd shot someone famous. His mind struggled to comprehend the magnitude of what he'd done. He'd shot that boy! And now the news was saying it was gang-related, saying it was a robbery. It was like he'd pushed over a domino that touched off a nuclear reaction. Every moment seemed to get worse than the next.

He didn't know what to do but he felt certain he should leave his cousin's house. He walked through the neighborhood, reeling. He kept expecting the cops to jump out and grab him at any time. What he wanted most of all was to talk to his mom.

The police picked Billy up at his aunt's house around midnight. They brought him to the station and interrogated him alone, asking if he was looking to rob someone that day. He said no. He told them what happened, over and over. But it didn't seem to matter what he said. The story was out of his hands. The dominoes had fallen. Finally, he asked for a lawyer. The police left the room and a lawyer came in. But it wasn't a defense attorney, Billy said; it was the prosecutor.

The prosecutor had a statement he wanted Billy to sign, one that said Billy had tried to rob Benji. The story was written before Billy got to tell it. Billy says he kept telling the prosecutor that it wasn't true, but the man said it was the only way he could see his mom.

Billy signed the statement. Now the prosecutor could charge him with attempted robbery, which would come with a longer prison sentence than manslaughter alone. The government wanted revenge, just like Jesse Jackson, just like Curtis, just like the whole city, and if the story didn't fit, the lawyers could make it fit.

After that, Billy was moved to a holding cell, where he could see a TV playing. That morning, there was breaking news once again. Billy watched through the bars, bracing himself.

It was over. Benji had died. The worst had happened. Billy sat in the cell, absorbing the truth. He had ended the life of a human being. Pain twisted through his chest like tiny shards of glass. He felt a kind of despair he'd never felt before, even after his own father had died. What God had created, Billy kept thinking, he had destroyed.

Billy and Omar were led, handcuffed, past TV news cameras and brought before a judge for a bail hearing. After the judge denied bail, an older female sheriff's deputy leaned in toward Billy. "You killed that boy!" she said. "I hope they give y'all the death penalty and they let me pull the switch on you muthafuckers!"

The Cook County State's Attorney's Office tried both Billy and Omar as adults. It took jurors just over an hour to find them guilty of murder and attempted robbery. "There was never any question at all," one juror said afterward. "It was very unanimous."

There was no mention of gangs at trial. The judge had ordered the lawyers not to refer to gangs because there was no evidence of their relevance. But the news media still brought them up in the coverage of the trial.

Billy served nineteen years and nine months in prison for killing Benji Wilson. Omar, who had not fired the gun, served sixteen years.

Billy's side of the story did not get told in the aftermath of the shooting. There was no robbery, no gangbanging, no sense to it all. The us-versus-them machine was hard to turn off. There were star athletes, and there were gang members. Stones and Disciples, Hatfields and McCoys.

Today, most of the violence on the streets of Chicago looks just like this: young men with fragile egos and powerful weapons. They may be gang members, even rival gang members, but that's rarely the whole story. That's just the part of the story that keeps the momentum going.

Come to think of it, Benji was wearing a skullcap that day, as Billy remembered it. Not a hat turned to the left. Or right. Or any which way.

"what if we had become friends thirty years ago?"

Curtis listened to Billy's story all the way to the end. The story felt, to him, deeply inadequate and entirely believable. He knew, in his gut, that Billy was telling the truth. He'd seen the same sad plot play out so many times in Chicago: one young man having a real bad day runs into another one, with a gun. It was sickening how familiar it was.

As Billy finished, Curtis had one thought, one he never could have imagined having before: "That could have been me." He could picture being a teenager and getting shoved just like that, and he could imagine refusing to back down, too, if he hadn't recognized Benji Wilson.

"I probably would've shot him, too."

It made Curtis dizzy, thinking about it. This encounter with Billy unraveled his narrative about the Disciples and Benji Wilson. The story that had ordered his life for so long was not true. And it never had been. There was no hat to the left. No gang storyline at all. The more he thought about it, the more he began to question every other assumption he'd had about this feud. It even occurred to him, suddenly, to doubt the very fundamentals. Basic premises he'd always assumed were true, without question.

Now he wondered: Was Benji Wilson ever actually a Stone? When he'd seen him playing basketball, his hat was to the left. That much Curtis knew. But now he felt a tremor underneath everything. Maybe Benji's hat had just got knocked that way when he was playing. Maybe it wasn't intentional. It was disorienting, like everything was up for grabs. Everything.

This is another peculiarity of high conflict. It can be one-sided. It can spiral out of a feud that lives mostly in our own heads. The other person may never even know they're in our high conflict at all. Which means that we all may appear in conflicts we aren't even aware of. How many feuds was Curtis featured in that he'd never known about? How many people dreamed of killing him? Probably quite a few.

By then, Curtis had already shifted out of high conflict. But Billy's story gave him another way to stay out. He and Billy were no longer enemies. They were in the same category, and they always had been. He could see that now. It was almost absurd, now that he thought about it. They'd come up in the same neighborhood, playing at the same park. Both of them were friends with Jesse, the back-flipping boy who had gotten killed selling hot dogs so many years before. Both of them had grieved Jesse's murder, without knowing it. "We had so much more in common than we had differences."

Curtis just wished he could have seen it all so much earlier. His brain started running through the "what if's," as he puts it. This happened a lot. "What if we had become friends thirty years ago?" Curtis asked himself. It was as if he was looking through a kaleidoscope, and all the shapes kept shifting.

It's hard to resist high conflict. But there are ways to boost our ability to hold on to complexity, even in us-versus-them conflict. The most well-studied strategy is through something known as contact theory, which is a way to help people recategorize one another by spending time together, under certain conditions. These encounters can interrupt the cascading assumptions we make about each other, essentially slowing down conflict and making space. Once people have met and kind of liked each other, they have a harder time caricaturing one another. A hat to the right may—or may not—mean someone is an enemy.

The effectiveness of contact theory has been illustrated in more than five hundred experiments, all over the world. It has worked on children in Chile, Belgian high school students sent to Morocco, and prison inmates in the U.K. Relationships change us, way more readily than facts. British people who had had meaningful interactions with Muslims *before* the 7/7 London transit terrorist attacks in 2005 exhibited less prejudice toward Muslims afterward.

It sounds obvious, but why does it actually work? On one level, relationships seem to complicate the stories we tell ourselves. When we get to know people, we can't reduce them to just one thing. This is why Father Pfleger and Curtis brought gang members together to play basketball: to build relationships that resist caricature. And this is why Billy's story, in all its complexity, was important for Curtis to hear.

If we try to caricature people we have come to know, it feels not only inaccurate but vaguely disloyal. We are social creatures, allied with all kinds of groups, and disloyalty is intensely uncomfortable. Knowing people as three-dimensional humans keeps us out of the Tar Pits. We might still believe a negative story about our opponent, and we will continue to disagree about many things. But usually, relationships make it harder to dismiss and dehumanize other people.

Remember the British environmentalist and writer Mark Lynas, the one who spent years protesting genetically modified food? In the first pages of this book, we saw how he eventually exited high conflict, even apologizing to the farmers he'd harassed years before. But how did he make that shift? Why then? Or ever?

After that night hiding in the field, Mark returned to his day job as an editor and writer. Over time, he began to interview scientists. In addition to his work fighting genetically modified food, he wrote books about climate change. Scientists were important sources for him. Eventually, he got to like some of these scientists.

The scientists he interviewed were trying to save the planet, just like he was. They had a lot in common. They traded personal stories, becoming colleagues, not just acquaintances. He came to admire their dedication to empirical evidence over ideology. And their willingness to admit when they were wrong. Soon he adopted their standards in his own writing. He worked to understand and incorporate rigorous scientific research, taking great care to footnote all of his arguments.

In 2008, one of Mark's books received the Royal Society Prize, Britain's most prestigious award for science writing. The prize was like his formal acceptance into the tribe of serious science writers. He hadn't been shamed or called out. He'd been welcomed, and it mattered. At the ceremony, Mark did not sound like a crop-killing activist anymore: "To be recognized by an institution like the Royal Society, which is one of the most important scientific institutions in the whole world, is a delight and a tremendous honor for me."

Three days later, he wrote that piece for *The Guardian* attacking genetically modified crops—the kind of piece he'd written many times before. But this was the first time that the criticism in the comments section bothered him. The accusations and the doubt could enter his bloodstream, because he'd had so many close encounters with serious scientists by then.

On the surface, Mark's campaign against genetically modified food had seemed like it was about nutrition and safety. And it was. But underneath all the crock pots, it was also about belonging, like many conflicts. For years, Mark had found a sense of purpose and identity as an activist, fighting the good fight against giant companies. It was energizing to be so right, so much of the time. But over time, he cultivated another identity, as a science writer. He found another way to belong, another group to call his own. Just like Curtis.

But his new identity clashed with his old one. For the next couple of years, Mark struggled to reconcile it all. He vacillated between his old conflict identity and his new one, not unlike Glenn Beck. Eventually, Mark felt he had to say something loudly and clearly about his evolution, if only to ease his own conscience. "It wasn't really defensible to just skulk around without being honest about it."

And so, fourteen years after hiding from those police dogs, Mark stood up in front of that conference of farmers and scientists in Oxford, England, and publicly admitted he'd gotten seduced by high conflict. He'd actively worked against the things he'd held dear.

"As an environmentalist, and someone who believes that everyone in this world has a right to a healthy and nutritious diet of their choosing, I could not have chosen a more counter-productive path," he said.

"I now regret it completely."

power

Contact theory is a delicate art. Interaction with the "other" side is not enough. Playing basketball together does not magically lead to more understanding, all by itself.

In some cases, contact can make conflict *worse*. In the 1940s, a researcher named Paul H. Mussen studied 106 White, low-income New York City boys who spent a month at an integrated summer camp alongside an equal number of Black boys. After the camp ended, about a quarter of the White boys showed a significant reduction in racial prejudice. But another quarter showed a significant *increase* in prejudice. For those boys, contact made matters worse.

In Northern Ireland, Catholics and Protestants knew each other. They'd spent decades inhabiting the same small country. And yet, starting in the late 1960s, they fought one another in spasms of high conflict that lasted more than three decades. There were some 37,000 shootings and 16,000 bombings attributed to the Troubles. Why didn't contact theory work in Northern Ireland?

Contact theory seems to require a few conditions. First, everyone involved in an encounter should ideally have roughly equal status, if not in the world then at least in the room and subculture in which an encounter takes place. This was rarely the case for Catholics in Northern Ireland, who were marginalized in politics, housing, and the workforce, and it remains rare among Whites and people of color in many parts of the United States.

Second, it seems to help if some kind of respected authority supports the get-together. Maybe it's a mosque or a church. Maybe it's the United Nations or another country's leader. Whatever the case, some official show of support seems to legitimize the encounter and induce some minimal level of trust in the process.

Third, it's ideal if people don't just talk but actually work together on some kind of common problem. This triggers our instincts for cooperation, rather than competition. It activates our desire to collaborate, rather than win. For Mark, he and the climate scientists shared the goal of saving the planet from global warming. This shared mission helped create a new, shared identity, which is much easier than trying to shed an old identity.

Finally, everyone involved should want to be there, in pursuit of some shared goal, whatever that is. This is as true in a divorce mediation as it is in a racial dialogue encounter. Motivation matters. If people *want* to stay in high conflict, if they want to dominate the other side or revel in contempt or righteousness, they will. And it can leave the other group vulnerable to emotional abuse or even violence. The study of the biracial camp in the 1940s found that the boys who ended up more prejudiced afterward were also the more rebellious, aggressive boys who expressed all kinds of frustrations and may have had other problems at home. The camp was, it seemed, an opportunity to unleash some of that hurt, to find a scapegoat.

Contact theory works best when everyone has enough motivation, stability, and power to take risks and withstand discomfort. These are pretty major requirements. In the case of Billy and Curtis, the necessary conditions were present in 2016, when they finally met. One was a Gangster Disciple and one was a Stone, but those identities had faded by then, and now both men were pursuing the same larger mission, trying to prevent more violence.

In many other situations, people do not *want* to let go of high conflict. This is what Mark has found as he gives talks to people all over the world about ways to solve climate change. "Some of the angriest responses I've gotten is when I challenge people's pessimism," he told me. Many people do not want a solution if it offends their other ideas of what is safe and pure—or if it means they will have to let go of an apocalyptic narrative that has become part of their identity.

"Put up your hand if you would like there to be a carbon fairy who could wave a wand and make all that fossil carbon just disappear," Mark sometimes says to large audiences. Usually, about 1 percent of people raise their hand, he's found. In his view, based on many years of research, nuclear power is the carbon fairy. It could help solve climate change, and it could be done safely. But many people, especially on the Left, don't even want to discuss it.

"Many people don't seem to want to just solve climate change," Mark told me. "They want to use climate change to turn the world into something they'd like to see." It's eerily similar to what happens when Halperin, the conflict researcher, asks Israeli audiences if they've heard of the Arab Peace Initiative, as described earlier in this book. Very few hands go up. This is how high conflict works. It puts us in a sort of trance, one that blinds us to many things.

Usually, people *want* to leave high conflict when they have reached a saturation point—or when they've developed other, competing identities. That's when contact theory can work well. But even then, contact theory is grassroots by definition. It cannot, on its own, transform institutions. Curtis and Billy's friendship didn't repair any of the root causes of gang violence. Real change requires putting sustained pressure on people and institutions that benefit from the current system. People with power don't generally give it up just because they become less prejudiced. They need to feel pressure, the kind that comes from organized political, legal, economic, and social action.

But here's the thing: pressure isn't enough, either. Lasting change requires shifts that happen up high and down low, in bank accounts and zoning laws, but also in people's hearts and homes. Otherwise, people will find ways to get around new laws. When Americans were forced to integrate schools for Black and White children in the 1950s, many White parents opened new, private schools or fled to the suburbs. There are stories like that all over the world, where laws changed but people didn't. The conflict burns on underground, where you can't see it.

"who is your why?"

In Chicago, the job that Curtis does today is formidable. The idea is to help gang members do what he did, finding a path out of high conflict, but to do it much faster. In months, rather than years. It is delicate, heartbreaking work, most of the time. But once in a while, it opens up an alternative reality, like a wrinkle in time, where boys don't kill boys over watches.

Chicago CRED, where Curtis works, was started in 2016 by Arne Duncan, the education secretary under President Obama. (CRED is short for Create Real Economic Destiny.) Duncan grew up in Chicago and played basketball with Benji Wilson, Curtis's boyhood hero. Duncan mourned his murder with the rest of Chicago. As an adult, he came home to Chicago from Washington and started CRED with a single mission: to dramatically reduce gun violence in Chicago by targeting the people most at risk of being shot or shooting someone else.

One of his first hires was Curtis, who had, by then, been working on disrupting violence in Chicago for more than four years. Other places he'd worked with had mentored high-risk youth and tried to separate people in times of intense conflict. But that was a short-term fix, he knew. The goal of CRED was to help people not just cease and desist—but to build a new identity altogether.

To do that, Curtis and his colleagues started mapping the conflict in the most dangerous neighborhoods of Chicago, block by block. Using crime data, they tracked the shootings and identified the eight most violent gangs and "cliques," as the smaller, contemporary gangs of Chicago are known. Then, for those eight groups, they identified their opponents or their "opps" as they are known—their rival gangs and cliques.

Once they had this list, they hired ten former gang members who were known and respected by various members of those gangs and cliques. Then they all went to work building more relationships. "It's a networking process," Curtis's colleague Jalon Arthur told me. They held basketball games, gave away book bags, and walked the streets. They identified the specific individuals who normally did the shooting in each group, and who made the decisions. These were the members they needed to know best. They offered them trauma counseling, stipends, and job training to join the CRED program, ideally with other members of their gang.

"Who is your why?" Curtis liked to ask these young men. What, in other words, do you care about that is bigger than this? Is it your son? Your God? Your grandmother? Just like the PLO marrying off the members of Black September, Curtis tried to find a way to revive an old identity or create a new one.

All the while, Curtis and the other CRED staff members waited for openings, brief pauses in the conflict, due to chance or a snowstorm or anything at all. These are the entry points, when they could potentially buy time and make space. "If we can go two weeks to thirty days without somebody on either side getting shot or killed, we gotta start having those conversations," Arthur said.

They couldn't just wait for guys to decide they'd reached a saturation point, the way Curtis did at his son's graduation ceremony. "If you're just waiting for people to just be tired, that can be decades," Arthur said. "No, you gotta intentionally look for those entry points, and even if it's met with resistance, you don't stop there. You look for another ripe moment to bring it back up."

In these ripe moments, they try to get people on both sides to agree to small, sensible commitments: like staying away from the other side's block; not posting their whereabouts on Facebook; and refraining from disrespecting their opps in their social media posts. This is exactly what negotiators try to do in conflict zones all over the world. They try to establish boundaries, to carve out a little time and space, from Venezuela to Afghanistan to Rwanda.

These days, the opportunities for disrespect are infinite. Gang members spend two to three more hours a week online compared to nongang members. They trade threats, insults, and boasts, just like gang members have always done. But they do it on social media with extreme efficiency: broadcasting disrespect to thousands of people all at once. Sparking violence with a word or an image, malice intended or not. That is where conflict ignites these days. So a big part of CRED's job is monitoring the social media accounts of the gang members they work with.

In the summer of 2019, in North Lawndale on the West Side of Chicago, a CRED outreach worker noticed a Facebook post around seven in the morning. There was a problem. The photo featured a young man from a gang in what is known as the K-Town section of North Lawndale (because all the street names there start with the letter "K"). But this young man wasn't in his own part of the neighborhood; he was standing on a block controlled by a rival gang, just east of K-Town. He had a gun in his hand, and he was bragging about the fact that he was there. His opps from the rival gang had left their block untended. (To avoid fueling further conflict, CRED requested that I withhold the names of the gangs.)

The thing is, these two groups had a nonaggression agreement in place, one that CRED had helped to negotiate. The agreement stipulated that gang members would not stray into each other's territory. Nor would they post inflammatory social media aimed at one another. So this particular individual had violated the agreement two different ways, which meant the other gang would feel compelled to retaliate. This is how feuds escalate. Just like with the Hatfields, the leaders can't control all their followers. Groups contain multitudes.

The outreach worker took a screen shot of the post and sent it around to the CRED team. The team categorized the threat as a Level 4 threat, the highest risk, based on the individual involved and the content of the post. The outreach worker called his contact in the rival gang, the one that had been disrespected by the Facebook post.

"We need you to wait for us," he said.

By nine o'clock that morning, CRED supervisor Jason Little had arrived on the block pictured in the photo. Sure enough, the gang members connected to that block had seen the post. They were armed and on their way out, locked and loaded. Ready to take revenge. He asked them to pause.

"Give me two hours."

For gang members, reacting to disrespect like this does not feel optional; it's an obligation. But these guys knew and respected Little and his team. Little had, as a younger man, lived their lives. Like Curtis, he was now a shield, someone who understood their conflict and could interrupt it. But every minute that post remained online boosted the odds of violence. It was literally a time bomb. "The more people who share it," Little said, "the more people who laugh at it, the bigger the threat."

By noon, the post was gone. CRED had reached out to another organization that was working with the K-Town gang. The gang took down the post, preventing a possible homicide just like that, with one click. "There's no question that woulda turned into another shooting," Arthur said.

That day, Little and his team seized the opportunity. They reinstated the nonaggression agreement. Both sides agreed not to make more inflammatory posts—and to stay off each other's blocks. Six months later, the agreement was still in place.

"None of these guys wanna die or go to jail," Little said. "They're not gonna say that, but a lot of them have been to jail, and they don't want to go back. And nobody wants to be the one whose picture is on a T-shirt." So if you have their trust, and you understand the conflict, you can slow it down.

Relationships, like these nonaggression pacts or any kind of peace treaty, create a tripwire. They establish a channel of communication, a mechanism that gets triggered when a violation happens. The more I've learned about peace agreements, the more I think they're misnomers. They don't make peace; they buy time, slowing down the conflict, which makes peace possible.

conflict hacks

Slowing down a conflict, with or without a peace treaty, requires enormous self-control. People like Curtis learn shortcuts to help them regulate their own emotions, creating time and space at the individual level. We all do this already, without consciously realizing it. The trick is to use these tactics purposefully, at the right time.

The first conflict hack is simple: avoid the fire starters. For Curtis, this meant moving to a new apartment. For the gang members he coaches, it can also mean relocating, if at all possible, or at least limiting their contact with the fire starters in their lives.

For someone trying to get out of political conflict, it could mean giving up cable TV and deleting their Twitter account. For people going through a divorce, it might mean spending less time with conflict entrepreneurs who urge them to fight at all costs. (Sometimes this person is their attorney, which means they need a new attorney.)

Other strategies apply when encounters can't be avoided. One tactic is to tweak the situation, so it doesn't have the same emotional power. For someone exiting gang violence, this might mean getting gang tattoos removed. Or turning your baseball hat to the middle when you go outside. For someone going through a divorce, it might mean preparing a short list of benign topics to discuss with your ex-husband, should you run into him at a friend's BBQ.

For everyone, in any high-emotion situation, the most tried and tested method is to practice rhythmic breathing. Taking slow, deep breaths is one of the few actions that influence both our somatic nervous system (which we can intentionally control) and our autonomic system (which includes our heartbeat and other actions we cannot consciously access). The breath is a bridge between the two. That's why breathing is used by Special Forces soldiers and by martial arts practitioners and by pregnant women in labor. Because it is the best tool we have in the moment.

Call it "combat breathing" or mindfulness, it's all related. But it takes practice, ideally under stress. (I once interviewed a police officer who practiced doing intentional breathing while listening to recorded siren sounds, until he learned to automatically breathe deeply every time he used his siren in his patrol car.) One version taught to many police officers works like this: breathe in for four counts; hold for four counts; breathe out for four counts; hold for four; start again. When all else fails, breathing slows down conflict, so you can think again.

Another simple but powerful tactic is distraction. Intentionally focus your attention on something else, even in the midst of conflict. Sometimes, Curtis imagines the young men he works with as they looked when they were small children, innocent and sweet. "I look at everyone and see my grandchild," he said. "That's the state I have to see them in." He recategorizes them in his mind. They are not gangbangers. They are people who were children once, who lost a first tooth, who needed help tying their shoes, who liked to dance.

The most long-lasting tactic may be reappraisal. This one is more like a Jedi mind trick. It means reframing the situation, changing how you think about it internally. Over time, Curtis learned to reframe his own conflict as one between all Black people and a corrupt system, as opposed to a conflict between the Stones and the Disciples. He recategorized his enemy by reframing the whole conflict.

The anthropologist and negotiator William Ury uses this technique in conflict zones all over the world. Years ago, he was working as a mediator between the Venezuelan government and the opposition. One night, on the precipice of civil war, then-President Hugo

Chávez kept him waiting for three hours for a scheduled meeting. Finally, at midnight, Chávez showed up. But as soon as Ury started talking, Chávez started screaming at him, right in front of everyone. He leaned in, close to Ury's face, and he yelled at him for a full half hour.

Embarrassed and incensed, Ury struggled to resist the pull of the conflict. He'd spent eighteen months working on this conflict, and he didn't want it to be for nothing. So he fought to reappraise the situation, in real time. To do this, he did something he calls "going to the balcony." He imagined himself watching the scene from "a mental and emotional balcony, a place of calm, perspective, and self-control where you can stay focused on your interests, keep your eyes on the prize."

Then he considered his options, from this mental distance. If he defended himself or counterattacked, he knew, he would only escalate the conflict. That would be like Gary writing the letter that infuriated his neighbors. It was a conflict trap, and from the balcony, he could recognize it as such.

So Ury tried to redefine the conflict. He told himself a different story about it. Maybe, instead of a humiliation, it was an opportunity to understand Chávez better. This story made it easier to control his emotion. "I just listened, giving him my full attention, trying to understand what was really going on for him," Ury said later. What he described is exactly what Gary teaches people to do with looping. Really listening, even when people are saying things you know to be false, can interrupt the spiral of conflict.

Finally, the anger left Chávez's voice, and his shoulders sagged, and he said, "Okay Ury, what should I do?" Like most people, Chávez had wanted to be heard, before he could listen.

Ury made a suggestion. Everyone needed a break from the conflict, he said. Christmas was fast approaching. What if Chávez proposed a truce, so people could spend time with their families in peace? And that's what Chávez did.

It's hard to imagine "going to the balcony" when someone is screaming at you. Ury is like an astronaut when it comes to remaining calm under pressure. But there's evidence that most of us can be taught to do a version of this in our own home. Surprisingly, it only takes about twenty-one minutes.

On average, married couples experience a slow decline in the quality of their marriage as the years go by. It's a depressing but well-established pattern. But when couples practice a version of going to the balcony, something unexpected happens. Social psychologist Eli Finkel and his colleagues directed a group of sixty married couples to spend seven minutes writing about their most recent fight *from a different perspective*. Specifically, "from the perspective of a neutral third party who wants the best for all involved."

They imagined a mediator like Gary in the room, in other words. "How might this person think about the disagreement? How might he or she find the good that could come from it?" Then they were asked to think about that person's perspective during their next fight. Every four months, for a year, they repeated this writing exercise.

The couples who did this marriage hack, reconsidering their conflicts from an imaginary third party's point of view, reported feeling less upset about their disputes than couples who hadn't done it. More importantly, the usual, slow loss of marital satisfaction *did not happen* for these couples that year. They still had conflict, but it didn't wear on them the same way. Because it was healthy.

"it looks so much smaller than I remember it"

In the fall 2019, Billy, Curtis, and I walked through Foster Park together. Billy pointed out where he'd played baseball. Curtis showed us the wall where he used to do back flips with his best friend, Jesse. "It looks so much smaller than I remember it," he said, staring at the low cement wall.

Right behind the wall is the basketball court, the one where he'd

Billy (left) and Curtis, walking in the fall of 2019 in Foster Park, where they'd both grown up, and where Benji Wilson had played basketball before he was killed. Amanda Ripley

seen Benji Wilson play. It, too, looked small, just a rectangle of asphalt at the far end of the park, by the playground.

After serving his prison term for Benji's murder, Billy got a job working for an organization that partners with CRED. Then CRED hired him outright. So he and Curtis are colleagues, in the same business of interrupting violence, sometimes on the same streets where they grew up. They go on peace marches together, and they talk at least once a week.

On that quiet, beautiful evening, it was hard to grasp how much violence the neighborhood had seen. The houses ringing the park were neat and tidy. The park was leafy and pleasant. Father Pfleger was still running the Peace League basketball tournaments each year. They'd gotten more elaborate. There were tryouts and even a draft. The chosen teams were made up of guys from all different gangs, which was its own small miracle. And yet, there weren't many kids out that evening. Foster Park remained a dangerous place, a place where shots could break the peace without warning.

In 2017, Billy's son was driving by the park when someone walked up and opened fire. Billy pointed out the spot to us that day, as we walked by. Billy had raced to the park, only to find the car draped in a sheet, surrounded by police tape. His son was still in there.

Seeing that sheet, Billy knew that his only child was dead. He stood there, weeping, holding his son's mother as she sobbed. And he thought, again, about Benji. He thought about Benji's mother. He thought about how he had caused someone to feel what he now felt, a pain worse than anything he'd ever endured. In that moment, he felt a kind of terrible certainty sink in. His son's death was his fault, he believed, his punishment for killing Benji. It was like he'd been waiting for this retribution to overtake him, waiting for thirty-three years.

Billy's son was shot sixteen times. It didn't take long for Billy to hear who might have been responsible. From what he learned, it may have been a case of mistaken identity.

Mistaken identity. That phrase sounds so benign, like an accident. But it's more than that. It's a uniquely human catastrophe. Sixteen times over.

How many homicides, I wonder, are essentially cases of mistaken identity, at some level? Identities threatened, identities presumed. Sometimes people shoot someone they didn't intend to kill. More often, people kill someone whose death will not bring them what they seek.

Curtis spent years chasing a vendetta against the Disciples, sparked by an identity story that *was not true*, as it turned out. Benji was not killed because he was a Stone, he now knows. Today, Curtis is not even sure that Benji *was* a Stone. Viewed from a balcony three decades away, many high conflicts start to look like cases of mistaken identity. Even wars.

Four years after the murder of Billy's son, no one had been arrested for the killing. Billy keeps hoping the young man who did the shooting will walk through the door where he works. He wants the chance to forgive him, the way he wants to be forgiven.

chapter 5

Gary walking near his home in Muir Beach, California, with his dog, Artie, in 2020. Trish McCall

making space

interruption

A narrow path leads from the ocean up a hillside to the Muir Beach Community Center. Walking there from Gary's house takes about five minutes. At the top, you get to savor one of the most sublime views in North America. Green velvet mountains frame the beach below, where waves sway back and forth, under a wide-open sky. As the sun sets, the distant San Francisco skyline lights up the Pacific like glitter.

On January 25, 2018, Gary did not notice any of that. He walked up those steps just before seven that night with the enthusiasm of a man headed to a colonoscopy. He had reached his saturation point not long before, when the Old Guard had trounced his allies in the election.

That loss had forced a pause in the conflict. Just enough of a pause for Gary to realize what had happened. He'd entered politics as a world-renowned expert in conflict mediation, intending to heal his town. Instead, he'd lost two years of his life to the Tar Pits. He'd disappointed his family, alienated his neighbors, and sacrificed his peace of mind. He had done all of this for an unpaid volunteer position. He felt humiliated.

Practically speaking, Gary had no idea what to do next: he could resign, giving up the last three years of his term in order to recover what was left of his old life. Or he could stay, diminished and embarrassed.

He struggled to decide. On the one hand, resigning felt weak, like a child stomping away in anger. It also felt permanent. At that point, his failure would be complete, unalterable. The crock pot would be lost forever.

If he stayed, on the other hand, he had a chance. Maybe he could redeem himself somehow. Maybe he could still help his community in some small way. But then again, he thought, wasn't that just more hubris? Didn't staying make it all about him—and about winning— yet again? Maybe resigning was the way to show humility. To admit that he, Gary Friedman, was human, too.

Either way, he had to show up at this board meeting—the last one under his leadership. It would have looked cowardly not to come. So he walked up the steps undecided, the ocean to his back.

At 7:03 p.m., Gary called the meeting to order. A fire crackled in the community center fireplace. People greeted one another, getting settled. If you didn't know better, it would have sounded almost convivial.

One minute later, the board held a vote to replace Gary as president with a member of the Old Guard. His marginalization was complete.

At this point, Gary did something surprising. He interrupted the cycle. He voted *with* the Old Guard for the new president. Then, two minutes later, Hugh, also of the Old Guard, got nominated to be vice president. This time, Gary *seconded* the nomination. This was, you'll remember, the same person to whom he'd written the infamous accusatory letter, just a few months before. Now he was voting to give him *more* power. Gary did all of this without much comment. Then he spent the next three hours trying to stay quiet and control the expression on his face. The meeting finally ended just before ten o'clock, an hour later than Gary would have ended it.

People who study conflicts like to map them out. Because conflicts are systems, a series of interlocking feedback loops that interact with each other. The forces are complicated and interrelated, like weather patterns. Which means that any change can affect the whole system, not always in ways we predict.

Electoral losses, like snowstorms or pandemics, can destabilize conflicts. There's a moment when the system is disrupted, and in that moment, huge opportunity exists. For things to get better. Or much worse.

By voting for his old enemies, Gary was disrupting the system. He was intentionally changing the one pattern in the conflict system that he could control. Granted, Gary's votes that night were largely symbolic; the Old Guard was going to win those positions either way. Gary was outnumbered. But symbolic concessions matter a lot in conflict. They disrupt the feedback loops and lower everyone's guard, creating space where there was none, at least for a moment.

When Egyptian president Anwar Sadat visited Jerusalem in November of 1977, he became the first Arab leader to visit Israel and issue a call for peace to Israel's leaders. This was the same man who had, just four years before, helped launch a surprise attack on Israel on the holiest day in Judaism, starting the Yom Kippur War (known to Arabs as the October War), which killed thousands of soldiers.

But by coming to Israel, visiting the Holocaust memorial, praying at the Al-Aqsa Mosque in Jerusalem, and calling for peace, Sadat disrupted the feedback loops of the conflict. "I sincerely tell you that before us today lies the appropriate chance for peace, if we are really serious," Sadat told Israel's parliament, the Knesset, in Arabic. "It is a chance that time cannot afford once again. It is a chance that, if lost or wasted, the plotter against it will bear the curse of humanity."

Sadat's gesture was a symbolic concession, not much more. But it paved the way for peace negotiations at Camp David a year later. Anniversaries of Sadat's historic visit are still memorialized in the Israeli news media, decades later.

The stakes were a touch lower in Muir Beach, needless to say. Zero lives were on the line. But the psychology was not radically different. Gary voted for the Old Guard that day not as an act of surrender but as a very intentional way to disrupt the conflict system. He realized that if he stayed on the board, he had to get out of the trap he was in. Which required a counterintuitive move. What if he could be something other than a rival? Imagine if John Adams had volunteered to serve in Jefferson's cabinet?

At the next meeting, the board voted to get rid of almost all of the subcommittees created under Gary's leadership. It was a painful rebuke. Those committees were Gary's legacy, his way of bringing

Egyptian president Anwar Sadat arrives at Ben Gurion Airport outside of Tel Aviv, Israel, on November 19, 1977. Moshe Milner/Israel GPO archive

everyone to the table, just like he had with the symphony mediation, years before.

But Gary voted for that, too. Again, it was a symbolic *and* purposeful concession. "I'm feeling much less righteous," he told me, "much more interested in figuring out what is productive."

Gary decided to stay on the board. He didn't know if it was the right choice at first, but he got more convinced with each passing day. At the same time, and this is important: he held fast to the understory, the thing that mattered most to him.

How did he do this? First, he took his own best advice, somewhat belatedly. He *investigated his own understory*. For Gary, meditation helped him do this. Sitting in silence, he could try to be more aware of his own emotions. Then he could notice those emotions more readily when they popped up during board meetings or walks through his neighborhood.

He had no interest in meekly complying with the new board just to reduce the conflict. He'd seen too many people do that in divorce mediations; it was always a mistake, one they regretted later. He didn't even use the word "compromise" in his mediations. Compromise feels like a surrender, like a collapse. And despite all his meditation, Gary was no pacifist. He believed conflict made us better. Or it could. He'd seen it happen. So he asked himself the same questions he asks divorcing couples: What's behind that? Why is that important to me? What would it be like if I got what I wanted here?

There was a lot of noise in his head and plenty of blame to go around. But eventually he realized that what he'd wanted most of all was to prove there was another way to do conflict, a better way. But pressuring people to adopt his worldview was never going to work.

He had to return to what he knew from forty years of mediating conflicts: "The kinds of changes that are significant don't really come about by coercion. They come about through understanding, and understanding is hard won, and it requires patience."

Understanding was Gary's understory. His identity depended on his ability to help his neighbors understand one another, even as they continued to disagree (or talked more than three minutes). That was the way to do conflict better, the thing that mattered most of all to him, and it became his true north, helping him decide when to speak up and when to vote yes.

Gary couldn't reinvent the Muir Beach governance structure, unfortunately. He couldn't make it like the Bahá'í elections, where no one was allowed to campaign and everyone owned every idea. But there were other things he could do to make politics less adversarial, and he could do them right away.

the magic ratio

For one thing, Gary worked to *break the binary* of the Old and New Guard. He mixed up the categories. He did this systematically, like training for a marathon. Every day, he did things to rehumanize and recategorize his opponents. Some days he voted with one member of the Old Guard; other days he voted his own way. He tried to re-individualize people, one-on-one. "When I pass the people who most hate me, I smile at them," he said. "I ask about their health. One's mother just died, and I asked about it."

The beauty of group identities is that we all have many of them, waiting to be lit up. No one is just a Tory or a Labour supporter, a White man or a Black man. We are also sports fans, churchgoers, dog owners, or parents. So Gary tried to revive the other identities in his own mind—and in everyone else. When he saw one particular member of the Old Guard, he talked about the roses in his garden. He activated the Gardener Identity in both of them quite intentionally, just the way a conflict entrepreneur activates our other identities.

One day, after he accidentally left his gate open, one of the Old Guard called him up to let him know that his dog, Artie, had wandered up to their house. That felt promising.

This ritual of making light, positive connections, outside of conflict, sounds obvious, but we neglect it all the time in our regular lives. These fleeting, pleasant encounters help expand the definition of *us*. Gary's neighbor may be one of *them* when it comes to the water rate debate, but she's one of *us* in the garden.

These interactions are small inoculations, which, taken regularly, protect us from making the errors in judgment and interpretation that can lead to high conflict. Psychologists Julie and John Gottman have studied conflict in some three thousand married couples over the years, and they've found that the couples most capable of keeping conflict healthy were the ones whose everyday positive interactions exceeded the negative by a ratio of 5 to 1. This is the "magic ratio," as they put it.

When sixty-five men who had spent the winter together at Antarctic research stations were asked about what had unified them, 40 percent mentioned the importance of singing and playing games together. It was the single most commonly cited unifying factor, way above drinking alcohol.

Remember Josh Ehrlich, the aspiring astronaut who spent almost eight months locked away with five strangers in a Mars simulation mission? His crew avoided high conflict partly because they made it part of their mission to create that magic ratio.

"We always ate dinner together. Every night," he told me. "We always exercised in groups. We tried not to single someone out." They did ridiculous things on purpose. They held "fort nights" on a regular basis, sliding all their mattresses out into the shared space and creating a giant fort using ropes and sheets, like seven-year-olds at a slumber party. They organized theme dinners and surprise parties.

"We exploited any special days—birthdays, anniversaries. We'd bake a cake and put up decorations." They considered "crew cohesion" part of their mission, and they did it every day, on purpose. That way, when conflict inevitably arose, it didn't spiral.

You know what this means, right? It means those after-work happy hours or birthday cakes for a colleague are not just awkward ordeals, forced upon us by corporate overlords. They are investments in our future sanity, a way to build up the ratio of positive exchanges to manage the negative ones sure to come.

In a similar way, Gary tried to expand his own definition of *us* to include the Old Guard by doing more of the chitchat he used to disdain. The thing is, Gary had to *mean* it, when he asked about a neighbor's garden. It wouldn't work otherwise. But this turned out to be okay. Because he really did care about gardening. It didn't feel phony; it felt like a good day's work.

"no fog, a full moon"

The other change Gary made, besides holding fast to the understory and breaking the binary, was to *distance himself from the fire starters* that had helped get him into the conflict to begin with. He was untangling the conflict, one knot at a time. He relied less on Tanya, his adviser in the first campaign, the one who had used words like "kill" and "beatdown" and "thugs." Those were his father's words, and they'd never worked for him.

He appreciated Tanya's help, and he knew she understood politics far better than he did. But that was not the game he wanted to play. "I don't want to hold hostility in my heart for people," he told her. "I don't like living that way."

They remained friends, and he turned to his wife for political advice instead. Sometimes, when he made calls about board business, he did it on speakerphone, so Trish could hear it in the background as she went about her day. Then he'd ask her for feedback: Was he too sharp? Too impatient? And she'd tell him. She was on the balcony, with a much better view.

This all took longer than he would have liked. As with every path out of conflict, it was nonlinear. To hold on to what mattered most, Gary had to let go of a lot. And letting go is intensely uncomfortable.

It required a lot of breathing deeply in board meetings, paus-

ing before he responded, resisting temptation. He spent a lot of time
managing his own ego. In his head, he'd ask himself three questions:

Does it need to be said?

If the answer was yes, then he'd ask himself:

Does it need to be said by me?

And if still yes:

Does it need to be said by me right now?

It was surprising how often the answer was No.

It was still important to Gary to be true to his own values. If he
thought a board member was doing something dubious, in violation
of the public trust, he still said so. But he spent a lot more time trying
to make what he said "hearable," as he puts it.

What is "hearable"? It depends on the audience—and what *they*
care most about. This is where Gary had to understand his neighbors'
understories. Looping was key. It helped him slow down time so that
he could learn what mattered most to them—and understand it, even
if he didn't agree.

Generally speaking, there are six moral foundations that shape
how we feel about politics, as social psychologist Jonathan Haidt described in his enlightening book *The Righteous Mind*. Those six foundations are care, fairness, liberty, loyalty, authority, and sanctity. These
are the keys that unlock most political behavior.

In the United States, liberals (and liberal members of the media)
tend to be highly sensitive to three of these foundations: care, fairness, and liberty. But they can be oblivious when it comes to concerns
about loyalty, authority, and sanctity. Conservatives and conservative
media, generally speaking, seem to engage with all six, with a particular focus on loyalty, authority, liberty, and sanctity.

If you understand the moral understory, you can make what you say
hearable. So, for example, if liberals want to convince American conservatives to take action on climate change, they'd get more traction talking
about the need to protect the *purity* of nature, as social psychologists
Robb Willer and Matthew Feinberg have found. But liberal politicians

almost always talk about *caring* for the planet. Like everyone, they automatically default to their own moral language, rendering much of what they say unhearable to large swaths of the country.

It's very hard to get outside of our own heads and speak the other side's moral language. It is counterintuitive. It requires discipline, humility, education, and empathy. In their research, Willer and Feinberg found that about 20 percent of liberals would not reframe their arguments to persuade conservatives, *even if it would work better*. This is a symptom of high conflict: when any concession, no matter how small, feels too threatening to contemplate, even when it would be in our own interest.

One day, a neighbor told the board she wanted them to pay for a turnaround space on her driveway during the construction of a new road. This would have been an expensive, time-consuming addition to an already massive project. Gary could have responded by arguing that her demand was unfair, since everyone should not have to pay for something only she wanted. That might have been a compelling argument to him and many other neighbors, but he didn't make it. It wasn't hearable. Instead, he made another point, which was also true. "You might just want to consider," he told her, "that if we did that, you'd have to allow other people to turn around in your driveway." She changed her mind.

Was this manipulative? Maybe. But is it manipulative to speak French when visiting France? Maybe it's just how you communicate, if you really want to be understood.

One interesting side note: Gary did not tell me this anecdote about the driveway turnaround. I heard it from his former nemesis, Hugh. As Gary changed his behavior, Hugh noticed. "He's more like a mediator now," Hugh said. "The tone has improved." Hugh no longer thought about moving out of Muir Beach. In fact, he told me, he felt pretty good about the community, and he routinely worked with Gary to get things done.

Gary still got riled up on a regular basis, complaining to Trish and his kids about how the new board was undermining everything he'd done (which was not untrue). But he also talked about how relieved he felt. He was alternately agitated and hopeful, resigned and energized. If you've ever known someone shifting out of high conflict, you might recognize these vacillations.

At one point, months into the new regime, Gary felt sure he had to call a special meeting because of the way a board member was circumventing the rules. But then he asked himself, "Who am I really calling the special meeting for?" And he had to admit he was calling it for himself, for his own need to feel right and good.

So he paused. He repeated a mantra he sometimes used on himself: "I am not important, and this is not important." He figured out how he could hold the board member accountable without humiliating the person in a special meeting.

On one of my visits to see Gary, well into his recovery from his "personal derangement," as he took to calling it, we went on a walk through Muir Beach. "My God, we're having a beautiful summer," Gary told me. "No fog, a full moon. Everything seems like small potatoes." It was good to hear Gary talking this way, a sign of how far he'd come.

One of the burdens of high conflict is that it doesn't allow for delight, for these little moments of joy. Curiosity is a prerequisite for delight. And it's impossible to feel curious in the Tar Pits.

Then, as we passed one particular house, Gary whispered: "These people hate me." But he was smiling when he said it. About another neighbor he said, "I don't trust him, but I like him." There was a new complexity in his language. He was "holding the tension," as he put it. Not collapsing into good versus evil, us versus them. He'd carved out enough space for complexity in his own mind. And this meant he was seeing the world more accurately, in full. After all, a person can be likable *and* untrustworthy. We all know people like that.

This is what Gary and Curtis have in common. They are different in so many obvious ways, from race to age to background. Gary's small, nonviolent neighborhood dispute is trivial compared to Curtis's gang conflicts. But if we could see inside their heads, we'd be amazed at the complexity they both can hold. About themselves and other people. They have cleared this space in their own minds in different ways, but both drew on wells of curiosity and humility—strengthened by their spiritual practices. For Gary, it was his meditation work, which he'd learned through a Buddhist center near his house. For Curtis, it was Islam, which he'd been introduced to through his gang affiliation. Different as they are, Curtis and Gary share a certain quiet strength, an ability to maintain the tension *without giving up* what they hold most dear.

"who's winning this marriage?"

One day, as I was riding in the passenger seat of Gary's green Mini Cooper, he got a phone call from Hugh. As a board member, Hugh was overseeing the construction of a fence in the neighborhood. One particular neighbor was complaining about its height.

> Gary: "Have you talked to her?"
> Hugh: "No."

Gary tilted his head. "What do you think she would say if you called her?" He asked this question in his curious voice, the one I recognized from his mediator trainings.

> Hugh: "Oh, you know, she is so hard to talk to . . ."
> Gary: "I know," he said, chuckling. Then he said something I
>   hadn't expected: "But you're a compassionate guy," he said.
>   "And it's people like her who really need our compassion the
>   most. Because imagine how rarely they get it."
> Hugh: "Yeah, that's true." There was a pause. "I figured you'd say
>   something like that. Okay, I'll call her."

It was a two-minute conversation, but when Gary mentioned it to Trish that night, her eyes filled with tears. He was bringing the magic.

Not long afterward, as Gary was biking toward home at the end of a long day at the office, one of his neighbors called out to him. His immediate reaction was dread. "Oh no, what's she going to complain about now?" But he smiled and waved.

She came running up to him in his driveway. "I just want to thank you," she said. Before the last board meeting, he had encouraged her to speak up about something that was bothering her about the road project. At the meeting, when she'd spoken, he'd looped her. He'd helped her feel heard. "I felt like I was treated as a person," she said.

These moments felt, to Gary, different from winning an election. They were not as heady, but they lasted longer. Because Gary's life was intertwined with his neighbors' lives. Like Jay and Lorna, the divorcing couple he'd helped in his first mediation case decades before, there was no real "winning" if either one lost.

Adversarialism depends on total, complete, and permanent separation. In the real world, no such thing exists, most of the time. There is no "Old Guard" and "New Guard." "Using those tactics is like asking, 'Who's winning this marriage?,'" as the negotiator Ury likes to say. The same is true for a neighborhood dispute—or a political fight. You can get a temporary dopamine hit from a "beatdown," to use Tanya's word. That feels good. It can be galvanizing. You might even win important legal or political victories that create institutional change, which make other changes possible. That's a big deal.

But it's also true that the next custody fight or election or gun battle is never far off. In the long arc of history, we've all got kids together, metaphorically or literally. All across the globe, we are more dependent on one another than ever before. If winning means your neighbors get humiliated, you haven't won. "Anger is not transformative," Ruth King wrote in *Mindful of Race*. "It's initiatory."

I have politically active friends who hate when I talk this way.

Sometimes *I* hate it when I talk this way. In the blaze of a conflict, it is a huge bummer to be told there's no winning. "There is a time to fight," these friends tell me, eyes bright with certainty. And they're right. There *is* a time to fight—to protest, to organize, to knock on doors. Most of us need more *good* conflict, not less. But the kind of conflict matters. Conflict without understanding is a half measure at best.

During the two years that Gary made his shift out of high conflict in Muir Beach, here are some things that happened: The road got repaired. The water rate got raised. The tone of the meetings improved. The neighborhood made progress, without coming apart. One day, a member of the Old Guard called and left a message on Gary's phone, thanking him for the way he'd handled a dispute at the last meeting. The neighbor told him how good it had felt to understand the two people and not have to choose sides. Gary played it for me over the phone. It meant a lot to him, rightly so.

It had been much harder than he'd expected. But Gary had helped his neighbors—and himself—understand one another a little better. He'd proven that politics can be done differently, eventually.

Watching Gary and Curtis has motivated me to try to hold the tension. Even in the trenches of political clashes. I try to remind myself: there's no winning this marriage. We've all got kids together, all of us, all over the world.

What then?

The Putumayo River, as seen from the peaks of the Sibundoy Valley in Putumayo, Colombia. Nicolò Filippo Rosso

chapter 6

reverse engineering

"Since wars begin in the minds of men, it is in the minds of men that the defenses of peace must be constructed."

—*Preamble to the constitution of UNESCO*

The helicopters appeared just before dusk. Three of them, hovering over the rainforest canopy, like UFOs. It was November 9, 2009, and Sandra Milena Vera Bustos and her boyfriend were packing, getting ready to walk through the Andean mountains at night. That's how they moved in the guerrilla group they belonged to, so they would not be seen.

She recognized the drone of the helicopter rotors instantly. It was a recurring thrum in the lives of guerrilla members all over Colombia, the soundtrack of this war. The noise came on suddenly this time, low to the ground, with purpose. She felt the vibration deep in her chest.

Looking outside, Sandra saw soldiers rappelling down ladders dropped from the helicopters. One, two, three, ten, fifteen. They just kept coming. Someone must have told them where they were. Now dozens of soldiers were fanning out, surrounding their group of just four guerrilla members. She looked around for her AK-47. It was in another room, and there was no time.

Sandra and Sebastián sprinted from the house, looking for cover down the mountainside.

This was what it looked like: the cat-and-mouse game played by the rebels and the military for half a century. It usually happened in rural parts of Colombia, just like this, violence slashing suddenly through fields or jungle, kicking up dirt, shredding roofs and scattering animals.

Sandra hid in the undergrowth behind a boulder, holding her breath. She heard the rat-tat-tat of gunfire, and then a scream. Was that Sebastián? It was, it had to be. Her heart contracted, like she'd been shot herself. She prayed furiously, silently.

In the distance, she saw another one of her fellow guerrilla fighters raise his rifle above his head in surrender. Maybe that was what she should do. It was time. She'd go to jail, but at least she'd live. What choice did she have?

But then she heard more shots, and the man crumpled to the ground. The soldiers had shot him anyway, with his hands above his head. So now she knew. There was no surrendering.

For hours, Sandra stayed frozen behind that rock, her heart pounding, her legs cramping, thinking about her daughter. She touched the silver dolphin on a chain around her neck, the necklace she'd worn day and night for years. Eventually, the sounds of the soldiers' voices began to fade, and she decided to make a run for it. She sprinted down the mountain, her black ponytail flying through the brush behind her.

But what was that? More voices. She slowed down. There were more soldiers down below. And more still above her. She was trapped in between, without food, water, or a weapon.

la desmovilización

We all live in two worlds: the external and the internal. They interact constantly. Formal peace treaties get signed by elites in the external world, when they get signed at all. And they are important. But this book is about something else—about what happens (or fails to happen) at the individual level when regular people attempt to make that *internal* shift out of high conflict.

Gary and Curtis made that shift largely on their own. They had to bushwhack their way out. Which is why many people, like Glenn Beck, do not make it out. There's no path. But what if there were? What if towns or even countries cleared a path to lead people out of high conflict?

Over the past few decades, more than sixty countries have tried to find out. The formal term for this experiment is Disarmament, Demobilization, and Reintegration. In the beginning, it mostly meant just disarming combatants: literally collecting and destroying their weapons. Over time, peacemakers and governments realized they needed to do more, or the conflict would just reignite. They needed to help people build new identities. Usually, they did this by giving them money, political power, and schooling.

This is a radical idea, if you think about it. Governments are spending millions of dollars on former enemies of the state, the same groups previously described (often by the very same government) as terrorists and insurgents, responsible in some cases for kidnappings, bombings, rapes, drug trafficking, and the recruitment of child soldiers.

These efforts can fail spectacularly, as you might imagine. In Sierra Leone, the reintegration program had *no measurable impact at all*. People who did not receive the support services were just as likely to successfully reintegrate into society as those who did. It is very hard to reverse engineer high conflict at scale. But it is one of the central questions of our time. How do you clear a path out of high conflict for not just one or two individuals, but for great crowds of us?

To find out, I went to a country that has accumulated unusual expertise on the subject. Colombia has been riven by conflict for more than fifty-seven years. This civil war, brother against sister, state against guerrilla force, has killed a quarter of a million people. (That's a hard number to grasp. As a point of comparison, if you add up all the people killed in the Arab-Israeli conflict in the past century, you end up with about half as many deaths.)

Colombia is a sprawling and mysterious place. It's the oldest democracy in South America. This is the country that gave us the writer Gabriel García Márquez, the artist Fernando Botero, and the singer Shakira. It is also the country that has supplied most of the cocaine sold in the United States, including cocaine sold by Curtis's gang in Chicago.

Partly because of the corruption and turmoil created by the narcotics trade, Colombia is a place with decades of experience in trying to get people *out* of conflict at scale. *La Desmovilización* has been epic by any measure—ambitious, expensive, and complicated. About 52,000 people have demobilized in Colombia through the government's reintegration programs since 2001.

In 2016, the government signed a fragile peace deal with the oldest guerrilla group, known as the Revolutionary Armed Forces of Colombia, or the FARC. But most of the ex-combatants left the conflict *before* that peace treaty was signed. One by one, they laid down their arms and tried to build new lives, just like Curtis. So far, most have not returned to the conflict or to crime, to the degree we can tell.

These days, Colombia's reintegration program spends tens of thousands of dollars per ex-combatant, more than quadruple the average for similar efforts around the world. This is a massive, unprecedented investment in helping people out of high conflict. And still today, Colombia has profound problems. The peace agreement has been shamelessly undermined by political and criminal conflict entrepreneurs, and it may not hold.

Sandra in a car in Bogotá, Colombia, in February 2020. Nicolò Filippo Rosso

Whatever happens, this much is clear: Colombia is home to millions of "conflict experts," official and otherwise. It is a real-world laboratory for how people get in and out of high conflict, en masse.

into the jungle

One day, when Sandra was about fourteen, a car pulled up outside her neighbor's house, carrying three men. Her neighbor came outside, holding her grandbaby in her arms, to see what the men wanted. This woman was known to everyone in the village. She was on the local council, called a *junta*, which meant she helped resolve disputes and negotiated with various armed groups that came through the village. She was a shield, like Curtis and Billy in Chicago. Or she was supposed to be.

Two of the men had their faces hidden behind balaclavas. While Sandra watched, a third man stepped out of the car and shot the grandmother in the head. He executed her, without a word. The grandmother collapsed. It felt, to Sandra, like it all happened in slow motion. When the grandmother fell, she dropped the infant, who hit the ground hard. The car drove away.

Sandra's parents belonged to a left-wing political party dedicated to helping the poor. The party had communist roots, which meant Sandra's family was always on the run. Right-wing groups had been systematically killing off the party's leaders and followers for over a decade, executing hundreds of them. Sandra moved at least ten times that she could remember. She finally dropped out of school at age fourteen. She couldn't stay in one place long enough to make it work.

It was around this time that Sandra watched the murder of her neighbor outside her house. She watched it in silence. Then she watched as the grown-ups came running. Later, she listened to them grieve. Both the grandmother and the baby died.

This was the moment Sandra decided to join the conflict. She was done watching. She'd start fighting instead. Fighting the paramilitaries who had run her parents out of town, who had executed anyone who jeopardized their control over power, land, and wealth. It was a moment of horror, which Sandra turned into a career.

Sandra left her family and joined the communist rebel army, the FARC. She was still a young girl, but that was not so unusual then, and it isn't now. Of the roughly 300,000 child soldiers fighting around the world today, about 40 percent are girls.

Like all the guerrilla fighters, Sandra chose a new identity, quite literally, selecting a nom de guerre. "Liceth" was the new Sandra, she announced. But because of her indigenous roots, her shiny black hair and her wide-open face, her comrades nicknamed her "Little Indian." Sandra would claim many identities, confused and overlapping, in the years to come.

"son, wait no longer"

After sixteen years of failing to qualify, Colombia made it into the World Cup, the most watched sporting event in the world, in 2014.

The team's best player was out with injuries at the time, so the expectations were muted. But a young, red-cheeked, breakout star named James Rodríguez stepped into the void, electrifying the nation, racking up five goals in the first four games.

On June 28, Colombia played Uruguay in the Round of 16, looking to advance to the quarterfinals for the first time in the country's history. Like almost every Colombian alive, Juan Pablo Aparicio was watching. He was a twenty-one-year-old college student, living in Medellín, holding his breath, hoping for a miracle.

In the 28th minute, Rodriguez scored one of the most beautiful goals in soccer history, a left-footed volley that arced just under the crossbar from a full 25 yards away. It was exquisite. Juan Pablo and everyone around him erupted in joy. It felt exhilarating, and strange, to feel so proud of his country. And to know all of Colombia was united, in this one moment.

In the middle of the game, there was a public service announcement. Not the kind most of us have heard, urging people not to smoke cigarettes or drink and drive. This message urged people to leave high conflict. "Son, wait no longer," the announcer said, speaking directly to the country's guerrilla fighters. "I'm saving you a seat to see the best plays. Demobilize."

It was the kind of propaganda ad that the government aired regularly at the time, trying to nudge rebel fighters to surrender. On that day, Juan Pablo noticed it and shook his head. Why did anyone think that would work?

Colombia's civil war started in the 1960s, long before Juan Pablo was born, when a narrow stratum of elites controlled land, wealth, and political power in Colombia. Demanding a more equitable society, Marxist groups like the FARC took up arms against the state. To defend themselves, wealthy landowners hired their own militia, known as paramilitaries. These paramilitaries included the men who killed Sandra's elderly neighbor. Fire starter leaders inflamed the conflict, exploiting old divides between urban and rural Colombians and rich and poor.

As the years ticked by, the Colombian military began to work alongside the paramilitaries to fight the FARC. It was sometimes hard to tell them apart. The U.S., meanwhile, helped to sponsor this civil war, providing financial and military support to the Colombian military. First, the U.S. got involved to fight a war on communism and then a war on drugs and finally a war on terrorism. Like most wars, nothing went as planned. Violence led to more violence. Polarization, corruption, and inequality metastasized.

All sides in this conflict did unspeakable things. The FARC committed a sickening number of kidnappings. The paramilitaries executed an appalling number of innocent people. The military murdered thousands of peasants and then claimed they were combatants, sometimes even dressing the bodies in fatigues and posing them with guns, just to boost the official count of guerrilla casualties.

Regular people on all sides ended up worse off, a sure sign of a high conflict. Eight out of every ten people killed in Colombia's civil war have been civilians. Nearly eight million Colombians have been forced out of their homes by the conflict, becoming refugees in their own country.

Like most Colombians, Juan Pablo had lived with the conflict all his life, always in the background, like a recurring cancer. His best friend's father had been kidnapped by a far-right paramilitary outfit. He never returned. His own father was on a FARC list of kidnapping targets, singled out because of his family's successful coffee business. These guerrillas were beyond redemption, as far as Juan Pablo could tell. In what universe would telling a bunch of brainwashed thugs to give up their weapons actually work? The propaganda seemed ridiculously naive.

On that particular day, Colombia won the game, making it to the quarterfinals. Rodríguez became a national hero. He was the best player in the tournament, even the opposing team's coach said so. Six days later, Colombia lost against Brazil, which was painful. But there was a feeling that lingered for Juan Pablo. A feeling that maybe Colombia was capable of more than everyone expected.

surrounded

By the time the helicopters came, Sandra had been in the FARC for nine years. She and Sebastián had just gotten transferred to a political posting in another location, and she was hopeful. The two of them would get to work together, like they had when she'd first joined, explaining the ideology of the guerrilla movement to people in small towns. This was what she loved: talking about ideas, justice, the Marxist revolutionary Che Guevara, a vision of a better, fairer world, as yet unrealized. She wouldn't have to do much of the ugly work, extorting people for money in what the FARC called its "financial" unit, the one responsible for raising revenue through any means possible, including kidnapping and narcotrafficking.

Unlike many of her comrades, Sandra didn't take pictures of herself profiling in her camo with her AK-47. That wasn't her style. She knew how to handle her weapon, but she had never had to kill anyone, thank God. She'd had to threaten people on occasion, and that was bad enough. She'd felt sick for days afterward. That's one reason she'd been trying for years to get back to a political post, like this one.

But there was another reason. FARC members were not allowed to have children. Female guerrilla members who got pregnant were often forced to have abortions. When she'd gotten pregnant with Sebastián's child, she had managed to get an exception to the rule and carry their baby to term. But one year after giving birth, she'd been called back to the jungle. She'd left their daughter with Sebastián's relatives in Bogotá. Now, Tamara was a sweet, round-faced four-year-old, and Sandra was consumed by the fear that she and Sebastián would both die, leaving Tamara an orphan.

Like Curtis in Chicago and the members of Black September in the Middle East, her identity as a parent was pulling her away from the conflict, changing her risk calculation. Every time it was her turn to take watch, she worried about being ambushed. Every time she got in a truck to drive somewhere, she imagined a bomb going off.

She still felt a sense of purpose in the FARC, a sense of belonging and duty. But she could not justify leaving her daughter alone in this world. She wanted her daughter to have one parent who was alive, at least. So she was so relieved to be heading to a less dangerous posting, closer to Tamara. That was the plan.

Then the soldiers surrounded them, killing Sebastián. For ten days after the ambush, Sandra wandered on that mountainside. As she got weaker, she lost track of time. She prayed to Santa Marta, the saint whose picture she carried in her pocket, a gift from her mother many years ago.

And she decided, like Curtis at his son's graduation ceremony, that she was done. If she survived this, she would leave the conflict and take care of her child. She would become Sandra again. This was a painful decision. Her comrades would consider her a traitor, she knew. In the FARC, desertion was punishable by death.

But she'd reached her saturation point. The losses had become too much to bear. Finally, she knocked on the door of a peasant family who gave her food and water. She recovered enough to contact her own family. She asked her sister to come get her. "I want to leave," Sandra told her. "I don't want any part of this anymore."

counterpropaganda

Four years after watching that thrilling World Cup victory, Juan Pablo was studying for his PhD in economics. For his research paper, his adviser told him to pursue the craziest idea he could think of, the crazier the better. At the time, Colombia had just qualified for the 2018 World Cup. And so Juan Pablo thought back to those ads. Did they have any effect at all, he wanted to know? Was it possible to nudge people out of high conflict with a thirty-second spot?

He sincerely doubted it. But he had one reason to be curious. He knew, by then, that the opposite was possible. In Rwanda. A 2014 study by David Yanagizawa-Drott had looked at the effects of a popular radio station that had called for the extermination of the Tutsi

minority during the 1994 Rwandan genocide. In that case, only vil-
lages with radio reception could have heard the messages. There were
natural control groups all over the country, wherever there was no
radio signal.

The results were shocking. As radio reception improved, killings
increased in Rwanda. In all, about one in every ten acts of violence
could be linked to the messages from this radio station. Tens of thousands of people were nudged into attacking their fellow countrymen by simple messages urging them to do so. Some fifty thousand
Rwandans may have been killed as a result of these radio broadcasts.
Words mattered. Conflict entrepreneurs started fires all over Rwanda
by broadcasting hatred at scale, on the radio.

So Juan Pablo wondered: Could words work in the reverse direction? Members of the FARC religiously listened to Colombia's
national soccer team games on radio, whenever they could, wherever
they were, as ex-guerrillas had acknowledged in published interviews.
They remained fiercely loyal to their country's soccer team, even as
they took up arms against the state. So the guerrillas were, by and
large, hearing these messages urging them to demobilize.

Meanwhile, the Colombian government keeps records of each
successful *desmovilizado*, so Juan Pablo could track how many people
had voluntarily left the conflict from the FARC each month between
2001 and 2017. It was a huge database of more than nineteen thousand desertions, a treasure trove of data.

Unlike Rwanda, all of Colombia enjoyed pretty decent radio coverage. Rain, however, varied a lot across Colombia's tropical climate
and landscape. And when it rained, radio reception was terrible, as it
turned out. So Juan Pablo could tell where FARC members had likely
heard the messages, based on the weather at the time of kick-off. And
then he could compare the postgame demobilization rates in those
areas to the rates in the rainy regions. It was a natural experiment.

To make sure the announcements were actually played in each
game, per government contracts with the broadcasters, Juan Pablo

asked the broadcasting company if he could access the two hundred or so archived national soccer games. They said no. He asked the government. Also no.

But Juan Pablo did not give up. It became a kind of obsession, at the intersection of soccer and country, two things he cared about deeply. So he put a message on Twitter offering to pay $1,000 to any soccer superfans who happened to have recorded those soccer games. It was a gamble, but Juan Pablo had a lot of faith in Colombia's superfans.

Within hours, he had a response. A superfan who ran a popular soccer meme site in Colombia met him at a mall in Medellín and gave him a pile of thumb drives with recordings for almost all of the games. Juan Pablo gave him $1,000.

For months afterward, Juan Pablo enlisted his parents and his younger brother to help him listen to the games. Soon he had a database of the demobilization messages. He used rainfall data from NASA's Tropical Rainfall Measuring Mission to figure out which of Colombia's 1,122 municipalities had radio reception during the national soccer team games. He also identified which games were played at dusk, when FARC members were most likely to be listening.

What he found astonished him. A soccer game played at dusk, with no rain interference, led to twenty extra guerrilla members demobilizing the day after a game. That was ten times the daily average for desertions. Demobilizations stayed up in these areas even a week after the game was played.

By comparison, the killing of a high-profile FARC leader drove about thirty-six additional demobilizations. But that kind of high-level execution happened only a handful of times during Colombia's civil war. The soccer messages were, according to Juan Pablo's data, much more impactful, since they happened far more often—and cost much less in lives and treasure.

No one really knows why the soccer ads seemed to have worked. Many forces must have interacted to spur those desertions. And counterpropaganda does not always work. Other Colombian ads have failed, even ones that seemed much more compelling, as we'll see.

But Juan Pablo has come to respect the power of creative messaging. "We can get people out of conflict without killing them," he told me, "and propaganda is a very good way to get people out." Over the course of the nine years that these ads aired, the soccer campaign demobilized more people than the formal peace deal signed with the FARC in 2016, according to his results.

There's a lot we don't know. One thing that we can say for sure, though, is that all of us, including guerrilla fighters, carry multiple identities in our hearts. And we want to do right by all of them.

"invisible citizen"

Sandra's sister arrived on a motorcycle to take her out of high conflict. They left together at dusk, driving nine hours through the mountains to Bogotá. Careening through the dark, Sandra felt like she was in a kind of trance. Afraid she might be killed by the army or, now, by the FARC, for desertion, she could not allow herself to think about Sebastián's death. She shut off that part of herself. She thought, instead, of Tamara.

Soon after they arrived in Bogotá, Sandra was reunited with her daughter, which was a relief. At first. But what then? Hiding out at her mother's apartment, Sandra felt the walls closing in. She had two terrible choices: she could wait for the authorities to arrest her, which would not take long, since she was living with her family in the city; or she could turn herself in to the government, which could mean she'd be killed. That is what the FARC had always told her: the government will squeeze you for intelligence and then kill you. There was, really, no option at all. Not if she wanted to raise Tamara.

In the jungle, Sandra had heard public service announcements on the radio, urging FARC guerrillas to desert, promising them a better life. But she had never trusted these messages. The Colombian military had killed her friends and helped the paramilitaries that had displaced her family and murdered her neighbor. Her comrades told her those messages were lies, and she believed them.

Now, living in tight quarters, trying to reconnect with her daughter, who didn't call her *mamá*, who barely knew her, Sandra felt desperate for a way out. She woke up each day and tried to concoct a plan. She wanted to get a job and support her family. She wanted to go back to school. But how?

It's striking how much Sandra's story echoes the stories of gang members in Chicago. Hiding out in relatives' houses, afraid to go anywhere, paralyzed. We'll never know the exact number, but it's safe to assume that there are, right now, millions of people living in high conflict who would leave, if only they could see a path out.

In January 2010, two months after Sebastián's death, Sandra did a Google search on her sister's computer. She looked up the name of the Colombian office responsible for what they called "reintegration." This was the word she'd always heard on those propaganda ads, urging guerrilla members to demobilize.

Then she clicked on "Reintegration Route," on the toolbar at the top. Rank-and-file guerrillas who turned themselves in would *not* be jailed or killed, she read. Instead, they would get services—to help them build a new life. She pursed her lips, skeptical.

There was a process, apparently, like applying for a job: 1. Find a demobilization office near you. 2. Sit for an interview. If you convince the government you were part of a guerrilla group, you will receive a certificate. 3. That certificate gives you certain rights. You will get a customized reintegration plan, based on your needs, including counseling and a monthly stipend to help you go back to school. Notably, the government cannot pressure you to inform on your comrades, the website claimed.

The more she read, the more curious Sandra became. She still did not trust the government, not at all. But for the first time, a sliver of space opened up in her mind. Maybe because she saw the steps laid out on the screen in official-looking font. Maybe because she had no other options. Whatever the reason, she did not reject the messages outright, as she had in the past. "In that moment," she said, "I felt hope."

This is the first lesson from Colombia: to help people out of conflict at scale, you must clear a path. And the path must be safe, legitimate, and easy to find. In a civil war, it might require a government agency with a transparent, step-by-step process. In a less violent high conflict, such as the political polarization afflicting America and many other countries in recent years, it may require a third party— or another legitimate, alternative, easy-to-find group for people who have reached their saturation points and need a new way to matter.

I visited an office of Colombia's reintegration program in Soacha, a downtrodden suburb just outside of Bogotá. There were tiny chairs and toys in the waiting area for kids. A mother was feeding her newborn baby. The list of things the agency has failed to do is long and meaningful. But its very existence felt important. It reminded me of CRED's office in Chicago, a safe place where gang members can go to cultivate a new identity.

Around the time Sandra was learning about the reintegration program online, an old childhood friend named Diego came to visit her. Now, he was a police officer. But he didn't come to arrest her. He came to try to persuade her to turn herself in. After a few days, Sandra agreed to let him accompany her to the office listed on the reintegration website. He became part of the community that showed her a path out of conflict, just like Curtis and Billy do for gang members in Chicago. Escorts are critical on the path out of conflict, it turns out. If we want people to take a perilous road, it's unreasonable to expect them to go alone.

The office listed on the website was on the bottom floor of a famous old hotel in Bogotá's financial district, the Hotel Tequendama. In early February 2010, Sandra headed to the hotel, with Diego at her side. "I was terrified," she said. She'd been out of the jungle for less than two months, and now she was making her way through a city of ten million people to meet the enemy. She walked past men carrying high-powered weapons, standing guard near the hotel. She felt her heart beating as she opened the door and walked through the marble lobby, to the office where she would turn herself in. She had to remind herself to breathe.

When she arrived, she was shown to a cubicle, where she waited. It was a very long fifteen minutes. She touched the dolphin on the necklace around her neck. Police and soldiers walked by, glancing her way. She felt naked, without her gun, in the enemy's house. Her hands were shaking. "It felt horrible. I had no clue what would happen next. I just hoped I was doing it right."

Eventually, a young clerk appeared to interview her. He was not in uniform, which was reassuring. He asked her a series of questions: "When did you join the FARC? Why did you stay as long as you did? Why do you want to leave now?" He took notes. He had to determine whether she really was a member of the FARC, so she could qualify for the program's benefits.

In Colombia and other countries, demobilization efforts have been exploited by fraudsters looking to game the system and claim benefits they don't deserve. So this step made sense. But it also put people like Sandra in a dicey situation. In a Defense Ministry office, a stranger was essentially saying to Sandra: "Prove you were my enemy. Tell me about the crimes you committed against the state. Convince me of your treason. Then I will give you money!"

There were things Sandra didn't tell him, in the end. But she told him enough to convince him that she had indeed been a member of the FARC. At which point, she should have been released into the fresh air, with the promise that she'd be certified to get reintegration services.

Instead, a colonel in the same office asked to talk to Sandra. The man was in uniform and armed. He asked Sandra to tell him where he could find her commanding officer, who also happened to be Sebastián's father and Tamara's grandfather. Sandra declined to tell him anything. At which point, he threatened to withhold her demobilization certificate. Sandra began to sweat through her civilian clothes. It was just as she had feared, after all.

Sandra could not betray what was most important to her. She'd joined the FARC to fight injustice, as she saw it. And then the FARC had become her family, literally. Giving them up to the enemy would have been a profound betrayal. Like Gary and Curtis, Sandra knew what she held most dear, and she would not surrender it.

"I know my rights," she said, more confidently than she felt. She quoted what she'd read on the website, almost verbatim. If he didn't sign off on her certificate, she said, she would file a complaint. She understood the process. She would give up her gun, but not her family.

This is the second lesson from Colombia. If you want to help people out of high conflict, don't ask them to betray their remaining identities, the ones that transcend the conflict. These are the identities they will need to stay out of the conflict. "When a man is denied the right to live the life he believes in," Nelson Mandela wrote, "he has no choice but to become an outlaw."

Three months after she faced down the colonel, Sandra got her demobilization certificate. The government kept its promise after all. Then she met with a reintegration worker who helped her design a plan, focused mostly around education and work. She would receive about $76 per month to help her live while she went to night school. She'd get another $76 a month, provided she met with a social worker twice a month as ordered. It wasn't much, but it was a start.

Around this time, Sandra got work in a market stall, helping with the books. She attended classes at night and went to the social worker, as ordered. All this time, her mother helped care for Tamara, making everything else possible.

This phase in Sandra's "reintegration" sounds like progress, and it was. But it was also profoundly lonely, just as it was for Curtis in the beginning. She was out of the jungle but hiding in plain sight. She could not tell anyone about her past. Not her neighbors, not anyone. When she applied for jobs, she explained away the previous decade by saying she'd been an *ama de casa*, a housewife. She was what researchers call an "invisible citizen." This is a solitary life. You put on a mask every day. It's hard to belong when you have to hide.

Despite all the violence Sandra had witnessed in her life, she received no trauma counseling. This was the biggest weakness of the process, she told me. And it's a failure of most reintegration processes I've seen, with the exception of CRED in Chicago, which includes this kind of help. For Sandra, the visits to the social worker were basically worthless for the first three years. Each time, she met with a different person, a stranger who knew nothing about her. It was more like a parole meeting than a counseling session.

But there were flashes of hope. Sandra finished her high school studies and got an associate's degree in business. She got a job in a factory making T-shirts. She eventually met a man named Sergio, who had not been involved in the conflict. She told him her story, and he listened. It came as a surprise that she could fall in love with someone outside of the FARC.

In 2012, they had a baby boy, whom they named Sergio Jr. Two months later, the Colombian government began to negotiate with the FARC in Havana, Cuba. The news leaked in the media, and the Colombian president confirmed that "exploratory talks" had begun with the leftist guerrilla group. Sandra began to let herself imagine a different future for her growing family.

Then her boss began to complain about her absences. Twice a month she had to leave work to attend those required social worker visits, but she couldn't tell him why. Finally, she told someone from the human resources department that she was "in a process," using a euphemism for her reintegration program. The next day, the HR person fired her.

"It's too dangerous to have you here," he said.

Sandra was adrift again, punished for her past identity, not her present. This, too, is a common experience of people who leave high conflict. Just when they start to find their place in a new group, they get suddenly banished. She left the factory feeling empty, hopeless.

She had to start over, yet again, and with a new baby at home, she needed money badly.

But she understood this man who fired her, she told me. All he knew of the FARC was what he'd seen on TV. She was the "other," a terrorist. She reminded herself that she'd felt the same way about the police and the military, not so long before.

She began looking for a new job.

operation christmas

Other forces motivated people to leave the conflict in Colombia, too. Darker forces, unrelated to soccer. For example, when the Colombian military went on the offense and successfully destroyed major FARC targets, more FARC members deserted.

Another pattern had to do with drugs and money. The FARC was one of the most powerful drug trafficking syndicates in the world, extracting "taxes" at every level of the supply chain, from coca farmers to buyers to truck operators. At its peak, the FARC made somewhere between $500 million to $1 billion off the coca economy, the Colombian military estimated in 2005. So whenever the Colombian peso got stronger compared to the U.S. dollar, the FARC made less profit. When that happened, more FARC members deserted, according to research by Enzo Nussio and Juan Ugarriza.

In other words, rebels left the conflict when they experienced hunger and misery, either from battlefield losses or revenue cuts. This made sense. Just like Curtis questioning his commitment to the conflict as the feds closed in on his fellow gang leaders, guerrilla members felt the pressure. As a general rule, no one wants to die. Not in Medellín or Chicago or Aleppo. And it's exhausting to be on the run, moving camp every night to escape the helicopters.

Saturation points can be caused by suffering, plainly put. If things get bad enough, the latent identities of guerrilla members may resurface, spurring them to leave high conflict.

Interestingly, other forms of propaganda did *not* work, according to Nussio and Ugarriza's study. For example, in 2010, a global ad firm working with the Colombian Defense Ministry decorated nine tall trees in the Colombian jungle with blue Christmas lights, next to banners that read, "If Christmas can come to the jungle, you can come home. Demobilize." It was a beautiful visual made for TV. The campaign, known as Operation Christmas, was featured in media reports all over the world, from the BBC to *60 Minutes*, and the ad agency claimed victory, citing significant spikes in the number of desertions.

But that's not what the researchers found. In the months during and right after the Christmas campaigns of 2010, 2011, and 2012, they found no statistically significant change in the amount of FARC desertions, after controlling for other factors. If anything, the campaign seemed to *negatively* correlate with desertions—meaning fewer FARC members demobilized after the campaign than would otherwise be expected.

Why would the soccer ads work if the Christmas trees did not? It's hard to say for sure, but it may have to do with the reach and potency of the soccer ads. It's possible that more guerrilla members heard the ads, first of all, just because soccer games were of great interest to guerrilla members.

It's also possible that the message itself worked better. The initial wave of soccer ads, designed by the government, were focused on the guerrilla's family, urging rebels to come home to see their mothers, for example. Later, the professional ad agency that was brought in tweaked the campaign to focus more on soccer itself—telling rebels they were part of Colombia's team. But the first message, focused on the family, seemed to work better, Juan Pablo found, spurring more desertions.

"It seems like the most effective campaigns are the ones that appeal to a family relationship," Juan Pablo said. It was a theme I heard again and again, in all kinds of conflict. Reviving latent family identities can help propel people out of high conflict—in divorce court or gang feuds or civil wars.

But that's only the beginning of anyone's exit from high conflict.

Military bombardments, currency fluctuations, and soccer ads may have spurred desertions, but they didn't defeat the FARC. Those who deserted were replaced by new recruits, many of them children. Meanwhile, military offensives killed thousands of civilians. All of which perpetuated the cycle of high conflict, seeding new under-stories for generations to come.

A saturation point, like a peace agreement, is only the first step in transforming high conflict—and maybe the simplest one. Everything depends on what happens next.

"this is you"

Mariana Díaz Kraus spent twelve years working on demobilization in Colombia, including at the government's reintegration agency, the one Sandra turned to after reaching her saturation point. The government's internal research confirmed that family was indeed often the catalyst for leaving, she told me. "Family pulls you out." But it's not enough.

The smartest way to help people *stay* out of high conflict is keep

Sandra and her son, Sergio Jr., at home in Soacha, Colombia. Nicolò Filippo Rosso

the new identity alive. Help them cultivate those newly revived roles. When the Royal Society awarded the environmentalist Mark Lynas its prize for science writing, it formalized his new identity as a scientific thinker. Intentionally or not, this gesture made it much harder for him to go back to his old identity, fighting genetically modified crops.

In Colombia, it helped to literally give people identity cards, the official government-issued documents that most ex-combatants did not have when they left the jungle. "The identity card was a very powerful tool," Kraus said, "in showing them, 'Here, this is you. Your picture, your name, your thumbprint. This is the citizen who has rights, who can demand things from the state in a legal way.'"

It sounds like such a small milestone, but it really mattered, practically and spiritually. In Colombia, that identity number is critical to opening up a bank account, voting, getting health care, even buying a pair of sneakers. Ex-combatants would show Kraus their new identity cards with pride. It was a badge of relevance.

Another powerful strategy was to directly help ex-combatants' families, Kraus said. Make sure the children are in school, help their partners find jobs, work on securing housing and health care for the family unit, not just the individual. "When you feel that your family is doing well, and it's because of the decision you made," Kraus said, "it makes it a decision you cannot easily undo."

Again and again in Sandra's story, her family reappeared. Sandra's sister literally drove her away from the conflict. She and their mother welcomed her home, despite having no money to spare. Without their support and love, it's hard to imagine what would have happened to her. "My family," she said, "was indispensable."

Sandra's story is the story of thousands, in this way. In 2016, Enzo Nussio and his colleague Oliver Kaplan compared a sample of 1,485 ex-combatants in Colombia with police and military records—to see which ones had been arrested by police or captured in military operations in the four to nine years since demobilizing. Most did not reappear on the police or military capture lists. But 14 percent did. Why did those particular people get caught up in crime or the conflict? Why did so many others stay off the lists?

Having children mattered a lot, it turned out. People with children were 40 percent less likely to return to illegal activities. Forty percent! In fact, strong family ties were more predictive of success than whether an ex-combatant had found a job, to the researchers' surprise.

Families are the reason many people leave high conflict to begin with, as we've seen. Family members can act as shields, drawing their loved ones out of conflict, away from the fire starters. Families can make people realize that they've reached their saturation points. Gary's wife and children did this, as did Curtis's son. When they're not generating it themselves, families compete with high conflict all over the world. Ideally then, anyone who wants to help people out of conflict should help their families, just like the PLO did when marrying off the members of Black September.

This is tricky to pull off, politically speaking. Conflict generates deep resentment and distrust, legitimately so. In the past, about eight of every ten surveyed Colombians said they did not trust ex-combatants. That level of fear and contempt makes it very hard to justify giving people like Sandra or her family money or assistance. Half of Colombians said former combatants should not receive any support at all.

Which means there's a third critical group to address when trying to help people out of conflict, beyond the ex-combatants and their families. That third group is the public. They, too, were part of the conflict, in different ways. Regular people matter. If they continue to see people like Sandra as the enemy, the conflict will continue. She will be isolated, resented, and ostracized.

In this way, Operation Christmas may have had some positive effect after all. Not because those ads convinced large numbers of guerrillas to leave the jungle but because they disrupted the binary for everyone else. Regular people noticed those ads, which got a lot of media attention. Regular people heard the voices of guerrilla members' mothers, asking for them to come home. This was not sufficient, not even close, but it was a start.

Here's the painful truth: communities have to welcome former combatants home, whether they are ex–gang members, ex-rebels, or even ex-pundits. Otherwise, they will go where they feel like they belong, which is usually back to the conflict.

el brexit colombiano

The year she got fired from her job, Sandra was assigned a new social worker, named Viviana, who remained her social worker for three years. The required visits went from being a chore to being useful. Viviana had no expertise in trauma counseling, but she was supportive and consistent, like a good coach. She encouraged Sandra to take hold of her own life, not to wait for the government or the FARC or anyone to lead the way.

In October of 2016, the Colombian people were asked to vote on the peace agreement that had just been signed by the government and the FARC. It was a referendum, with two sides: yes or no. This step was not necessary to the peace process, but it had seemed like a good way to get public buy-in.

In reality, it was a dangerous gamble, given the power of the binary. It collapsed half a century of civil war into a single up-or-down vote, making it easy for political conflict entrepreneurs to exploit. Still, everyone thought the referendum would pass. All the pollsters said so.

Sandra voted for the peace agreement. Late that night, she got into bed to watch the results on TV, with her children and her husband under the covers with her.

The results shocked the world. The peace agreement failed—by less than half a percentage point. Most of the people directly victimized by the war had voted for it; but two thirds of Colombians hadn't voted at all. Hearing the results, Sandra's heart dropped. She and her husband locked eyes. They'd been ready to celebrate, but instead they just sat there in the bed, holding their children, tears running down their faces. "I felt like hope had been taken away."

Looking back on it, the failure of Colombia's peace referendum shows how important it is to work on conflict from the bottom up, not just the top down. Leaders can start the process by signing a peace treaty or reforming the justice system. But that's the external world. What about the internal world of regular people?

The internal world gets neglected most of the time. The Christmas tree ads were a nice start, but many Colombians resented and feared ex–guerrilla members and thought of them as subhuman. And why shouldn't they have? For decades, politicians had demonized the FARC to suit their own ends. And the news media had covered the conflict mostly from the perspective of the government. So regular people grew up thinking of the FARC as the enemy of civilization.

This is another toxic legacy of conflict entrepreneurs. They vilify *them*, the very people who will need to join *us* for high conflict to end one day. This creates a huge challenge. Just as the enemy got dehumanized, they must be rehumanized.

There are lots of ways to rehumanize people, but one way is through great storytelling. It can be more powerful than any peace treaty. In Macedonia, the nonprofit Search for Common Ground produced a children's TV show in which families from four ethnic backgrounds live in the same magical, talking apartment building. The show included all the languages from the different ethnic groups, which was unusual. It was a huge hit. Nine out of ten Macedonian children said they'd watched at least one episode, and almost half said they'd talked about the show with their parents. Before viewing the show, only 30 percent of children would have invited a child from another ethnic group into their home. After eight episodes, 60 percent said they would.

Rehumanizing the enemy takes time. It's hard to do well. But it is just as essential as the peace talks. It was neglected in Colombia, as it is in many places.

The only time I saw Sandra get emotional was when she talked about the night of the referendum vote. Telling the story, years later, her eyes filled with tears. "I felt scared that my children would grow up in the same Colombia, of hatred and fear." She was, I could plainly see, still scared. You can get yourself out of the Tar Pits, but you can't take your country with you.

The referendum's failure, sometimes referred to as *El Brexit colombiano*, led the government and the FARC to hastily return to the negotiating table. They made some changes to the peace agreement, and then they signed it again. But the vote had undermined the deal, doing profound damage to the peace. Just like Brexit, it forced everyone to pick sides, and there were only two.

Not long afterward, Iván Duque Márquez, a politician who had campaigned against the peace agreement, was elected president of Colombia. His government systematically ignored or undercut many of the promises outlined in it. Meanwhile, since the peace treaty was signed, an estimated one thousand social activists and local advocates have been killed, executed in much the same way as Sandra's neighbor decades ago. New understories take root every day. Dissident FARC outfits have recruited about four thousand Colombians to return to the conflict.

The next year, Sandra officially finished her reintegration process and got a job working at the reintegration agency. She'd come full circle, helping people find a path out of the conflict, just as she'd been helped.

It was the first time she could go to work every day and be herself, not hiding who she was but using her past to help other people. She still felt powerless to further the peace process, given the political realities. But like Gary and Curtis, she had found a way to hold on to what mattered most to her, to the understory of her conflict. She was still fighting for justice for Colombians.

One day, ten years after her exit from the guerrilla forces, Sandra was assigned to run a workshop for local businesses in a neighborhood near her home. The idea was to explain how the reintegration process works and encourage business owners to consider hiring ex-combatants, something Sandra knew was critical to sustaining the peace.

But there was more. She'd be working with a former paramilitary fighter, she was told, a man named Jaime who had once been part of the same group that had murdered her neighbor, so many years before. It left her cold, the idea of working beside such a person. She knew the workshop was important, so she couldn't back out. But she dreaded going, as the date approached.

On the day of the workshop, Sandra and Jaime met. They exchanged stories, which were familiar and yet different. He had demobilized a year before her, as it turned out. He seemed like a human, Sandra had to admit.

It came as a relief, in a way. After all these years, it was the closest she'd ever gotten to an ex–paramilitary fighter. It was disorienting and liberating, all at once.

A year later, Sandra and Jaime were still exchanging text messages and helping one another professionally from time to time. They were not friends, exactly, nor enemies.

preventive measures

People do break free from high conflict. We've seen it happen. In different ways, Gary, Curtis, and Sandra recognized their own saturation points and then interrupted the conflict cycles in which they were trapped. They investigated the understories, the deeper roots of their conflicts. They broke the binary of the groups to which they and their enemies belonged. And they distanced themselves from the fire starters in their lives, quite purposefully.

To help crowds of people move out of high conflict and stay out, governments, families, and neighbors can help or fail to help, as Sandra experienced in Colombia. They can ease the way by building a

legitimate and clear path out of high conflict and by bolstering identities that reside outside of the conflict, the roles of parents, citizens,
employees, neighbors, or basketball players.

Of course, most of us are not embroiled in a civil war or a gang
vendetta at the moment, happily. But we have to navigate conflicts all
the same, in all parts of our lives. In a survey across nine countries,
85 percent of us said we encounter conflict at work. Some of that
conflict was healthy and good. But one in four people reported workplace conflicts that escalate into personal attacks. Close to a third
dealt with conflict "always" or "frequently." Certain professions seem
particularly prone to unhealthy conflict. Nine out of ten nurses said
they'd experienced verbal abuse in just the past month. Usually, the
abuse came from a physician.

Then, at home, there is often even more conflict. Family estrangement is surprisingly common and long-lasting. Over a quarter of
American adults say they are currently estranged from a relative. That
translates into about 67 million people, more than the number of
Americans who suffer from allergies. Half of these estranged adults
have had no contact for four years or longer. Most of these rifts came
between parents and children or between siblings. Almost everyone
in a rift says the estrangement is upsetting to them.

Sometimes estrangement is the only good option. Especially
when there's a history of abuse or when the other side has no desire
to make the conflict healthier, which happens. But usually, estrangement freezes high conflict. The understory never gets investigated.
Misunderstandings multiply. Story lines harden, like the asphalt in
the Tar Pits. No one learns or grows as a result of the conflict. People
suffer from the loss, especially children.

In the United States, the conflict-industrial complex still domi-
nates the legal system, including family law. About a quarter of divorces can be labeled "high conflict," give or take. That translates into
roughly 195,510 high conflict divorces per year, just in America. If
you could bottle all that pain, you could destroy a small city. Other

couples never divorce but spend decades locked in high conflict any-way. They are what therapists call "conflict-habituated."

Of course, humans don't even have to live with each other to get trapped by high conflict. Consider all the political junkies in living rooms all over the world. Each morning, they scroll through the headlines, checking the scores. Who is winning the marriage today? They are conflict-habituated, too.

High conflict is not all that rare. It draws us in. There are ways out, but it's a grinding and lonely journey, as Sandra can attest.

The best way to escape the Tar Pits should be clear: never set foot in them at all. Once we get captured, it's hard to get out.

The B'nai Jeshurun synagogue in New York City. REUTERS/Keith Bedford

chapter 7

complicating the narrative

"we leaned into it"

On the Upper West Side of Manhattan, there is a mega-synagogue called B'nai Jeshurun, known as "BJ" to its members. It was founded by German and Polish Jews in the early 1800s. Over the centuries, it became one of the most influential Jewish communities in the United States. Today, the Moorish-style sanctuary, located just off Broadway on West 88th Street, is the spiritual home to about 2,400 New Yorkers.

Just shy of its two hundredth birthday, BJ nearly came undone, torn apart by a political controversy that seemed, on the surface, very far away. It all started in late 2012, with a United Nations vote to upgrade Palestine to a nonmember observer state. This change was mostly symbolic, but it did allow the Palestinians to participate in General Assembly debates.

American and Israeli politicians objected to this upgrade in status. But BJ's left-leaning rabbis celebrated it. "The vote at the U.N. yesterday is a great moment for us as citizens of the world," the rabbis wrote in an email to all congregants, noting that Israel itself had received United Nations recognition of its right to independence sixty-five years earlier. "Every people has the right of recognition."

The backlash to the rabbis' email crackled around the city, landing on the front page of *The New York Times*: "Cheering U.N. Palestine Vote, Synagogue Tests Its Members," the headline read. "It's very shocking to many of the congregants that this position was taken publicly and this e-mail was sent around," Eve Birnbaum, a member of the congregation for fifteen years, told the newspaper. "I am very dismayed . . . that the rabbis and the board would take a position that is contrary to what many members believe."

Some people withheld their donations. Others threatened to leave the synagogue altogether. The rabbis were stunned. "It was like an earthquake: the hostility, the animosity," said BJ's senior rabbi, José Rolando Matalon, known to all as Roly. "People whom I loved and respected and thought respected me were saying terrible things."

Rabbi Roly is a gentle presence in most rooms. He wears horn-rimmed glasses and speaks with the lilting accent of his home country of Argentina. He loves to play the oud, the Arabic lute. Over the years, he's helped BJ become known around the city for its joyful Friday night services, luminous with singing, clapping, and dancing. He'd led the synagogue for three decades by that point, but all of a sudden, he was questioning how well he really knew his own congregation.

The rabbis held emergency meetings with the congregation. They released another letter, which also made the *Times*. "We regret the feelings of alienation that resulted from our letter," they wrote. "We are unequivocally committed to Israel's security, democracy and peace."

Then the rabbis did what most of us do after encountering unexpected, unsettling conflict. They tried to move on. They hoped the turmoil would die down and everything would go back to normal. They still wanted to be able to express their opinions about Israel, of course. But they hoped the congregation would support them, as it had in the past.

Just over a year later, Rabbi Roly and another BJ rabbi named Felicia Sol signed onto a short letter criticizing the mayor of New York City for having pledged his loyalty to a powerful pro-Israel lobbying group. And just like that, the conflict flared up all over again, this time making *The Washington Post*.

Once again, the rabbis were accused of disloyalty to Israel. This time, Birnbaum, whose children had held their bar and bat mitzvahs at BJ, left the congregation. "We felt like outsiders," she said.

Sam Levine, a twenty-five-year member of BJ, left, too, calling the rabbis' actions "unforgiveable, inexcusable." The rabbis "took advantage of their extraordinary platform and instead of strengthening the Jewish people, they do the opposite."

These accusations cut Roly deeply. He had lived and studied in Israel. He'd organized countless educational programs on Israel and led many BJ trips there. The reason he criticized certain Israeli government policies was *because* he cared so much about Israel. And now he was being called "anti-Israel"? It was mind-boggling.

Families that had raised their children and buried their loved ones in the BJ community were refusing to return. It had the potential to become a high conflict: an unexplored understory, a powerful, reductionist binary, for Israel and against, fueled by cycles of blame and defensiveness.

So Roly considered his options. He could leave BJ. That was one option. He could find a new congregation, one more aligned with his views on Israel. Or he could stand his ground. Keep fighting until everyone who disagreed with him left, until the congregation became more like him. That was his second choice. His third option was to keep his mouth shut. He could stop sharing his own beliefs on Israel and other controversial issues, as many religious leaders do. In a 2013 survey of over five hundred American rabbis, almost half said that they had refrained from publicly voicing their views on Israel in the past three years.

But none of those options felt right. Not leaving, fighting, or censoring himself. "I didn't want to have a congregation where every opinion was the same," he told me. "I want to be in a place where there is controversy."

Part of his job was to challenge his congregants' thinking. Disagreement was necessary for any kind of growth. Or so he'd always thought. "I think to be a religious leader is to live in that tension all the time," he said. But in this spiral of conflict, more tension was not leading to more growth. To the contrary. "If we kept speaking our mind in this way, it was going to destroy everything."

A rabbi named Marshall Meyer had preceded Roly at BJ. He was a legend in Argentina for his role in fighting for human rights. Meyer had defied the military junta, risking his own life, and infuriated the conservative Jewish establishment with his social-justice activism. Now Roly felt the full weight of his mentor's legacy. How could he be courageous, too, without making everything worse?

the fourth way

After months of agonizing, Roly agreed to a fourth option. He would not leave, fight, or surrender into silence. Instead, he would try to keep his congregation together by going deeper into the conflict. "We leaned into it."

To do this, Roly knew he needed help. A congregant urged him to bring in mediators who had worked with Israelis and Palestinians in the Middle East. Surely BJ's problems would be simpler, right? Melissa Weintraub, a rabbi and the cofounder of the dialogue organization Resetting the Table, sensed the tension in the synagogue on her first visit. "People were sitting with their camps, had a lot of assumptions about each other, and were no longer speaking to each other," she said. "It felt like a kind of microcosm for polarization."

First, Weintraub surveyed 750 of BJ's members and discovered that a third had relatively hawkish views on Israel—far more than the rabbis had realized. Many were younger members. Nearly half said they "frequently" or "sometimes" kept their true feelings about Israel to themselves to avoid tension with other members or the rabbis. This was a loss for everyone involved, Weintraub knew from experience. When people do not talk about their differences, they miss the opportunity to be stretched—intellectually and emotionally—and to come out the other side stronger and wiser.

Then Weintraub talked with BJ's members in depth. It was a daunting experience, even for a veteran of intractable conflict. She did fifty interviews, and the situation seemed dire. "It did feel like it could be impossible," Weintraub said. "There were so many divergent voices who wanted such different things." But most of the people she interviewed also seemed to appreciate the importance of trying, given how influential BJ is among American Jews. As one member put it:

> If we can't resolve the differences in our own community, how are we going to resolve our differences with the Palestinian people? We have to be able to live together. I am not going to eliminate them, nor will they eliminate me. How are we going to be one community?

It was just like Jay and Lorna, the divorcing couple. They were stuck with each other. So what then? Over the course of the next year, the mediators organized twenty-five programs at BJ. There were structured workshops reaching hundreds of congregants, intensive staff trainings, in-depth sessions with the rabbis and the board. "There was a lot of skepticism," said Irv Rosenthal, a member of the synagogue's board, "about whether the rabbis were serious and whether it would help."

In groups of forty, the congregants shared personal stories about their connections to Israel, about feeling torn between their sense of justice and their sense of duty. "It was hours and hours and hours of meetings, days and nights," Roly said. "It was hard."

But over time, something shifted. The congregation began to peer underneath the crock pot. Israel wasn't just about Israel. It was about loyalty, history, and their children's future. One woman explained how, since so many of her relatives had been killed in the Holocaust, she'd been raised to believe that criticizing Israel was sacrilegious. "There were people whose views on Israel I disagreed with pretty profoundly," Irv said, "but when I heard their life stories, I could have some understanding."

It became clear that many people wanted the same end goal: for Israel to be stable and secure *and* for the Palestinians to have independence and dignity. What they disagreed about—profoundly— was how to get there.

The other revelation was that there were not just two schools of thought. Some people took extreme positions but many more had ambivalent feelings. They struggled to reconcile it all. Their answers might be different from one day to the next, depending on how the question got asked. That's because there was no easy answer. The conflict was internal as much as external.

Eventually, they got to a place where they could express their own views *and* "tolerate the discomfort of someone else's opinion," as Roly put it. They could hold the tension, like Gary and Curtis. They'd discovered the fourth way.

We can't avoid conflict. We need it in order to defend ourselves and to be challenged. In order to be better people. As Mahatma Gandhi said, "Honest disagreement is often a good sign of progress." But it's so easy to slip into *dishonest* disagreement, into high conflict, given the right conditions.

The secret, then, is to avoid those *conditions*. To build guardrails in our towns, our houses of worship, our families and schools, the kind that lead us into worthwhile conflict but protect us from slipping into high. This means setting up a conflict infrastructure, the kind that preempts high conflict before it starts by helping us investigate the understory, reduce the binary, and marginalize the fire starters in our world. It means cultivating curiosity in conflict, on purpose.

Building this infrastructure creates conflict resilience, an ability to not just absorb conflict but get stronger from it. But conflict infrastructure requires serious time and dedication. "Many communities invite us in to lead a workshop and want everything to change," Weintraub said. "BJ dedicated the staff time and resources to *really* do the work. This doesn't happen from a single workshop or even seven."

BJ's conflict infrastructure would be tested again and again, as we'll see. Like physical fitness, conflict resilience requires perpetual maintenance. But in time, learning to tolerate the tension was oddly liberating. It didn't resolve the conflict but it made everyone smarter about what the conflict actually was. And it made each disagreement more interesting, more like an enigma, less like a violation. As one congregant put it:

> I had largely stopped talking about Israel with any but selected friends. . . . The power of the workshop and the initiative for me has been reengaging with the subject of Israel—realizing I want to talk about it, that I can initiate conversations with people, and they don't have to be horrible. It made me *curious* rather than anxious about the thought of talking to people who . . . don't necessarily share my views.

the difficult conversations lab

Two miles up Broadway from the synagogue, there is a hard-to-find, windowless space called the Difficult Conversations Lab. Here, researchers at Columbia University pair up strangers who disagree on hot-button issues including, as it happens, Israel. They put them in a room together and let them argue about a given controversy for twenty minutes, while being recorded.

"It is hard to study real-life, intractable conflict as it happens," social psychologist Peter T. Coleman told me. "This is an attempt to get as close as we can." He started the lab with a group of colleagues over a decade ago. To date, the lab and several sister labs around the world have analyzed some five hundred charged encounters.

It does not always go well. Some conversations have to be shut down before the twenty minutes end, to avoid lawsuits or violence or other unpleasantness. People can quickly sink into frustration and blame.

But then there are *other* conversations. In these encounters, Coleman noticed, people still felt waves of frustration and blame, but they cycled through other emotions, too—like curiosity and even flashes of humor or understanding. They asked questions, more questions than people in the stuck conversations. They experienced positive emotions and then negative and then positive again, demonstrating a flexibility that was missing from the stuck conversations. This is what good, healthy conflict looks like. It's fluid.

Afterward, the people still disagreed. And this is important. No one changes their mind about a deeply held belief based on a twenty-minute conversation with a stranger. That's not how the human brain works.

But over time, after more conversations like this with more people, particularly people they trust, they might change their minds. Or they might not. But curiosity is a prerequisite to change. Like sunshine and water, it doesn't guarantee growth, but you can't get meaningful, internal change without it.

The Difficult Conversations Lab was inspired, in part, by the Love Lab in Seattle, where psychologists Julie and John Gottman studied thousands of married couples. One lab studies love and the other studies hate. But in a way, both labs are studying the prevention of high conflict, in love and in war.

So what made the difference? For one thing, it helped if the number of positive interactions was greater than the number of negative interactions. That's the magic ratio we learned about earlier. Like the gardening conversations that Gary had with his neighbors, or the birthday celebrations during the Mars simulations, these sparks of warmth create a buffer against unhealthy conflict.

In real time, looping accomplishes this beautifully. Every time you attempt to show someone you've heard them (and ask if you got it right), you boost the magic ratio. "People need to have some balance of feeling like they're heard, like that was an interesting point they made," Coleman told me. "Then they stay in the more complex, nuanced place, where they can see different sides."

At BJ's workshops on Israel, the mediators trained everyone in active listening, just as Gary did with the striking musicians in San Francisco. These skills should be taught to every child in elementary school, I'm convinced. Listening and checking for understanding is probably the single best way to keep conflict healthy, all through life. That's why it is practiced by everyone who navigates high conflict with grace. Wherever you find a wise minister, psychologist, salesperson, or hostage negotiator, you will find someone who knows how to loop, even if they don't call it that.

But we aren't born with these skills, and they take practice. Most people have never been taught to listen well, and they aren't good at it. And while it's a good idea to bring trained mediators into organizations to help with conflict, it's not always practical or affordable. So what then? Is there a way to nudge people into having better conflict anyway?

To find out, Coleman and his team tried an experiment. Right before the strangers met for their difficult conversations, they were each given a news article about some polarizing issue. One version of the article laid out both sides of a given controversy, similar to a traditional news story, arguing the case for gun rights, for example, followed by the case for more gun control. It was the kind of binary framing we're used to seeing in our adversarial culture: pro and con, us-versus-them.

Another group got a different version of the article. This version contained much of the same information, written differently. It emphasized the complexity of the gun debate, rather than describing it as a binary issue. For example, the article explained that many Americans support requiring background checks for all gun owners. Still, the article noted, background checks would not prevent violence committed with stolen guns. Meanwhile, other people worried about how background checks could violate their privacy. In other words, the article explained many different points of view. It read less like a lawyer's opening statement and more like an anthropologist's field notes.

It turned out that the different articles mattered. In the difficult conversations that followed, people who had read the more simplistic, adversarial article tended to get entrenched in negativity. They asked fewer questions and left less satisfied. But those who had read the more complex articles asked more questions, came up with higher quality ideas, and left more satisfied.

Complexity is contagious, in other words. This is a big deal. People can be primed to see the world as a less binary place. When that happens, they become more curious and more open to new information. They listen, in other words.

One fundamental lesson for anyone who wants to cultivate healthy conflict is to complicate the narrative early and often. For a leader of a school or business, this might mean listening to everyone and then amplifying the contradictions and nuances you've heard. Point out the variance *within* groups of people, which are often greater than the differences between them. Get curious. It is infectious.

In politics, this might mean voting for leaders who reject adversarial, us-versus-them language. Who repeatedly expand *us* to include *them*. (Notice that this is not the same as a "moderate" or a "centrist." A politician can support dramatic change *and* reject us-versus-them binary language.) Or it could mean passing reforms to create space for more than two political parties, since most people don't fit into two categories. There are many ways to create conflict guardrails in politics, and we practice almost none of them at the national level in the United States today.

In journalism, I've found, complicating the narrative means doing the reporting. Going out and talking to people I don't know or understand and really listening to them. This is hard to do. At first, it can feel dangerous. If I listen to someone who seems wrong or bigoted, aren't I part of the problem? Shouldn't I be calling them out, shaming them for their ignorance?

But that's more magical thinking. No one, ever in history, has changed their mind because some reporter they don't know called them out. That's not how humans work. Shame rarely has the desired effect, even with people we know. It never works outside of your own tribe, and reporters are almost always on the outside.

Listening doesn't mean agreeing. It doesn't mean legitimizing or amplifying what other people say. I still decide what to put in the story—and what to keep out. Listening deeply does not mean creating false equivalencies. The rush to assume it *does* comes from a superficial understanding of conflict. Instead, investigating the understory means going deeper in a conversation alongside people, getting curious about what lies underneath what they've said.

How did they get to be so sure about vaccines? Or the Democrats? Whenever there's blame, there's usually some kind of vulnerability lurking underneath, as Gary learned. Which vulnerabilities are they protecting? What do they think their life would be like if they woke up tomorrow and had, miraculously, "won" this marriage? I want them to walk me through that day, step by step.

Understanding people doesn't change them. It's not nearly enough. But almost no one changes until they feel heard. That's the third paradox of conflict. People need to believe you understand them, *even as they realize you disagree*, before they will hear you. Many disputes devolve into a game of chicken because of this paradox. Who is going to dare to listen first?

In my own work, complicating the narrative has also meant finding space for the quotes and details that don't fit the story I originally thought I was telling. The ones that show ambivalence or contradiction, but are still true. That's the kind of thing I used to cut from my drafts. Now I try to keep it in there. Readers can handle a lot more complexity than most journalists think.

Twenty years ago, an editor told me that all great stories required conflict. I repeated this mantra for decades, never really questioning it. But journalists' definition of conflict has narrowed to a sliver. There are, in real life, many kinds of tension, including the internal kind. Often, the better story comes from looking for a *complication*, not a conflict.

Still, the word "complicate" makes people nervous, I've learned. After all, some things are not complicated. They are simple. Sometimes there is a villain and a victim, justice and injustice, good and evil. That's true. Complexity should not be used to obfuscate, to reject accountability. Not all conflicts are complicated.

But all people are complicated. And in high conflict, there is almost always false simplicity lingering somewhere in the narrative. And in that simplicity, no one hears what they don't want to hear. In those cases, complicating the narrative can spark curiosity, where there was none. And curiosity leads to growth.

The idea is not to mask the truth. It's to tell the truth, in full.

investigating a mystery

One year after the Israel workshop ended at BJ, the rabbis started making people uneasy, once again. This time, they wanted to consider whether it was possible to conduct interfaith marriages, a practice long forbidden in Conservative synagogues. (Although officially unaffiliated with any specific denomination, BJ has ties to the Conservative branch of Judaism.) For years, younger members who had grown up at BJ, who considered it their home, had been asking to be married in the synagogue to people who weren't Jewish, and the rabbis had said no. This led people to leave BJ, which was heartbreaking. It was time, they thought, to at least talk about whether this still made sense.

It was a sort of test: could the community control the burn of this conflict? Or would it erupt into personal attacks and permanent estrangement yet again?

It wouldn't be easy. "To me, Israel is important, but when BJ turned to interfaith marriage, it became very personal," said Irv's wife, Ruth Jarmul, who has wrestled with the challenge of interfaith marriage in her own extended family. "It is very painful for me. I love my extended family very much, and I cherish our relationships. I also want Judaism to not just survive but thrive."

In other synagogues, rabbis have simply declared new policies on interfaith marriage, by fiat. But given their recent experience leaning into conflict, and their desire to stay out of *The New York Times*, BJ's rabbis decided to bring the mediators back. They set up more difficult conversations, sharing stories in small groups in people's homes. It was less efficient but much more interesting.

This time, there was a little less skepticism. Many BJ members now knew there was a fourth way, more satisfying than running away, fighting, or staying silent. This fourth option felt more like launching an investigation, less like launching an attack.

To begin, Rabbi Roly did exactly what the Difficult Conversations Lab might have advised. He primed people for complexity. In a webinar early in the process, he explicitly rejected the binary and recognized the many different understories of the conflict. He told the truth, in other words:

> We're dealing here with a very complex issue. There are a lot of emotions about this, a lot of anxieties, also a lot of hope in some people. Some have personal lived experience with the issue of intermarriage. Some don't have a formed opinion yet. "Who should be counted in?" "Who should be counted out?" "Should we be counting people in or out?" I mean, all of these things are questions for which we don't have simple answers.

BJ congregants discussing interfaith marriage in the synagogue on May 17, 2017. Nomi Ellenson/
Resetting the Table

The conversations continued for one full year. Everyone was invited into the room, just as in Gary's mediation with the San Francisco
Symphony. There were lectures about what it means to be an American Jew today, small discussion groups in people's homes, and online
dialogues. Many people were startled by the range of views within the
congregation—and even within themselves. As one person put it:

> The most powerful moment for me was when I heard myself
> expressing a deep hurt and disappointment that "my Rabbi"
> would not marry my daughter and her fiancé, who was not
> Jewish. I'd never realized consciously how distancing, alien-
> ating, that was for me. How "not part of the group, even the
> community" I became as a result of not "qualifying" for this.

Sometimes, it's not just that other people don't understand us.
It's that we don't understand ourselves. If your house of worship
refuses to marry your child and the person she loves, that rejection

induces a wave of social pain, whether you admit it to yourself or not. Often, the more social pain there is, the deeper the understory gets buried.

After months of listening and talking and trying to *understand*, rather than persuade, the rabbis presented their own thoughts and options at a forum with hundreds of congregants. Then everyone gave the rabbis feedback, in conversation and in writing, which helped the rabbis make their final decision.

Going forward, BJ's rabbis announced, they would preside over interfaith marriages, provided couples agreed to create a Jewish home and raise any children they had in the Jewish faith. In explaining their decision, they carefully acknowledged the many specific points of disagreement in the congregation. "Not everybody agreed," said Roly, the senior rabbi, "but people felt heard and respected." Just as Gary proved in Muir Beach, people didn't have to agree to make progress, but they had to feel heard. That is the key to conflict resilience, I am convinced.

No one left the congregation this time around. Not even the people who continued to disagree, who considered the policy change a tragic mistake. The conflict strengthened the community, rather than fracturing it. "I think we handled it beautifully," said Ruth. She sounded proud when she said it. There was a purpose in just understanding other people, even as she continued to disagree. The fourth way was becoming part of the identity of the synagogue and its members.

"they were only stereotypes to me"

In November of 2016, most of BJ's members, including Ruth and her husband, Irv, voted for Hillary Clinton. So did almost everyone they knew. In Manhattan, 86 percent of voters chose Clinton. Everyone just assumed she would win.

Trump was a New Yorker, and not well liked by other New Yorkers, by and large. He was seen as a phony. "Clown Runs for Prez," the New York *Daily News* proclaimed when Trump announced his campaign.

On Election Day, when Trump and his wife arrived at their local poll-ing place to vote, people booed. "You're going to lose!" one man yelled.

Trump's victory stunned many of BJ's congregants. They were deeply distressed by his rhetoric about immigrants and women and fearful about what he might do in office. They felt themselves slipping back into conflict, this time with Trump supporters.

By this point, many BJ members understood good conflict better than most people. They weren't afraid of leaning into controversy. But how could they do that with people they'd never met? "I didn't know anybody I could have had a conversation with," said Martha Ackels-berg, a BJ member. "They were only stereotypes to me."

For a year, they had no answers. Ruth, Martha, and many other BJ members channeled their energy into politics, attending protests outside Trump Tower. Martha joined a committee on racial justice at BJ. But it didn't feel like nearly enough.

One day, a fellow New Yorker and community organizer named Simon Greer came to BJ for a birthday party. Having grown up Jew-ish in Manhattan, he'd been to the synagogue many times and knew the rabbis through his social justice work. At the party, he told one of the rabbis about a group of conservatives he was working with in Michigan. They were corrections officers, mostly Christian, and they were really interesting, thoughtful people, he said. And most of them had voted for Trump.

"I have a crazy idea," he said. "Why don't we bring some BJ mem-bers to Michigan to meet them?"

The rabbi laughed. Just imagine it: a bunch of progressive Jewish New Yorkers go on a pilgrimage to rural Michigan to hang out with conservative Christians who work at a prison. It sounded like the beginning of a joke. Not a very good one.

Simon flew back to Michigan and mentioned the idea to Andy Potter, the executive director of the Michigan Corrections Organiza-tion, the corrections officers' union. Andy had a lot to worry about at the time. The prisons were overcrowded and understaffed, and many state lawmakers distrusted unions. But something about the idea resonated. It might be a chance to show some liberal elites that corrections officers were real people, professionals who had a lot of ideas about how to reform the criminal justice system, if only someone would ask.

A couple months later, back in New York, Simon asked BJ's rabbi again. Why not go to Michigan, toward the conflict, not away? Isn't this what BJ was all about?

"I'll do it"

When the call came, Caleb Follett was working the night shift, as usual, from 10 p.m. to 6 a.m. in a housing unit on the grounds of the prison where he worked outside of Lansing, Michigan.

Corrections officers aren't allowed to bring their phones inside the prison. Or anything else really. So Caleb returned the call the next day from his desk in the basement, while his kids were upstairs with his wife.

"We're doing a sort of cultural exchange program with some New Yorkers," the man from his union said, "and we'd like you to participate."

"A cultural exchange—?"

"Yeah, well, we're basically going to host this group of liberal Jewish people from New York City. For three days. In our homes."

Caleb is a large, muscular man with a shaved head. He has an intensity about him that he's learned to contain. He loves to debate politics, religion, philosophy, you name it. His brow furrows, and he delights in the back-and-forth. It energizes him. But at his job in the prison, he doesn't get to talk about these things very often.

Listening to the union man, he realized he knew no Jews and very few liberals. None who could really challenge his ideas. Now someone from the Michigan Corrections Organization was offering him the chance to host liberal Jews in his own home.

"You know what," Caleb said, coming alive to the idea, "I'll do it."

On one level, Caleb fit the stereotype that many BJ members had about Trump supporters. He's a White Christian heterosexual who not only voted for Trump but campaigned for him. Caleb likes the idea of a border wall. He has a small arsenal of weaponry in his rural Michigan home, including an AR-15.

Caleb is also taking psychology classes on the side and has considered becoming a therapist. He is married to a Filipino woman who immigrated to the U.S. not long ago, and they had two young children and a third on the way. He is in the Marine Corps Reserve. He has a personal mission statement that he reminds himself of often: "to impact people by way of truth and love."

Right away, he started thinking of questions he'd like to ask these visitors. For example, he'd heard, growing up in an evangelical Christian family, that Jews were God's chosen people, and so he was taught to hold Jews in esteem. But he also knew that most Jews were liberal politically. It didn't make sense. How could they be God's chosen people if they were liberal? "It was a quandary for me."

"I want to host as many people as possible," he told the union man.

"why would I want to do this?"

The rabbis announced the trip to all BJ congregants in their regular newsletter. Roly and fellow Rabbi Shuli Passow would be leading a "study exchange" to rural Michigan that spring. "We will only heal the widening rifts that run across our country by opening our hearts and minds," the invitation read.

When Irv heard about the trip, he signed on immediately. He saw it as another opportunity to go deeper into conflict, just like the workshops on Israel and interfaith marriage. It was the fourth way all over again. When he asked his wife, Ruth, to join him, she was less excited. But she agreed to go.

"We're going to live in their homes, and they're going to live in our homes. We're not going to a hotel," Rabbi Roly explained when people asked him about it. He reminded everyone what they'd learned during the workshops on Israel and interfaith marriage: "The search for truth lies in controversy, not agreement."

At first, Martha was uninterested. "Why would I want to do this? What would be the point?" She could see this controversy from New York. She didn't need to get on a plane. She could go to Staten Island to find Trump voters right here in New York. She had no plans to do so, but still.

In some ways, Martha fits the stereotype that many Republicans have about liberals. She's an Ivy League–educated academic. Before retiring, she was a professor at Smith College, where she helped start the women's studies program. She uses words like "intersectionality" and "White supremacy" in everyday conversation. She is also a lesbian with short hair who wears sensible shoes and carries a faded, pale blue backpack.

Martha is also very religious. She loves to sing in synagogue, and she keeps kosher and observes the Jewish sabbath, which means she attends services and refrains from working from Friday night until sundown Saturday. Her parents were the first in their families to go to college. As a child, she often felt lonely, one of very few Jewish kids in her New Jersey town.

"Well, it might connect to your racial justice work," Rabbi Shuli told her. "You're passionate about reforming the criminal justice system, and it might be useful to hear from corrections officers." Apparently, these Michigan conservatives wanted to reform the criminal justice system, too, or so Rabbi Shuli said.

That got Martha's attention. She had thought a lot about the perspective of the inmates in the criminal justice system, but not at all about the people who worked there. For reasons she couldn't totally articulate to her partner or even to herself, she agreed to go.

She'd be staying, alongside two other women from BJ, with Caleb Follett.

"not happening"

"No way," Mindi Vroman said when the union man called.

The man talked about the chance to learn about political differences and Judaism.

"Not happening," Mindi said.

She didn't know any Jewish people. She'd always assumed Jews were a "snobbish, rich, kind of Amish tight-knit community." As for politics, she didn't spend too much time thinking about it. She'd voted for Obama, hoping he'd shake things up, and he hadn't. So then she'd voted for Trump, hoping for the same thing.

Mindi has blue eyes, freckles, and short, dirty blond hair. Her father and her aunts had worked in the corrections system, and so, after studying criminal justice at the local community college, she'd gotten a job there, too. She had three kids and often had to work double shifts in the prison. She had no time for "study exchanges" or whatever this was, she told the union man. She tried to speak bluntly, something she prided herself on doing:

"We live on a farm. We own guns. I drink. We swear. I know nothing about 'Judaism.' I didn't even know that was a word."

For some reason, the union man kept talking.

"Well, you know, the exchange works both ways," he said. "If you host these people now, then in a couple months, you get to go on an all-expense-paid trip to visit them in New York City."

Silence.

This phone call kept getting weirder. She reminded herself that she'd never been to New York.

"I'll talk to my husband, but don't count on it."

unsafe

It was around this time that I interviewed Rabbi Roly about the synagogue's challenges with conflicts, to hear what he had learned. In our conversation, he mentioned that he would be leading this excursion to rural Michigan soon, and he was unsure how it would go. That's how I first learned about this trip, right before it happened.

Naturally, I asked if I could go along. What better way to see BJ's approach to conflict up close?

All the participants agreed to have me join. I would be staying, I was told, with two other BJ women in the rural home of the grand-mother of one of the corrections officers. The group had generously offered to include me in the hospitality.

Suddenly, this all felt a little strange. Usually, as a journalist, I stay on the outside, in hotels, where I have some professional distance. My own bathroom. Sure, I wanted to watch other people do this exchange, but did I really want to join it myself?

One way journalists try to remain independent is to keep their distance from the people they write about, and sometimes that makes sense. You shouldn't be best pals with the police chief you are covering. But other times, this tradition is just a cop-out, a way of avoiding vulnerability. And I could tell that this was one of those times. Maybe my reluctance to stay in a rural farmhouse with a bunch of strangers was a sign that I needed this exchange as much as they did.

In New York, meanwhile, Ruth was starting to have serious doubts about her decision to join her husband and thirteen other people from BJ on the trip to Michigan. "I was thinking crazy thoughts," she told me. "'Are they going to hurt me? Are they going to shoot me?' I was very anxious."

Meanwhile, Martha worried about what to pack. What hostess gift do you bring for someone with whom you have nothing in com-mon? "It was tricky." Finally, she picked out a potholder and a dish towel with New York City icons on it. The Statue of Liberty, the Empire State Building. That seemed safe.

"I was definitely anxious," she said. People asked her why she was going. "I didn't really have great answers." She knew she couldn't change the minds of the people in Michigan, and vice versa. So what was she doing? The night before the flight, she didn't sleep well.

Meanwhile, in Michigan, Caleb tried to reassure his wife. "She could see I was excited about it, but she had a lot of reservations," he told me. She was nervous about having three strangers from New York City in their home. "She felt unsafe."

A friend of his told him he was out of his damn mind to be participating in this exchange. "I think he was afraid of liberals, because of what he sees on the news, all these Antifa protesters," Caleb said.

Both groups felt afraid. It was striking to hear them say the same things about each other. They were all White Americans who lived in the same time zone. But both expected intolerance and maybe aggression from one another. The Michigan group members seemed mostly wary of being misunderstood, belittled, or mocked. "I was afraid they were going to judge me and my lifestyle," Mindi said. They expected condescension.

The New Yorkers seemed mostly afraid they'd run into a wall of ignorance or hate, or that just by going there, they would be betraying their deepest ideals. They expected bigotry.

Martha didn't feel frightened for her physical safety so much, she told me. She knew how to take care of herself, and she'd be with other BJ members. She was more worried that she'd feel the need to hide who she was, something she'd stopped doing a long time ago. She was afraid she was making a mistake, trying to talk with people who would not take her seriously, and with whom she would not really be able to be honest. What was the point?

For Americans reading this, it's worth imagining such a thing happening somewhere else. What if you heard that two groups of people in, say, Poland, were planning to meet. One lived in the countryside and one in the city, but they were citizens of the same nation who spoke the same language and shared many cultural traditions. And yet they were afraid of one another. It might seem odd, from afar. How had these Poles become frightened of each other? Who had brainwashed them? Come to think of it, for these Americans, it might have been much more comfortable for them to host people from Poland.

The day before the New Yorkers arrived, Caleb found out he'd be hosting three older women, including Martha Ackelsberg. This news put his wife's mind at ease. How dangerous could three older women be? Then he started Googling. "I found Martha," he said. He read about her research on feminism and power, and her book about an anarchist women's group in Spain. "She's like a little famous, so it's kind of intimidating." He may have been the straight White man in this situation, but she was the one with the PhD from Princeton.

On April 29, 2018, everyone met at the union's office in Lansing. "It was like a first date," Irv said. They mingled and exchanged names and small talk. "I've seen you on YouTube!" Caleb told Martha. Rabbi Roly wore a black, pinstriped beret and a North Face fleece. He looked less like a rabbi than he did in New York.

In the back of the union office where they met, there were mannequins wearing corrections officer uniforms. There was also a case filled with weapons that had been confiscated from inmates over the years. Homemade shanks, daggers, razors. Ruth's eyes kept returning to it. "I sensed a lot of anxiety on both sides," she said.

Simon Greer, the organizer who had brought them together, laid down three ground rules.

"We're going to take seriously the things everyone holds dear," he said.

"We're not going to try to convince each other we're wrong."

And finally, "We're going to be curious."

I wonder, looking at this list, what a political debate might look like with these same ground rules. It's inconceivable, really. But then again, so was this whole scene.

Finally, Simon reminded everyone to practice active listening. Summarize what the other person says and ask if you got it right.

People need to feel heard to create the magic ratio. It's the shock absorber for conflict.

When all else fails, he told them, just say this: "Tell me more!"

With that, this unlikely group left for their first bonding activity: visiting a firing range. It came as a surprise to the liberals that it was on the campus of Michigan State University. But it was also oddly reassuring. They shot .22 caliber pistols, which Mindi did not consider "real shooting." She called it "plinking," but she went along with it. Caleb gave Martha some tips, and she did well, surprising herself. It was more fun than she'd expected. For the first time in her life, she could understand why people enjoyed shooting guns.

After dinner at a local brewery, everyone went to their respective host families. The farmhouse where I was staying was rambling and peaceful, and the grandmother, our host, was warm and welcoming. There was nothing to fear. I felt lucky to have been included. And I felt embarrassed, thinking back on my initial reluctance.

Meanwhile, back at his home, Caleb introduced the three BJ women to his family and showed them where they'd be sleeping. The kids had moved to the parents' room, and Caleb had moved to the basement. "Everybody had completely given up their space," Martha noticed. Something about this gesture touched her more than she could explain.

Caleb seemed thrilled to have the visitors in his home, and his enthusiasm was hard to resist. After the kids went to bed, Caleb turned to the New Yorkers.

"Would you like to see my guns?"

"Tell me more!" Martha said.

They headed to the basement, where Caleb unlocked his gun cabinet and took out two shotguns. One he used for hunting and the other was a present from his grandmother. This idea that guns held sentimental value was hard for the New Yorkers to understand, but they heard it again and again on this trip.

Then he took out his AR-15 and asked if they wanted to hold it. "No, thank you," Martha said. It looked just like all the AR-15s she'd seen on TV, in news stories about mass shootings. It was a weapon of war. A civilian version of the military's combat rifle. Not for hunting, not for heritage. She felt short of breath.

"What do you use this for?" she asked him.

"Number one, for self-defense," he said, "Number two, for sport. And number three, worst-case scenario, for self-defense against a tyrannical government."

"What kind of tyrannical government?"

"Well, there are lots of examples from history of governments taking away people's guns and oppressing people and even genocide," Caleb began.

"Okay, but in this country, we had a revolution, and we created a Constitution and a representative government," Martha said. "We don't need to fight the government because the government is us."

Caleb tried to explain. Just because he worked for the government didn't mean he had blind allegiance to it. He felt safer knowing he could protect himself and his family, no matter what. But it was hard to communicate all of this, and he could tell she wasn't hearing him.

He could also tell she was upset by the guns, so he put them away. He was surprised how much it bothered her. Pretty much everyone he knew had owned guns for their whole lives. It was normal. The opening of hunting season was a holiday, something he looked forward to every year. He knew AR-15s were very dangerous, but he also knew how to use one.

Martha had a hard time sleeping. She felt shaken by the quantity of guns Caleb owned. What did it mean that a man who worked for the state and served in the Marine Corps Reserve, who actually *was* the government, felt the need to arm himself against the government? It was hard to understand.

The other problem was that she was starting to like this person, which she hadn't really expected. Caleb was generous and open, even in disagreement. And so it bothered her, to feel so much distance between them.

That was the tension. Maybe the whole point, she started to realize, was to find a way to hold all these things in her mind together.

complications

For the next two days, the mostly male conservative Michigan Christians drove me and the mostly female New York liberal Jews around in their trucks. We visited Cell Block 7, a prison museum in a decommissioned facility. We got Superman ice cream, a tricolor flavor popular in Michigan and Wisconsin but never before seen by most of the New Yorkers. We went to a park in Jackson, Michigan, where, in 1854, over a thousand people had gathered to protest against the expansion of slavery. The event marked the beginning of the Republican Party in America. This was news to pretty much everyone.

At the prison museum, the officers told stories about their jobs. One talked about his oldest stepson, who was in prison himself. Another explained how, growing up in that part of Michigan, he'd gone to work for Oldsmobile, which had at one time employed twenty thousand people in Lansing. It was a solid middle-class job. But then, after waves of downsizing, he'd switched to corrections. Prisons turned out to be a lot more stable.

They described how the prison food had become almost inedible after the food service was privatized to save money, and how the officers had successfully pushed for change, in agreement with the inmates. They described the overcrowding in Michigan's prisons and how they frequently had to work a second shift without advance notice, sometimes with no one to take care of their kids at home. They talked about how it feels to be in a prison yard with eight hundred inmates and no firearm. (They aren't allowed to carry guns when they're among the inmates, out of a concern their weapons could be used against them.) One officer told a story about getting drenched with urine or worse, and not being able to find out if the inmate who threw it had any communicable diseases, due to privacy protections.

They thought the whole system was broken, just like the New Yorkers did. But they knew a lot more about it. "I've been in prison forty hours a week, fifty weeks a year, for almost eight years," Mindi said. "I've seen more penises than a urologist."

The New Yorkers listened to all of this, without shock or revulsion. They didn't roll their eyes. "I was surprised," one of the corrections officers said, "by how little pretentiousness there was." These New Yorkers were more real than they'd thought liberals could be.

Then the pizza came, with a side of Ranch dressing, another Midwestern tradition. Caleb ate his lunch with Martha. "This feels therapeutic," he said. He seemed relieved to have been taken seriously.

"I know for us conservatives, we have watched mainstream news outlets, comedians, and Hollywood misrepresent us," he told me later. This time with the New Yorkers felt different. "Essentially what occurred, I think, is that our voice was being heard, and we knew it and felt it."

Just like the feuding couples in Gary's office, everyone wanted to be heard. What puzzled Martha was why Caleb had not felt heard before. Weren't his views represented on Fox News? And by Trump, the president he'd voted for, whose voice echoed on every social media platform, every day?

Why was it important for Caleb to be heard by Hollywood, too? Or by these strangers from New York? She struggled to understand him as she simultaneously delighted in his company, bouncing around in the passenger seat of his Chevy Equinox SUV, debating the Constitution, explaining Judaism, trading questions and theories. "There's a kind of exuberance and naïveté about him that I found really compelling," she told me, "and at other times difficult."

The conversations continued all that day and the next. The New Yorkers told stories about ancestors who had died in the Holocaust. They explained how Trump's attempt to ban all Muslims had reminded them of Nazi orders targeting all Jews.

This was not an analogy that Mindi had thought of before, and it bothered her. She mentioned it to me multiple times afterward. The corrections officers asked the New Yorkers all kinds of questions, about 9/11 and Israel. They noticed how gingerly the New Yorkers talked about Israel's policies toward Palestinians. It was a reminder that the divisions within a group can be greater than you'd expect.

There were organized conversations, too, one focused on Trump, another on guns. It was notable how bad almost everyone was at anticipating each other's positions. The Michiganders kept assuming the New Yorkers wanted to take away their guns. The New Yorkers kept saying they didn't.

There were flashes of agreement. "We both think Trump should not have Twitter," Mindi said, gesturing to herself and Rabbi Shuli. Many of the New Yorkers, including Martha, agreed it was important for the country to have a border, to Caleb's surprise.

And there were vast oceans of disagreement, like when Caleb tried to explain his support for Trump. "He's not really racist. He's not any of these things!" he said smiling at the absurdity of taking Trump so literally. "He's like a wrecking ball. He blows through political correctness."

The New Yorkers did not smile. Nor did they erupt in outrage. They pushed back on each point. "He says things that legitimize bigotry," Rabbi Shuli said.

It was a strange encounter to behold, slightly contrived but less awkward than it sounds. I had left Washington, D.C., where the cable news pundits and politicians remained locked in combat, to watch these Americans doing something much more interesting. They had come together with a sense of possibility, copious misunderstandings, and many questions. They were strangers in their own country.

But despite everything, in defiance of the entire conflict-industrial complex, they wanted to make sense of each other. It reminded me of the first paradox of conflict all over again. Humans have the capacity to simplify and demonize, but we also crave harmony. We are animated by conflict, and we're haunted by it. We want out, and we want in.

"It's hard to explain," Mindi said, "but I'm really starting to like these people."

During another conversation, Caleb said that a baker should not be forced to make a cake for a gay wedding, that it would be a denial of religious freedom. Hearing this, Martha quietly got up and walked outside. She didn't feel indignant. She felt sad. "He had no conception that there might be freedoms on the other side and people with feelings on the other side," she said. She knew she would talk to him about all of this, but not just yet. "So I just cried and breathed for a few minutes."

On the last day, the group sat around a big table at the union office, next to the confiscated weapons case, and marveled at how connected they felt. "I was moved by this experience in a profound way," Caleb said. "Thank you for listening, to put it simply."

"I'm just so grateful for how you opened your home, turned your home inside out, for us," Martha said. "It's really been an incredible thing to have the experience of really coming to care deeply about you and realizing that there are things we're going to continue to disagree about, and that's okay."

Next came Mindi, a woman who rarely got emotional in public. "I appreciate the education. I was naive," she said, looking around the room. "We asked each other open questions. We didn't get angry." She grabbed a napkin to dry her eyes.

Andy, the head of the union, said he'd been amazed by the vulnerability everyone had shown, including his own members, who were usually very guarded. These were people who wouldn't reveal their home addresses to their own union. Some used pseudonyms on Facebook, out of concern for their safety. And yet here they were, crying into napkins, hosting strangers in their own homes. "The overall lesson is, Don't allow a narrative to be the grounds on which you made a decision about people," Andy said. "Allow yourself the vulnerability it takes to really get to know someone."

. Rabbi Roly spoke last. "It was transformational for me," he said quietly. "I feel a profound sense of healing, that we generated together." It occurred to me then how little sermonizing he'd done the entire visit. He'd seemed happy to be there, at ease with the discomfort, intrigued by everything that he didn't understand. But of course, by then, he'd been practicing leaning into conflict for years. He knew how to do it.

cannoli and yarmulkes

Over the past century, the United States has gotten much more politically segregated, making encounters like this extraordinarily uncommon. Since 1973, the rate of politically mixed marriages has declined by about half. Neighbors, too, are more likely to agree on politics than they were when I was a child. Back then, nobody seemed to know who had voted for whom in my neighborhood. Nobody seemed to care, either. But after the 2016 election, everyone in my son's public school in D.C. seemed to know which kid's parents had voted for Trump. That family moved to Florida soon afterward.

Separation can lead to prejudice, just as it does with racial or religious segregation. "Separation triggers a series of interlocking processes that inflame group conflict," the social psychologist Thomas Pettigrew wrote. "Negative stereotypes are magnified; distrust cumulates; and awkwardness typifies the limited intergroup interaction that does take place."

The surge in political animosity in America over the past two decades can be traced in part to this segregation. Couples who agree on politics tend to judge their political opponents more harshly. Their children suffer, exposed for decades to a narrower, less accurate story about the political "other." The home has be-

Rabbi Roly (in hat) with Caleb and other members of the New York–Michigan exchange, at a subway stop in New York City. Amanda Ripley

come the ultimate echo chamber, every bit as powerful as Facebook or YouTube.

People in politically *mixed* marriages, on the other hand, tend to have more complicated views of the other party and its candidates. The diversity of families, in the very same household, has a huge impact on polarization nationwide.

All over the world, knowing people who think—or look—differently seems to deradicalize humans. It reduces the risk of high conflict, and leads to fuller, richer lives for everyone involved. That kind of conflict resilience requires new infrastructure. Which means building relationships and institutions that generate meaningful relationships *in* conflict, not in spite of it.

Two months after the New Yorkers went to Michigan, the Michigan conservatives flew to New York City, as planned. Everyone met at a kosher pizza place by Wall Street. Once again, I was included in the hospitality. Robin Kerner, a New York psychologist, gave up her bed for me while she slept on the couch in her Upper West Side one-bedroom apartment. She wouldn't have it any other way. That's what the Michigan hosts had done, and so would she.

There were hugs and photo sessions. There was none of the awkwardness of the initial encounter. This time, the main thing the Michiganders were nervous about was New York City itself.

"I cried for three nights before coming here," Mindi told me. She was worried about finding her way on the subway, about the crowds, about the strange food she might have to eat. This is a woman who works in a prison, remember. Who routinely supervises large men convicted of serious, violent crimes. But traveling on her own to New York City? "I almost chickened out," she said.

Caleb had been brushing up on issues, he told me, in preparation for the trip. The agenda would include hard conversations, this time on gay marriage and immigration, and he wanted to be prepared. "It's a little nerve-wracking to know I'm going to talk about LGBT with Martha," he said.

That night, the whole group attended Shabbat services at the synagogue, led by Rabbi Roly.

"They were strangers," Roly said in his sermon, introducing the visitors to the congregation. "They were 'them.' They're now 'us,' and they're friends. We have very, very wide gaps in terms of opinions about all sorts of things, but we have something that is powerful in common, that is our humanity. And when you discover someone's humanity, you cross that bridge—between the 'us' and the 'them.'"

Then the music began, and Robin, my host, leaned over to me and Caleb and whispered, "It's time to dance." Caleb, wearing a white yarmulke on his shaved head, immediately got up and held hands with the New Yorkers, circling around the sanctuary and singing, as did I. It felt weird and kind of wonderful.

Over dinner afterward, Caleb marveled at the reunion, his first trip to New York City, his first yarmulke. "It's surreal. That we're all here—with these hats. What are they called?"

Martha was excited to host Caleb at her apartment in lower Washington Heights. She knew how important religion was to him, and so she hoped he'd enjoy talking to her partner, a religious studies scholar and teacher. She was thrilled to see him again, and also apprehensive. She knew they were going to talk about gay marriage, and she knew they would disagree.

That night, as she showed Caleb to her study, where he would be sleeping, she felt self-conscious about the size of the apartment. Three bedrooms was not big for Michigan, but it was huge for New York City. She tried to explain that the neighborhood was less expensive than other parts of New York, but when Caleb asked what rents were like, she had to admit she didn't know. It had been so long since she'd looked. "That was an embarrassing moment for me," she told me later, "of recognizing my privilege."

That night, Caleb did not sleep well. His brain just kept spinning, thinking about all the things he'd seen, the points he wanted to make. It was the same thing that had happened to Martha her first night in Michigan, lying in Caleb's house, unable to shut off her whirling mind.

That weekend, the group of liberal Jews and conservative corrections officers went to Central Park and ate vegan kosher food in Chinatown, which was better than anyone had expected. They got cannoli from the famous Ferrara bakery in Little Italy. The Michigan visitors were amazed that everyone lived in apartments, and that some of them had no TV—by choice. There was a flurry of excitement when they learned that Irv and Ruth were neighbors to Kimberly Guilfoyle, the girlfriend of Donald Trump Jr.

On the second day, a group of the corrections officers asked to go to Trump Tower, where they spent a gleeful twenty minutes taking photos and buying souvenirs in the gift shop. The New Yorkers waited outside, looking chagrined.

Everywhere we went, Mindi struggled with all the smells. The smell of urine in the elevator at Penn Station, the smell of raw fish in

Chinatown. "Keep going so I don't vomit," she told me when I paused to point something out.

New Yorkers, she noticed, did not obey traffic signals. "There's less respect for law and order," she concluded. But overall, the Michigan visitors seemed pleasantly surprised by the exceeding civility of New York. "I haven't felt threatened once," one of the corrections officers told me, his voice rising in amazement. "Eight and a half million people and not a bad word!"

By almost any measure, New York City was a very safe city at that time, as it had been for years. The homicide rate was about half what it was in Lansing, Michigan, the city closest to their own homes. But that reality had gotten lost in translation somehow. They had all expected some amount of mayhem.

It was nice to see their relief, but it was heartbreaking, too. How had this happened? How did Americans who lived just four states apart get to be so foreign to one another?

"we must stop this"

On the last full day together, the group held a difficult conversation about gay rights, as planned, in a side room of the synagogue. To begin with, there was falafel and hummus and only a little confusion about the synagogue's gender-neutral bathrooms. "How does this work?" one Michigan man asked another. "Like any other bathroom, man."

To start the conversation, Simon had everyone stand in a line to show the range of views. Stand on one end if you felt no conflict between your religious views and gay marriage and on the other end if you felt a lot of conflict. Martha and the rest of the New Yorkers stood on the end, with no conflict. Most of the Michigan visitors stood in the middle.

There was Caleb, all alone on the far end, with the most conflict. "I almost felt bad for him," Martha said. Then they all sat down to talk about a recent Supreme Court decision on gay marriage. Martha took the lead, describing in an intellectual way the problems she had with how the court framed the case. They went back and forth, not resolving anything, but listening and talking and repeating. Then he and Martha embraced. It was painful for both of them, and yet it felt better than keeping their differences hidden.

Later, someone asked Caleb how he reconciled his friendship with Martha with his belief that homosexual acts were sinful.

"You love 'em," he said. Same way you treat anyone you care about who sins, he said, and we all sin.

After the long-awaited gay-marriage conversation, Martha could relax. The hard part was over. But it was also a little anticlimactic. "It was hard for me not to think, 'Did we change anyone's mind?'" That question violated the rules, she knew, but she couldn't help it.

She knew she'd changed her own mind on some things. She now appreciated the importance of involving corrections officers in reforming the criminal justice system, for one thing. And she had changed the way she categorized conservatives in her mind. There were many kinds of conservatives, just like progressives. It got harder to caricature her political opponents, and she could tell that change was mutual. "They were able to see us as fuller, complicated people who weren't dismissing them and whom they didn't need to dismiss. And we felt the same way."

On the last day, after a visit to the Tenement Museum, the group brainstormed ways they could expand on their exchange. "I know it's a fantasy," said Ruth, "but I really wish the whole country could go through this experience. I wish we could be Congress. I don't want to just go home and think about the great Chinese lunch we had."

Simon, the organizer who had brought all these people together, watched these final moments with wonder. Something had happened here that was important, even without Congress. "What was unusual was seeing that many people being curious," he said. "There was a critical mass of curiosity."

The group said their goodbyes. There were tears from people who rarely cried, just like in Michigan two months before. Rabbi Roly had traveled all over the world and met all kinds of people, but there was something about this that was different. "In my life, I've had very few experiences like this. Your story is now my story, and my story is now your story," he said.

Four months later, on October 27, 2018, a man shouting "all Jews must die" opened fire inside a Pittsburgh synagogue, killing eleven people gathered for services. The man was armed with an AR-15 assault rifle and three handguns, all of which he had bought legally.

Three days later, the Michigan and New York groups got on a conference call to share support and grief. Everyone sounded shaken. They'd sat together in services just like the Pittsburgh one, not long before. "All the other shootings that occurred, it never affected me like this did. This was close to home," Caleb said. "I get really emotional in this group. I don't know why. I am not this emotional in every part of my life." And, he also said, he hadn't changed his mind on gun control.

Afterward, the Michigan group decided to write a letter of solidarity to their New York counterparts. They crafted it together, and it was signed by Caleb, Mindi, and all the participants in the exchange. Two weeks after the shooting, Andy and two of his colleagues, Jeremy Tripp and Mike Lennox, flew to New York City to deliver the message in person, reading it aloud at BJ's Shabbat services.

> We are writing today as conservative, patriotic Americans. . . . We believe America is indeed an exceptional place that has served as a unique symbol and model to the world. As such, we have seen enough of the divisive politics that separate our country and are calling for an end to any rhetoric that confuses hate and fear mongering with patriotism. . . . We must stop this before America stops being America.

It took the Michigan men about nine minutes to read the full letter. Afterward, the entire BJ congregation stood in applause. It was a small moment of grace, a circle of liberal Jewish New Yorkers surrounding three conservative men in borrowed white yarmulkes, all of them wanting more for their country. It wasn't nearly enough, everyone there would agree, but it was more than many of us imagine possible in America today.

Over the next two years, the group created a shared Facebook page and kept in touch, for a while. Martha and Caleb texted and talked a couple of times. Separately, both of them told me they'd toned down their Facebook posts because of their experience. "I have no patience for people who write obnoxious, angry, dismissive tweets or postings about people who support Trump," Martha said. "It's now profoundly clear to me that it's really counterproductive. It doesn't work."

Then came the pandemic, the killing of George Floyd in Minneapolis, and protests around the world, followed by the 2020 election. The memories faded, as memories do. Some of the Facebook pages became more extreme again, I noticed, including Caleb's posts. The adversarial assumptions roared back to life. There was an *us* and a *them* again, for many of the group members.

The conflict-industrial complex is powerful. To keep conflict healthy in an adversarial world, the encounters can't end. The research is pretty clear on this, and the Michigan–New York exchange confirmed it. Conflict infrastructure has to be made of steel, built for the long term. Otherwise, the effects erode with time, as everyone returns to their adversarial echo chambers.

But keeping the conversation going is a huge challenge in a country where people increasingly live, date, and marry in their own political tribes. As in any segregated society, encounters won't happen naturally.

For now, BJ continues to lean into other conflicts. The rabbis were starting another exchange program, this one with an Orthodox synagogue right in Manhattan, on the other side of Central Park. They hoped to have uncomfortable conversations about the Israeli-

Palestinian conflict and about Trump, whom many Orthodox Jews supported.

Meanwhile, Simon worked with BJ and the Michigan Corrections Organization to start another exchange, this one between college students. In early 2020, students from liberal Oberlin College in Ohio did an exchange with their counterparts at Spring Arbor University, a conservative, evangelical school in Michigan. Eight other colleges were planning on adopting the program.

When I last talked to Martha, she said she often wondered what Caleb might be thinking. She thought of him whenever she read the news about the coronavirus spreading in prisons or about protests in Michigan. "How is Caleb seeing all of this?" she'd ask herself.

She probably wouldn't like the answers, she knew. But she didn't assume she knew what they were. And that was huge. She'd set that false confidence aside. She was still curious, two years later.

"I feel like this brought out the best of me," Martha told me, and I knew exactly what she meant. I have had the same feeling, a sense of being fully alive in good conflict. Arguing, wondering, revising, awakening to something I hadn't understood before, without surrendering what I held dear.

Once you've had that sensation, you want to feel it again. That sense of wonder that comes from discovering our common humanity, in good conflict. Martha got to experience that feeling on both exchanges, in Michigan and New York. But in normal life, it's become vanishingly rare.

"I wish I could appear everywhere in my life the way I felt called to appear those two times," she said. "Present, open, able to be surprised."

Amen.

author's note

My deepest debt is to Gary Friedman, Curtis Toler, Sandra Milena Vera Bustos, José Rolando "Roly" Matalon, Caleb Follett, Martha Ackelsberg, Mark Lynas, and all the conflict survivors featured in this book. It takes a special kind of strength to pull yourself out of the Tar Pits of conflict and tell your story publicly. It has been a privilege to try to convey their wisdom, vulnerability, and humility.

This is my third book, but only now am I noticing what they have in common. In each case, I found myself baffled and demoralized by some quagmire I was covering as a reporter. Finally, the only way to make sense of it, for me anyway, was to rely on regular people who had experienced some kind of transformation in the quagmire.

After covering terrorism and disasters, survivors of all kinds of catastrophes taught me what they wished they had known, what they wanted the rest of us to know. Not just about suffering but about grace and resilience. Then, after covering education, American teenagers transplanted into the best education systems in the world helped me understand the problems and possibilities of our own schools, from afar.

Conflict is different from classrooms and hurricanes, of course. It's a deep and mysterious part of the human condition. We can understand it better (much better) but never completely. So this time around, I needed a lot of help. More help than seems reasonable, looking back on it.

The Emerson Collective fellowship gave me the financial freedom to go down absurd rabbit holes and come back out. To do the kind of enterprising work that very few journalists get to do these days. It also gave me courage. Every conversation I've ever had with Laurene Powell Jobs, Stacey Rubin, Peter Lattman, and Amy Low pushed me to think bigger. To do riskier, more original, audacious work. At a time when journalists were under relentless pressure to think smaller, this kind of talk was miraculous, borderline subversive. I will always be grateful.

I would be lost without my brilliant and kind editor, Priscilla Painton, and her intrepid colleagues at Simon & Schuster, including Jonathan Karp, Richard Rhorer, Hana Park, Megan Hogan, Phil Metcalf, Jackie Seow, Elise Ringo, Chris Lynch, Christina Zarafonitis, and Elizabeth Gay Herman. Their faith in an admittedly amorphous idea at an extremely uncertain time is hard to explain, honestly. But I dare not question it. Thank you for believing.

For challenging me to reimagine the traditions of journalism in high conflict, I am profoundly grateful to the Solutions Journalism Network. Samantha McCann, David Bornstein, Hélène Biandudi Hofer, Tina Rosenberg, Michael Davis, and their brave colleagues are reinventing this craft, making the news "hearable," as Gary might say.

In the three years I spent reporting this book, many wise people helped me see what mattered—and what didn't. Too many people to name in the body of the book. Thank you to John Paul Lederach, Catherine Conner, Rachel Brown, Andrew Hanauer, Samantha DiScala Iraca, and everyone who generously shared some knowledge along the way.

For helping me decide which stories to tell (and not tell, most importantly) and for alerting me to the La Brea Tar Pits and so many other treasures, thank you to the ingenious editor Robin Dennis. For shaping this idea and finding it a good home, I am very grateful to my literary agent, Esmond Harmsworth. It feels like just yesterday that we went to lunch in New York, and you suggested I write a book. Thank you for nineteen years of conspiring together to tell great stories.

This book required intensive on-the-ground reporting in California, Illinois, New York, Michigan, and Colombia. In every case, local fixers, historians, and researchers helped me find my way. Thank you to Joe Parkin Daniels in Bogotá for finding Sandra and other ex-combatants, for guiding and translating our often meandering conversations, and for tracking down the answers to all manner of questions about Colombia's conflict, past and present. Thank you also to Nicolò Filippo Rosso, the gifted photographer who took the Colombia photos in this book. In Chicago, I am indebted to everyone at CRED and to Stephanie Kearns, a private investigator who never quit in her attempt to help me track down long-lost criminal court records. (She is still looking for some of them, last I heard.) Thank you also to David Rugendorf, who helped me make sense of some of these court records, and to Joe Figini, who explained how high conflict can operate in family-law cases.

Thank you to Kim Pate, David Plotz, and Joan Strickler for helping to clean up early drafts. Caleb Follett spent hours reviewing the manuscript to help me correct for some of my own biases about Trump supporters. We spent about ten hours on the phone, over the course of several days, going back and forth, trying to understand one another. We laughed a lot, learned new things, and continued to disagree, which was just fine. Thank you, Caleb.

For nudging me to come out from my cave and keep writing about all kinds of things, thank you to Michael Duffy, a fine editor and lovely human, at *The Washington Post*. For a masterful job fact-checking and improving the book in the final months, thank you to my research assistants, Emma Francois and Dina Williams. Our Team Conflict virtual huddles kept me going in the darkest days of quarantine. For helping me get curious about the understory of my own conflicts, thank you to Leila Bremer.

I am grateful to Scott Stossel, Sarah Yager, Ta-Nehisi Coates, Jeff Goldberg, David Bradley, James Gibney, Vernon Loeb, Denise Wills, Don Peck, Vann Newkirk, Adrienne LaFrance, and everyone at *The Atlantic*, past and present, for giving me the opportunity to write complicated narratives for the past decade.

My good friend Lisa Green and her wonderful colleagues at L&M Policy Research gave me a room of one's own, which is the only way to write a proper book. Thank you to Russ Tisinger for chatting about hyper-partisanship and the media, when all you were trying to do was pick something up at the printer. Suzy Wagner, thank you for ignoring the sirens, the masks, and everything else you had to do to take pictures and share a laugh with me. And many thanks to Jessica Sandham Swope and Sabrina Tavernise, who happily brainstormed with me about the human condition on many Dupont Circle lunch breaks.

My dear friend Catherine Brown, what can I say? Our Sunday runs got me through this book, just like the last one. Thank you for listening to me talk about listening, even when you didn't want to, from several states away, while chasing a very strong dog. Your friendship has given me joy, opened my mind, and saved me from making many bad decisions in conflict since middle school.

Our families are the place where our worst (and sometimes our best) conflict instincts reveal themselves. Thank you to my husband, John, and my son, Max, for putting up with a lot of looping lessons, for forgiving me when I fail to listen, and for making me—and this book—better.

There are times when we have really good conflict in our house. Not always. But sometimes, we manage to speak hard truths to each other, listen with curiosity, and discover something we didn't know. That feeling of being stretched and coming out the other side, with grace, is something everyone should experience. I want to get better at it, and I hope I'll spend the rest of my life trying.

"When the soul lies down in that grass," the poet Rumi wrote, "the world is too full to talk about."

appendix I

how to recognize high conflict in the world

language to listen for . . .

- Do people use sweeping, grandiose, or violent language to describe this conflict?
- Are rumors, myths, or conspiracy theories present?

actions to watch for . . .

- Do other people withdraw from the conflict, leading to the *appearance* of just two binary extremes?
- Does the conflict seem to have its own momentum?

High conflicts can be violent or not. They can last for decades or much less. They can even be unrequited, when the conflict lives in just one person's head, unbeknownst to the other side. And yet, despite all that variety, it's not hard to recognize a high conflict when you see one, in my experience.

Let's take one example from Europe. For two hundred years, no wolves had been seen at all in Denmark. Then, in 2012, birdwatchers spotted a wolf trotting along in the countryside, having crossed over from Germany. Soon, a few more wolves were spotted, including a female wolf. In 2017, seven wolf puppies appeared, romping across the land, like they belonged there. Now that qualified as a "pack."

Very quickly, people began to argue about the wolves, which began appearing all over northern Europe, in places where they had not been seen in many years. Farmers resented them for attacking their sheep and livestock. So did hunters, who were not allowed, under European Union law, to hunt the wolves, even though the wolves killed their hunting dogs and competed with them for large game. Other people, especially (but not exclusively) environmentalists, defended the wolves. They pointed out that wolves rarely attacked humans. Bears pose more danger to humans, statistically speaking. These people protested any attempts to harm the wolves.

This sounds pretty straightforward, right? Like a fairly healthy conflict over natural resources. But is it?

language to listen for:

Do people use sweeping, grandiose, or violent language to describe this conflict?

Remember how Gary described his election victory in Muir Beach as an "unprecedented landslide"? It was an odd way to describe the results of an unpaid, volunteer community election. His adviser, Tanya, talked about "good people" and "bad people." She and Gary routinely compared the Old Guard to President Donald Trump and the New Guard to President Barack Obama. When Gary's ally lost the next election, Tanya used words like "kill" and "beatdown" to describe the loss.

Whenever you hear language that seems disproportionate to the

conflict, pay attention. A high conflict "exceeds itself," as Danish social scientist Hans Peter Hansen told me. "Everything is magnified."
In Sweden, a wolf-conservation advocate compared the anti-wolf
sentiment to racism in an interview with *The New York Times*: "The
hate against an animal, against a species such as the wolf, is like racism
in people—it is absolutely the same process in the mind." In France,
farmers brought 250 sheep to the Eiffel Tower in a show of protest.
One farmer described the threat of wolf attacks as "omnipresent and
oppressive."

It's not that these people are exaggerating. The emotion is real,
just as it was for Gary. At a deeper level, the wolf conflict has to do
with people's sense of the world and their role in it, the Norwegian
scientist Olve Krange told me. For some, the wolves (and the rules
against killing them) undermine not just their income stream but
their sense of self. These are people who think of themselves as
self-sufficient, who protect their land, livestock, and family from
all manner of natural forces. In their minds, nature is to be controlled by humans, not the other way around. The wolves' protections, in this view, represent yet another example of elites telling
them what to do, with complete disregard for the realities of their
lives. "The wolf is a sort of a symbol of café lattes and all of that, an
urban intruder into rural life," Krange said. In this way, some people see the wolves the way others saw mask mandates during the
pandemic—as an affront to their freedom. And even their masculinity. "Real men shoot wolves," one Norwegian bumper sticker
declared.

For other people, the wolves represent the purity of nature, of a
lost utopia. The animals' return to Europe offers a glimmer of hope,
in this view, a sign that Mother Nature may yet recover from human
harm. Any attempt to hurt the wolves represents yet another man-
ifestation of human arrogance and destruction, much like genetically modified crops. It's an affront to the sanctity of nature. This,
too, resonates with a much deeper narrative. Notice these groups are

responding to totally separate story lines. That is a sign of a high conflict.

Are rumors, myths, or conspiracy theories present?

In Denmark, a van was said to have crossed the border from Germany and released the wolves on purpose. Another myth claimed that the animals were not in fact real wolves. They were some kind of hybrid animal, between a dog and a wolf, and therefore could be shot legally.

High conflicts tend to erupt in places with low trust. When there is low trust, it is very hard to create a consensus about the facts. People become so suspicious of one another that they can believe anything. This makes it easy for conflict entrepreneurs to inflame the conflict further. And every attempt to end the conflict, by, for example, prosecuting people who shoot wolves, fuels more distrust. This is the trap of high conflict.

actions to watch for

Do other people withdraw from the conflict, leading to the appearance of just two binary extremes?

The wolf conflict often gets described in the news media as an urban-versus-rural conflict, but that is a false binary. In fact, within rural areas, there are people on all sides of the divide, researchers have found. The conflict is about many things including identity, resources, respect, and fear. But just like on Twitter, the most extreme people are the most vocal ones, and so the complexity collapses, leading the most helpful people to flee the scene.

Does the conflict seem to have its own momentum?

In Norway, the government authorized the culling of some of the wolves, to protect the sheep population. In response, a hundred or so

protesters set up camps and began sabotaging the hunt, crisscross-
ing the land on skis before dawn, erasing wolf prints in the snow.
The original dispute faded into the background. The us-versus-them
dynamic took over, as we've seen happen so many times in other conflicts. In Denmark, the head of an anti-wolf group called "Wolf-Free
Denmark" quit his post after receiving death threats. In 2015, fifty
angry French farmers kidnapped the head of a national park in the
Alps, holding him overnight and demanding that six wolves in the
park be killed.

Actual differences of opinion on the wolves became less important than the conflict itself, which gradually became its own reality.
Back in Denmark, two naturalists were filming the country's only
female wolf from afar in 2018 when a man driving by leaned out of
his window and shot the animal to death. The resulting video went
viral online, sparking outrage around the world.

This was a high conflict, and it was in charge. (To learn how one
Danish town shifted out of high conflict and into good conflict over
the wolves, check out Appendix III.)

appendix II

how to recognize high conflict in yourself

Here are some of the characteristics I've noticed in both good, healthy conflict—and in high conflict. It's not a comprehensive list, but it can be helpful to see these qualities in opposition to each other, since that is how they often feel, in our own minds.

good conflict	high conflict
humility	certainty
fluidity	rigidity
many different emotions	same emotions
complexity	simplicity
novelty	predictability
passion	righteousness
spikes in stress hormones, followed by recovery	chronic stress hormones, rumination, sleep disturbances

good conflict	high conflict
Curiosity	Assumption
Questions	Monologues
All sides want to find a solution	One or all sides do not want to find a solution. They want to fight.
Feelings of sadness when bad things happen to other side	Feelings of happiness when bad things happen to other side
Non-zero-sum thinking	Zero-sum thinking
Violence unlikely	Violence more likely

This is not a precise science. Humans are complicated, and charts and quizzes are not. But if you are in an intense conflict and wondering if it might be a high conflict, here are some questions that might help. Sometimes (not always) questions help us to buy some time, make some space, and consider a conflict from a little distance.

1. Do you lose sleep thinking about this conflict?
2. Do you feel good when something bad happens to the other person or side, even if it doesn't directly benefit you?
3. If the other side were to do something you actually agreed with, some small act, would it feel very uncomfortable to acknowledge this out loud?
4. Does it feel like the other side is brainwashed, like a cult member, beyond the reach of moral reasoning?
5. Do you ever feel stuck? Like your brain keeps spinning, ruminating over the same grievances, over and over again, without ever uncovering any new insights?
6. When you talk about the conflict with people who agree with you, do you say the same things over and over—and leave the

conversation feeling slightly worse than when you started talking?

7. Has someone who knows you very well told you they don't recognize you anymore?

8. Do you ever find yourself defending your own side by pointing out that the other side does the same thing—or worse?

9. Do you see different people on the other side as essentially interchangeable? If your conflict is with just one other person, is it hard to conjure a visual of that person as the small child they once were, even if you try?

10. Do you use words like "always," "good," "bad," "us" and "them," or "war" when you talk about the conflict?

11. Do you find it hard to remember the last time you felt genuine curiosity about the other side's thoughts, intentions, or actions?

If you answered yes to five or more of these questions, you may be in a high conflict. And I'm guessing you have very good reasons for feeling the way you do. And as we've seen with Gary's story, our own hardwiring as humans (along with the conflict-industrial complex) can make it damned near impossible to resist the pull of high conflict.

The question then is, do you want to *stay* in high conflict? Some people do. Maybe for you, right now, high conflict is the best option, the only option. It's useful to notice this. And to check in with yourself, every so often, to notice the toll it may be taking on you and the people you love. Make a list. Is the cost still worth the gains? If an opening appears to disrupt the conflict—maybe an emergency of some kind or a chance to make a symbolic concession, as Gary did when he voted for his rival—consider seizing it.

Conversely, if you answered yes to four or fewer of these questions, then you probably are not in high conflict. That means you have a lot more choices now than you might later. You can see possibilities and details that will vanish if the conflict escalates. That is a valuable gift. If it's not already, there's a chance this conflict could become good conflict, which makes us better people. It can be more valuable than no conflict at all.

Try to stay in that space. Take every opportunity to make deposits of goodwill, upping the magic ratio, as the astronauts did. Go to the balcony, as Ury does. Breathe. Resist binary categories and keep fire starters at a distance.

how to prevent
high conflict

It is undeniably possible to shift out of high conflict. We've now seen it happen, again and again. But it is much easier to prevent it altogether. To create a culture that is conflict resilient.

Here are some of the ways that the people in this book have found to build that infrastructure in homes, neighborhoods, synagogues, and space stations.

1. investigate the understory

What is the crock pot really about? It's hard to get anywhere until you start talking about the understory of any conflict.

One way to excavate the understory is to find a good mediator. These people are like the firefighters of the conflict world. They can help keep conflict healthy and get underneath the usual talking points.

Many cities have Community Dispute Resolution Centers to help people manage everything from noise complaints to landlord issues to assaults. Some work in the court system, and some are separate. Many will help people regardless of their ability to pay.

Remember the wolf controversy from Appendix I? In western Denmark, in a rural town near the home territory of the wolf pack, Hans Peter Hansen and a couple other social scientists invited everyone in the community to come to a meeting about the wolves in 2017. Fifty-one people showed up, including farmers, students, and hunters. There was a mix of ages, backgrounds, and opinions.

Then, all together, they started to dig deeper into their understories. What bothered people about the wolf situation, Hansen asked? People called out every complaint they had. The wolves were destroying people's livelihoods. The politicians didn't understand the hunters. The farmers were exaggerating the danger. Hansen and his team wrote each lament in big letters on posted sheets of paper. "Instead of avoiding the conflict, we confronted it," he said, sounding just like Rabbi Roly in New York.

Slowly, people started to feel heard, so they could listen. Importantly, no experts or politicians were invited to that first meeting. Those people were not trusted, not yet. Regular people are the experts in their own lives, and so they were asked to tell personal stories, not intellectual or political ones. No one other than the facilitators were allowed to interrupt anyone else.

Everyone then identified the one or two concerns that bothered them most. This helped clear out some of the noise. Slowly, they started to see underneath the crock pot. Many people were afraid to let their kids play in the woods. Others were afraid for the future. "Anxiety and fear were a much bigger issue than we thought from the beginning," Hansen said. That's usually the case in high conflict. (Blame almost always masks vulnerability, as Gary taught me.) Afterward, more than 80 percent of the people signed up to continue participating in the conversations, known thereafter as the Wolf Dialogue Project.

(To find a Community Dispute Resolution Center, try searching the member locator at the National Association for Community Mediation [www.nafcm.org]. You can also find a private mediator through the Locate a Mediator Directory at www.mediate.com. Other people turn to family therapists, clergy members or even mutual friends to mediate family conflicts. Whomever you consider, whether it's a professional mediator or a trusted member of the community, it's important to interview a number of people. Ask if they typically meet with everyone together, in the same room. That's what Gary has found to work best, but many mediators do not do this. For more on how to choose a mediator, see Gary's book, *A Guide to Divorce Mediation*.)

2. reduce the binary

Try not to form unnecessary groups. If groups are necesary, have more than two. And create traditions and routines that automatically scramble the groups, however many there are.

In a political system, this might mean using ranked-choice voting and third parties. In a newsroom, it might mean the reporters switch places with the editors once a quarter. At a school, it could mean the principal also teaches a class every semester, and the students are given responsibility for many more decisions. (It should definitely mean that groups are fluid, and kids in the "lowest" reading group quickly move up to a different group as they improve.) In meetings, try using the Bahá'í concept of consultation, where no one owns an idea after it gets proposed. Don't let complexity collapse into competition.

If you notice someone trying to shift out of high conflict, like Glenn Beck, recognize how excruciating that process can be. It may be tempting to punish these people, to ostracize them for their past mistakes. That feels good, I know. But if you really want to cultivate good conflict and create lasting change, consider (just consider) welcoming them instead, the way scientists welcomed the environmentalist Mark Lynas.

In Denmark, Hansen and his colleagues started the wolf workshop by reminding everyone of their shared identities, alongside their differences.

"We have two things in common," he said.

Everyone listened, wondering what these things could possibly be.

"First, we have nature in common. We all breathe the same air."

No one disagreed. "And the future. The future is something we have in common."

It was hard to argue with him. People may have arrived thinking of the conflict as a binary one, between the wolf haters and the wolf lovers, but the conversation complicated that assumption. There were not two sides. There were many. And some of them overlapped.

3. marginalize the fire starters

Notice who around you delights in the conflict. Who tries to bond with other people over their shared loathing of a coworker or a mother-in-law? Which leaders use the language of war to motivate their followers, when there is no war?

I've become much less interested in which politicians are "moderate" and much more interested in which are conflict entrepreneurs. Which ones divide the world cleanly into us-versus-them, good-versus-bad? Which ones frame losses as a humiliation?

Create some distance from these people. These are fire starters. In Curtis's case, he literally moved to a new apartment to get some space from the conflict entrepreneurs in his life. In Gary's case, he stopped relying on Tanya for political advice. For other people, this means finding a new lawyer. Or a different source for political news. Try to rely instead on people (and news sources) who are unafraid of complexity, ones who are more curious than righteous, most of the time. (And if you cannot marginalize the conflict entrepreneur in your life—if you must work or share custody with one—you might find it helpful to check out the very practical books on managing high-conflict people, written by mediator Bill Eddy.)

4. buy time and make space

When I was in high school, I read the novel *Lord of the Flies*, and maybe you did, too. The book describes how a group of schoolboys survived a plane crash only to devolve into violence and cruelty on a remote island. It's quite convincing.

In real life, a group of boys actually were shipwrecked on a remote Polynesian island in 1965, as Rutger Bregman described in his book *Humankind*. What happened in this true story? The kids hollowed out tree trunks to catch rain water. They worked in pairs, drawing up a schedule of chores to ensure that gardening, cooking, and guard duty all got taken care of. They started a fire and kept it going for 15 months, until they were rescued.

How did they manage such remarkable cooperation? Whenever they got into conflicts, they had a ritual. Each boy would go to opposite ends of the island to calm down. They created time and space, in other words. Then, after about four hours apart, they'd come back together and apologize.

They did something else, too, those marooned boys. Maybe just as important. They made a guitar out of a piece of driftwood, a coconut shell, and six steel wires scavenged out of the ruins of their boat. And they started and ended each day with songs and prayers.

Remember the magic ratio for conflict resilience. People need to have five positive interactions for every negative one in a marriage, as we've seen. Outside of marriage, the same principle applies. The positives must outweigh the negatives. That's why grown adults in a simulated Mars mission built forts for slumber parties. It's why humans like to break bread together. Before each meeting of the wolf project in Denmark, over the course of several years, the group ate dinner together. On purpose. Food is something we all enjoy, like air. It's an easy way to create a shock absorber. Then, when conflict arises, it doesn't escalate as quickly. Humor also works. (For a charming book on how to use humor to make life and conflict easier, check out *Humor, Seriously* by Jennifer Aaker and Naomi Bagdonas.) If you're not using food, music, and humor to boost the magic ratio in your workplace or your home every chance you get, please start. That's the low-hanging fruit.

Another way to buy time and make space is through looping or other forms of active listening. If you get a chance to go through training for active listening, *do it*. I am an impatient person, someone who does not like trainings in general. But this one is worth it. Because it's bigger than it sounds. Getting better at listening means getting more curious—and making people around you more curious. It is more than a skill; it's a skeleton key.

"As soon as you articulate the other side's point of view, they are a little surprised," Chris Voss, a former FBI hostage negotiator, said. "You've made them really curious to hear what you are going to say next." (There are lots of books and articles on how to listen better. One good list of resources can be found on the website for Oscar Trimboli, an author and podcaster focused on listening: www.oscar trimboli.com.)

Another way to slow down conflict is to "go to the balcony" in your own mind, as the negotiator William Ury does (or the opposite end of the island, if you happen to be on one). Remember the marriage hack? Couples made conflict healthier in their own relationships just by writing about an argument from a neutral third party's point of view. It sounds so simple but these tricks interrupt the spiral of conflict, so we can think again. (If you're a parent or a teacher, consider trying this trick with kids to develop the habits that lead to good conflict.)

In Denmark, after everyone listed out their complaints, they were asked to imagine a better scenario. Anything was possible! The crazier the better. What would they do? People came up with wild ideas. Maybe they could create a zip line into the wolf territory and make money off the tourism. Or implant chips in the wolves so all the locals could tell where they were through an app on their phone. Or maybe they could make the wolves vegetarian (my personal favorite). Then everyone would be happy! In this way, the group created a little breathing room. In that space, they could get more practical, and they did.

People did not have to like each other, Hansen kept reminding the wolf project participants. The goal was understanding, not friendship. They are not the same thing.

Want to convince other people that you are right and they are wrong? Stop trying to do it on social media. Or through shame, in any medium. It will backfire. Persuasion requires understanding, and understanding requires listening.

(There are bridge-building organizations all over the world that deploy trained facilitators to help people communicate across political, religious, geographic, or racial divides. Internationally, the non-profit Search for Common Ground works to end violent conflict in more than thirty countries. Examples in the U.S. include Braver Angels, Essential Partners, the One America Movement, Resetting the Table, and the Village Square. To find more, check out the members of the Bridge Alliance: www.bridgealliance.us.)

5. complicate the narrative

"Be suspicious of simple stories," as the economist Tyler Cowen has said. In difficult conflict, simplicity can blind us. And the cure is curiosity, in my experience. It is contagious. If you can get curious, really curious, about people who disagree with you, it can make conflict healthier, almost immediately, depending on the situation.

Curiosity requires some baseline level of security, of course—real and perceived. It's impossible to feel curious when you feel threatened. But curiosity also requires humility, which is especially rare right now.

One way to spark curiosity is to notice and amplify contradictions that you see in real life (something journalists covering controversy should do far more often). In the Wolf Dialogue Project, some participants told the organizers that they had stopped talking about the wolves in public because they didn't want to be labeled one way or another. "There was a kind of ambivalence," Hansen told me. Which he took as a very good sign. No one fit perfectly into one group. No one ever does.

Another way to incite curiosity is by asking questions. As they talked, the Wolf Dialogue participants collected a list of fifty questions they wanted answered—about the biology and behavior of the wolves, the details of the relevant laws, and all manner of things. They researched the answers themselves or agreed upon experts who could be trusted to help them find the answers. Ideally, local news media can help people answer questions, though that requires trust. (Spaceship Media and Trusting News are two organizations that work with newsrooms to bring people together, build that trust, and help answer people's questions.)

Questions, asked with genuine curiosity, can make conflict suddenly interesting again. Here is a list of some of my favorite questions to ask when I interview people in all kinds of conflict, drawn from the wisdom of many people, including the ones in this book:

1. What is oversimplified about this conflict?
2. What do you want to understand about the other side?
3. What do you want the other side to understand about you?
4. What would it feel like if you woke up and this problem was solved?
5. What's the question nobody's asking?
6. What do you want to know about this controversy that you don't already know?
7. Where do you feel torn?
8. Tell me more.

Six months after the Wolf Dialogue Project began, the group organized a public meeting and presented what they'd found to the wider community. Over a hundred people came, including several TV news outlets. "It was very beautiful," Hansen said. "Not that every-thing was just 'peace and harmony,' but we'd managed to find a way forward." They were not stuck in the Tar Pits anymore.

Next, the group invited policy makers from the national level to come meet with them. It took some time, but the officials did even-tually make the trip out to this remote town for not one but two different meetings. As of 2020, the Danish government was working on a new wolf management plan, and ideas from the wolf project had made their way into that national process.

The wolf project was never meant to change people's minds. It was about creating a common sense of responsibility for the problem— and the solutions—even as people continued to disagree. It was about shifting out of high conflict and honoring good conflict.

I'd love to hear about your own favorite questions—and your ex-periences investigating the understory and trying to get (or stay) out of high conflict. My favorite books are the ones that never really end.

So please, tell me more. I can be reached on email at amanda@amandaripley.com.

selected bibliography

Abrams, Dominic, Julie Van de Vyver, Diane Houston, and Milica Vasiljevic. "Does Terror Defeat Contact? Intergroup Contact and Prejudice Toward Muslims Before and After the London Bombings." *Peace and Conflict Journal of Peace Psychology* 23, no. 3 (2017).

Agence France-Presse. "Sheep Flock to Eiffel Tower as French Farmers Cry Wolf." *Telegraph*, November 27, 2014.

Ahler, Douglas J., and Gaurav Sood. "The Parties in Our Heads." *Journal of Politics* 80, no. 3 (July 2018).

Al Jazeera. "Nearly a Dozen Deaths Tied to Continuing Unrest in U.S." June 3, 2020.

Allport, Gordon W. *The Nature of Prejudice*. Cambridge: Addison-Wesley, 1954.

Anderson, Benedict. *Imagined Communities: Reflections on the Origin and Spread of Nationalism*. London: Verso, 2006.

Anderson, Shayne R., Stephen A. Anderson, Kristi L. Palmer, Matthew S. Mutchler, and Louisa K. Baker. "Defining High Conflict." *American Journal of Family Therapy* 39, no. 1 (2010).

Aparicio, Juan P., Michael Jetter, and Christopher Parsons. "For FARC's Sake: Demobilizing the Oldest Guerrilla in Modern History." Forthcoming 2021. Working paper shared privately with author in August 2020.

Associated Press. "China Didn't Warn Public of Likely Pandemic for Six Key Days." April 15, 2020.

_____. "Nixon Sisters Debate Library Fund." *Florida Today*, August 7, 2002.

_____. "Rev. Jesse Jackson Eulogizes Ben Wilson." *Rock Island Argus*, November 25, 1984.

Bar-Tal, Daniel. *Intractable Conflicts*. Cambridge: Cambridge University Press, 2013.

Barrett, Lisa Feldman. *How Emotions Are Made*. Boston: Houghton Mifflin Harcourt, 2017.

Basner, Mathias, David F. Dinges, Daniel J. Mollicone, Igor Savelev, Adrian J. Ecker, Adrian Di Antonio, Christopher W. Jones, Eric C. Hyder, Kevin Kan, Boris V. Morukov, and Jeffrey P. Sutton. "Psychological and Behavioral Changes During Confinement in a 520-Day Simulated Interplanetary Mission to Mars." *PLOS ONE* 9, no. 3 (2014).

Bass, Gary J. "What Really Causes Civil War?" *New York Times Magazine*, August 13, 2006.

BBC News. "Coronavirus: Donald Trump Wears Face Mask for the First Time." July 12, 2020.

_____. "Coronavirus: Trump's WHO De-funding 'as Dangerous as It Sounds.'" April 15, 2020.

Beck, Glenn. *Addicted to Outrage*. New York: Threshold Editions, 2018.

_____. "Glenn Beck Doesn't Care if He Alienates Trump Voters." Interview by Peter Kafka. *Recode Media with Peter Kafka*. *Vox*, March 10, 2017.

_____. Interview by Megyn Kelly. *The Kelly File*, Fox News, January 21, 2014.

_____. Interview by Samantha Bee. *Full Frontal with Samantha Bee*. TBS, December 19, 2016.

_____. Interview on *Fox & Friends*. Fox News, July 28, 2009.

_____. "What You Do Will Be a Pivot Point." Interview by Krista Tippett. *On Being with Krista Tippett*. The On Being Project, May 11, 2017.

Beisser, Arnold. "The Paradoxical Theory of Change." In *Gestalt Therapy Now*, edited by Joen Fagan and Irma Lee Shepherd. Palo Alto: Science and Behavior Books, 1970.

Berg, Kara. "With Homicide Rates Down, Here's Where Each Lansing-Area Case Stands." *Lansing State Journal*, January 2, 2019.

Bergeron, Jasmin, and Michel Laroche. "The Effects of Perceived Salesperson Listening Effectiveness in the Financial Industry." *Journal of Financial Services Marketing* 14, no. 1 (2009).

Bernstein, Elizabeth. "Worried About a Difficult Conversation?" *Wall Street Journal*, June 14, 2020.

Berreby, David. *Us and Them*. Chicago: University of Chicago Press, 2008.

Bober, Natalie S. *Thomas Jefferson: Draftsman of a Nation*. Charlottesville: University of Virginia Press, 2007.

Bond, Paul. "Glenn Beck's TheBlaze to End on Linear TV." *Hollywood Reporter*, November 6, 2019.

Bregman, Rutger. *Humankind: A Hopeful History*. New York: Little, Brown, 2019.

Bridgeport Post. "Jury Awards $5,500 to Woman in Crash." May 11, 1973.

Briggs, Jean L. *Never in Anger: Portrait of an Eskimo Family.* Cambridge: Harvard University Press, 1971.

Brusset, Emery, and Ralf Otto. "Evaluation of Nashe Maalo." Channel Research, December 23, 2004.

Butigan, Ken. "Chicago's South Side Rises Up Against Gun Violence." *Waging Nonviolence*, June 28, 2013.

Butler, Patrick. "A Million Volunteer [*sic*] to Help NHS and Others During Covid-19 Outbreak." *The Guardian*, April 13, 2020.

Carey, Benedict, and James Glanz. "Hidden Outbreaks Spread Through U.S. Cities Far Earlier than Americans Knew, Estimates Say." *New York Times*, April 23, 2020.

Carlson, Margaret. "Nixon Daughters Bury the Hatchet." *Time*, May 6, 2002.

Castle, Stephen. "Wolves, Resurgent and Protected, Vex Swedish Farmers." *New York Times*, August 15, 2015.

CBS DC. "Glenn Beck Says Media Are 'Rat Bastards,' Obama Is a Dictator." April 3, 2014.

Chenoweth, Erica, and Maria J. Stephan. *Why Civil Resistance Works.* New York: Columbia University Press, 2011.

Chernow, Ron. *Alexander Hamilton.* New York: Penguin, 2004.

Chicago. "You're the Inspiration." By Peter Cetera and David Foster. Recorded 1983–1984. Track 7 on *Chicago 17.* Full Moon/Warner Brothers.

Christakis, Nicholas A. *Blueprint: The Evolutionary Origins of a Good Society.* New York: Little, Brown Spark, 2019.

CNN.com. "N. Ireland Process: Where Did it Go Wrong?" October 22, 2003.

Cohen, Steven, and Jason Gitlin. "Reluctant or Repressed?" Jewish Council for Public Affairs, October 8, 2013.

Coleman, Peter T. "COVID Could Be the Shock That Ends Our Deep Divisions." *Daily Beast*, June 7, 2020.

_____. *The Five Percent: Finding Solutions to Seemingly Impossible Conflicts.* New York: PublicAffairs, 2011.

Conti, Richard P. "Family Estrangement: Establishing a Prevalence Rate." *Journal of Psychology and Behavioral Science* 3, no. 2 (2015).

Corkery, Michael, and Annie Karni. "Trump Administration Restricts Entry into U.S. from China." *New York Times*, January 31, 2020.

Cowen, Tyler. "Be Suspicious of Simple Stories." Filmed November 2009 at TEDxMidAtlantic.

CPP Inc. "Workplace Conflict and How Businesses Can Harness It to Thrive." Global Human Capital Report, CPP, July 2008.

Crary, David. "Keen Interest in Gentler Ways to Divorce." *Pantagraph*, December 18, 2007.

Dagher, Sam. *Assad or We Burn the Country*. New York: Little, Brown, 2019.

Dahlburg, John-Thor, and Stuart Pfeifer. "For Feuding Nixon Sisters, Finally a Peace with Honor." *Los Angeles Times*, August 9, 2002.

Davidson, Jean, and William Recktenwald. "Bullets End Benjy's Fight to Be the Best." *Chicago Tribune*, November 22, 1984.

DeBono, Amber, and Mark Muraven. "Rejection Perceptions: Feeling Disrespected Leads to Greater Aggression than Feeling Disliked." *Journal of Experimental Social Psychology* 55 (November 2014).

Drutman, Lee. *Breaking the Two-Party Doom Loop: The Case for Multiparty Democracy in America*. New York: Oxford University Press, 2020.

Duverger, Maurice. "Public Opinion and Political Parties in France." *American Political Science Review* 46, no. 4 (1952).

Edholm, O. G., and E. K. E. Gunderson, eds. *Polar Human Biology*. Sussex: William Heinemann Medical Books, 1973.

El Consejo Ciudadano para la Seguridad Pública y la Justicia Penal (The Citizen Council for Public Security and Criminal Justice). "Metodología del Ranking (2018) de las 50 Ciudades Más Violentas del Mundo." March 12, 2019.

Estes, Carol. "Radio Soap Operas Teach Conflict Resolution." *Yes!*, May 3, 2006.

Fattal, Alexander L. *Guerrilla Marketing*. Chicago: University of Chicago Press, 2018.

FBI: UCR. "Crime in the United States: Table 6." Uniform Crime Reporting Program, 2018.

Fearon, James D. "Civil War and the Current International System." *Daedalus* 146, no. 4 (2017).

Fearon, James D., and David D. Laitin. "Ethnicity, Insurgency, and Civil War." *American Political Science Review* 97, no. 1 (2003).

Feinberg, Matthew, and Robb Willer. "From Gulf to Bridge: When Do Moral Arguments Facilitate Political Influence?" *Personality and Social Psychology Bulletin* 41, no. 12 (2015).

Felter, Claire, and Danielle Renwick. "Colombia's Civil Conflict." *Council on Foreign Relations*, January 11, 2017.

Ferguson, R. Brian. "War Is Not Part of Human Nature." *Scientific American*, September 1, 2018.

Fernandez, Manny, and Audra D. S. Burch. "George Floyd, from 'I Want to Touch the World' to 'I Can't Breathe.'" *New York Times*, July 29, 2020.

Finkel, Eli J., Erica B. Slotter, Laura B. Luchies, Gregory M. Walton, and James J. Gross. "A Brief Intervention to Promote Conflict Reappraisal Preserves Marital Quality over Time." *Psychological Science* 24, no. 8 (August 2013).

Fischer, Sean, Hye-Yon Lee, and Yphtach Lelkes. "The Impact of Electoral Systems and Outcomes on Mass Attitudes: Experimental Attitudes." Draft submission to the *British Journal of Political Science*, Cambridge University Press, 2020.

Fisher, Max. "The One Map That Shows Why Syria Is So Complicated." *Washington Post*, August 27, 2013.

Fisher, Roger, and William Ury. *Getting to Yes*. New York: Penguin, 1981.

Flinn, Mark V., Davide Ponzi, and Michael P. Muehlenbein. "Hormonal Mechanisms for Regulation of Aggression in Human Coalitions." *Human Nature* 23, no. 1 (March 2012).

Franklin, Jon. *Writing for Story*. New York: Plume, 1994.

Friedman, Gary. *A Guide to Divorce Mediation*. New York: Workman Publishing Company, 1993.

_____. *Inside Out*. Chicago: American Bar Association, 2014.

Friedman, Gary, and Jack Himmelstein. *Challenging Conflict*. Chicago: American Bar Association, 2008.

Friedman, Thomas L. "The Humiliation Factor." *New York Times*, November 9, 2003.

Frijda, Nico H. "The Lex Talionis: On Vengeance." In *Emotions: Essays on Emotion Theory*, edited by Stephanie H. M. van Goozen, Nanne E. Van de Poll, and Joseph A. Sergeant. New York: Psychology Press, 2014.

Geiger, A. W. "For Many Voters, It's Not Which Presidential Candidate They're for but Which They're Against." Pew Research Center, September 2, 2016.

Gibson, Sam Ling. "Reintegration or Segregation? How Perceptions of Ex-Combatants and Civil Society Affect Reintegration (and Peace) in Colombia." MA diss., University of London, April 15, 2016.

Giles, Jim. "Maths Predicts Chance of Divorce." *Nature*, February 14, 2004.

Gilligan, James. *Violence: Reflections on a National Epidemic*. New York: Vintage, 1997.

Gilovich, Thomas, Kenneth Savitsky, and Victoria Husted Medvec. "The Illusion of Transparency." *Journal of Personality and Social Psychology* 75, no. 2 (1998).

Gold, Herbert. "Easy Living in Marin." *New York Times*, October 7, 1984.

Gordon, Amie M., and Serena Chen. "Do You Get Where I'm Coming From? Perceived Understanding Buffers Against the Negative Impact of Conflict on Relationship Satisfaction." *Journal of Personality and Social Psychology* 110, no. 2 (February 2016).

Gottman, John, with Nan Silver. *Why Marriages Succeed or Fail.* New York: Simon & Schuster, 1994.

Greater Chatham Initiative. "History: Auburn Gresham." Chatham Center Chicago. Accessed August 27, 2020.

Griffin, Dale W., and Lee Ross. "Subjective Construal, Social Inference, and Human Misunderstanding." *Advances in Experimental Social Psychology* 24 (1991).

Gross, James J., ed. *Handbook of Emotion Regulation.* New York: Guilford Press, 2014.

Grossman, James R., Ann Durkin Keating, and Janice L. Reiff, eds. *The Encyclopedia of Chicago.* Chicago: University of Chicago Press, 2004.

The Guardian. "Text: Bin Laden's Statement." Translated by the Associated Press. October 7, 2001.

Haberman, Maggie, and Eric Lipton. "Nobody Waved Goodbye." *New York Times*, November 2, 2019.

The Habitat. "Episode 3: Why Are We Like This?" Gimlet, April 18, 2018.

Hagedorn, John, Roberto Aspholm, Teresa Córdova, Andrew Papachristos, and Lance Williams. "The Fracturing of Gangs and Violence in Chicago: A Research-Based Reorientation of Violence Prevention and Intervention Policy." Great Cities Institute at the University of Illinois at Chicago (January 2019).

Haidt, Jonathan. *The Righteous Mind.* New York: Vintage, 2013.

Halperin, Eran. *Emotions in Conflict.* New York: Routledge, 2016.

Hartney, Michael T., and Leslie K. Finger. "Politics, Markets, and Pandemics: Public Education's Response to COVID-19." *EdWorkingPaper* 20–304 (October 2020).

Hatfield, Capt. Anse. "Letter to the Editor." *The Tennessean*, March 23, 1891.

Hawkins, Stephen, Daniel Yudkin, Míriam Juan-Torres, and Tim Dixon. "Hidden Tribes: A Study of America's Polarized Landscape." More in Common, 2018.

Hedges, Chris. *War Is a Force That Gives Us Meaning.* New York: PublicAffairs, 2014.

Hirt, Edward R., Dolf Zillmann, Grant A. Erickson, and Chris Kennedy. "Costs and Benefits of Allegiance: Changes in Fans' Self-Ascribed Competencies After Team Victory Versus Defeat." *Journal of Personality and Social Psychology* 63, no. 5 (November 1992).

Hoffman, Bruce. "All You Need Is Love." *Atlantic*, December 2001.

Hofstede, David. *Planet of the Apes: An Unofficial Companion.* Toronto: ECW Press, 2001.

Humphreys, Macartan, and Jeremy M. Weinstein. "Demobilization and Reintegration." *Journal of Conflict Resolution* 51, no. 4 (2007).

Illinois Medical Examiner-Coroner. "Death Certificate for Rita Henderson." File 605962, March 24, 1989. Copy in possession of author.

Ingraham, Christopher. "There Are More Guns than People in the United States, According to a New Study of Global Firearm Ownership." *Washington Post*, June 19, 2018.

Itzchakov, Guy, and Avraham N. Kluger. "The Listening Circle: A Simple Tool to Enhance Listening and Reduce Extremism Among Employees." *Organizational Dynamics* 46, no. 4 (June 2017).

Iyengar, Shanto, Tobias Konitzer, and Kent Tedin. "The Home as a Political Fortress: Family Agreement in an Era of Polarization." *Journal of Politics* 80, no. 4 (2018).

Jamieson, Alison. *The Heart Attacked: Terrorism and Conflict in the Italian State.* London: Marion Boyars, 1989.

Jensen, Trevor. "Thomas J. Maloney: 1925–2008." *Chicago Tribune*, October 22, 2008.

Jewish Virtual Library. "Vital Statistics: Total Casualties, Arab-Israeli Conflict." Last updated April 27, 2020.

Jones, Jeffrey M. "Illinois Residents Least Confident in Their State Government." Gallup, February 17, 2016.

Kaplan, Oliver, and Enzo Nussio. "Explaining Recidivism of Ex-Combatants in Colombia." *Journal of Conflict Resolution* 62, no. 1 (2016).

Karlberg, Michael. *Beyond the Culture of Contest.* Oxford: George Ronald Publisher, 2004.

Kaur-Ballagan, Kully, Gideon Skinner, and Glenn Gottfried. "BBC Global Survey: A World Divided?" Ipsos MORI Social Research Institute, April 22, 2018.

Kiernan, Samantha, Madeleine DeVita, and Thomas J. Bollyky. "Tracking Coronavirus in Countries With and Without Travel Bans." *Think Global Health*, April 7, 2020.

Kim, Sung Soo, Stan Kaplowitz, and Mark V. Johnston. "The Effects of Physician Empathy on Patient Satisfaction and Compliance." *Evaluation & the Health Professions* 27, no. 3 (September 2004).

King, Ruth. *Mindful of Race.* Boulder: Sounds True, 2018.

Klein, Ezra. *Why We're Polarized.* New York: Avid Reader Press, 2020.

Kleinfeld, Rachel. *A Savage Order.* New York: Pantheon, 2018.

Klien, Gary. "Muir Beach Election Pits Old Guard Against New." *Marin Independent Journal*, October 15, 2017.

Kugler, Katharina G., and Peter T. Coleman. "Get Complicated: The Effects of Complexity on Conversations over Potentially Intractable Moral Conflicts." *Negotiation and Conflict Management Research* (2020).

Kusy, Mitchell, and Elizabeth Holloway. *Toxic Workplace!* San Francisco: Jossey-Bass, 2009.

Leach, Katie. "Glenn Beck Dons MAGA Hat: I Will 'Gladly' Vote for Trump in 2020." *Washington Examiner*, May 19, 2018.

Lee, Amber Hye-Yon. "How the Politicization of Everyday Activities Affects the Public Sphere." *Political Communication* (2020).

Lesy, Michael. *Murder City: The Bloody History of Chicago in the Twenties*. New York: W. W. Norton, 2008.

Liberatore, Paul. "Longtime Residents, Relative Newcomers Vie for Seats on Muir Beach CSD." *Marin Independent Journal*, October 23, 2015.

Lindner, Evelin G. "Genocide, Humiliation, and Inferiority." In *Genocides by the Oppressed*, edited by Nicholas A. Robins and Adam Jones. Bloomington: Indiana University Press, 2009.

———. "Making Enemies Unwittingly." Human Dignity and Humiliation Studies, 2005.

Lynas, Mark. "GM Won't Yield a Harvest for the World." *The Guardian*, June 19, 2008.

———. "Lecture to Oxford Farming Conference." Filmed January 3, 2013, at Oxford Farming Conference, Oxford, England.

———. *Seeds of Science*. London: Bloomsbury Sigma, 2018.

Mackie, Diane M., Angela T. Maitner, and Eliot R. Smith. "Intergroup Emotions Theory." In *Handbook of Prejudice, Stereotyping, and Discrimination*, edited by Todd D. Nelson. New York: Psychology Press, 2016.

Mandela, Nelson. *Long Walk to Freedom: The Autobiography of Nelson Mandela*. New York: Little, Brown, 1994.

Margolick, David. "Burger Says Lawyers Make Legal Help Too Costly." *New York Times*, February 13, 1984.

Martelle, Scott, Stuart Pfeifer, and Jerry Hicks. "Bequest Leads to Deep Rift for Nixon Kin." *Los Angeles Times*, March 15, 2002.

Matalon, Roly, Marcelo Bronstein, Felicia Sol, Hazzan Ari Priven, Jeannie Blaustein, Steve Goldberg, and Orli Moss. "B'nai Jeshurun Leadership E-mail on Palestine." Reprinted in *New York Times*, December 4, 2012.

Matalon, Roly, Marcelo Bronstein, and Felicia Sol. "Second B'nai Jeshurun

Leadership E-mail on Palestine." Reprinted in *New York Times*, December 6, 2012.

McDermott, Jeremy. "Criminal Activities of the FARC and Rebel Earnings." *InSight Crime*, May 21, 2013.

McGhee, Heather C. "Racism Has a Cost for Everyone." Filmed December 2019 at TEDWomen, Palm Springs, California.

McGuire, Meagan Anne. "Verbal and Visual Symbolism in Northern Irish Cultural Identity." Thesis, Washington State University, May 2004.

Mehari, Yeabsira. "The Role of Social Trust in Citizen Mobility During COVID-19." SSRN, May 20, 2020.

Merriman, Scott. "Gilmore v. City of Montgomery." *Encyclopedia of Alabama*, July 9, 2015.

Milbank, Dana. *Tears of a Clown*. New York: Doubleday, 2010.

Mitchell, Chip. "Chicago's Dismal Murder Solve Rate Even Worse When Victims Are Black." NPR, October 9, 2019.

Mnookin, Robert, with Gary Friedman and Joel Cutcher-Gershenfeld. "A New Direction: Transforming Relations Within the San Francisco Symphony." *Harmony* 13 (October 2001).

Moore, Billy. *Until the Lion Speaks*. Not-yet-published memoir shared privately with the author in December 2019.

Moore, Natalie Y., and Lance Williams. *The Almighty Black P Stone Nation: The Rise, Fall, and Resurgence of an American Gang*. Chicago: Lawrence Hill Books, 2011.

Moore-Berg, Samantha L., Lee-Or Ankori-Karlinsky, Boaz Hameiri, and Emile Bruneau. "Exaggerated Meta-Perceptions Predict Intergroup Hostility Between American Political Partisans." *Proceedings of the National Academy of Sciences* 117, no. 26 (June 2020).

More in Common and YouGov. "COVID-19: Polarization and the Pandemic." Hidden Tribes, April 3, 2020.

Morrison, Toni. *The Bluest Eye*. New York: Vintage, 2007.

Muir Beach Community Services District. Accessed website for audio recordings, board minutes, and meeting agendas. Last updated 2020.

Mussen, Paul H. "Some Personality and Social Factors Related to Changes in Children's Attitudes Toward Negroes." *Journal of Abnormal and Social Psychology* 45, no. 3 (1950).

Myers, Linnet. "A Bump, a Taunt—then Death." *Chicago Tribune*, October 10, 1985.

———. "2 Teens Convicted in Murder of Ben Wilson." *Chicago Tribune*, October 12, 1985.

National Center for Complementary and Integrative Health. "Meditation: In Depth." Last modified April 2016.

Newheiser, Anna-Kaisa, and Kristina R. Olson. "White and Black American Children's Implicit Intergroup Bias." *Journal of Experimental Social Psychology* 48, no. 1 (2012).

Newton, Elizabeth Louise. "The Rocky Road from Actions to Intentions." PhD diss., Stanford University, 1990. (Accessed October 27, 2020, through the Internet Archive's Wayback Machine.)

New York *Daily News*. "Clown Runs for Prez." June 17, 2015.

Nussio, Enzo. "Ex-Combatants and Violence in Colombia: Are Yesterday's Villains Today's Principal Threat?" *Third World Thematics: A TWQ Journal* 3, no. 1 (2018).

Nussio, Enzo, and Juan E. Ugarriza. "Why Rebels Stop Fighting. Organizational Decline and Exit from Colombia's Insurgency." *International Security*. Forthcoming (2021).

NYPD. "Historical Crime Data: Seven Major Felony Offenses," 2000–2019.

OECD. "Better Life Index." Accessed December 3, 2019.

Ortaliza, Jared, Kendal Orgera, Krutika Amin, and Cynthia Cox. "COVID-19 Preventable Mortality and Leading Cause of Death Ranking." *Peterson-KFF Brief*, December 2021.

Otterman, Sharon, and Joseph Berger. "Cheering U.N. Palestine Vote, Synagogue Tests Its Members." *New York Times*, December 4, 2012.

Oxford Mail. "Science Writer Wins Award." June 27, 2008.

Paarlberg, Robert. *Starved for Science*. Cambridge: Harvard University Press, 2009.

Parker, Nealin. "Lexington Came Together After the Red Hen Incident. Can America Do the Same?" *Washingtonian*, June 21, 2019.

Parkin Daniels, Joe. "Colombian Army Killed Thousands More Civilians than Reported, Study Claims." *The Guardian*, May 8, 2018.

Pillemer, Karl. *Fault Lines: Fractured Families and How to Mend Them*. New York: Avery, 2020.

People of the State of Illinois v. Walter Henderson, Indictment for First Degree Murder, Circuit Court of Cook County, Criminal Division, No. 89 CR 8361, April 19, 1989. Copy in possession of author.

Pettigrew, Thomas F. "European Attitudes Toward Immigrants." In *Identity Matters: Ethnic and Sectarian Conflict*, edited by James L. Peacock, Patricia M. Thornton, and Patrick B. Inman. New York: Berghahn Books, 2007.

Pettigrew, Thomas F., and Linda R. Tropp. "A Meta-Analytic Test of Intergroup Contact Theory. *Journal of Personality and Social Psychology* 90, no. 5 (2006).

Pew Research Center. "Partisanship and Political Animosity in 2016." June 22, 2016.

Pfeifer, Stuart, John J. Goldman, and Phil Willon. "Views Emerge in Rift Between Nixon Sisters." *Los Angeles Times*, March 20, 2002.

Post-Conviction Petition and Order re: People of the State of Illinois v. Walter Henderson, Circuit Court of Cook County, Illinois, Criminal Division, No. 89 CR 8361. Petition filed *pro se* on September 23, 1993. Copy in possession of author.

Pyrooz, David C., Scott H. Decker, and Richard K. Moule Jr. "Criminal and Routine Activities in Online Settings: Gangs, Offenders, and the Internet." *Justice Quarterly* 32, no. 3 (2015).

Rabin, Roni Caryn. "First Patient with Wuhan Coronavirus Is Identified in the U.S." *New York Times*, January 21, 2020.

Rauhala, Emily. "Chinese Officials Note Serious Problems in Coronavirus Response. The World Health Organization Keeps Praising Them." *Washington Post*, February 8, 2020.

Reardon, Patrick. "Redlining Drains City, Aids Suburbs." *Chicago Tribune*, August 11, 1986.

Ripley, Amanda. "Complicating the Narratives." Solutions Journalism Network, June 27, 2018.

_____. "The Least Politically Prejudiced Place in America." *The Atlantic*, March 4, 2019.

Roman, John. "The Puzzling Relationship Between Crime and the Economy." CityLab, September 24, 2013.

Rosenblatt, Gary. "Fuel for Debate over Rabbis' Role." *New York Jewish Week*, February 24, 2014.

Rovenpor, Daniel R., Thomas Christopher O'Brien, Antoine Roblain, and Laura De Guissmé. "Intergroup Conflict Self-Perpetuates via Meaning." *Journal of Personality and Social Psychology* 116, no. 1 (2017).

Sadat, Anwar. "73 Statement to the Knesset." Translated by the Office of the President of Egypt. From Israel Ministry of Foreign Affairs, Historical Documents, Volumes 4–5: 1977–1979, November 20, 1977.

Sahoo, Niranjan. "India: Infections, Islamophobia, and Intensifying Societal Polarization." Carnegie Endowment for International Peace, April 28, 2020.

Sánchez, Miguel García, Juan Carlos Rodríguez-Raga, and Mitchell A. Seligson. "Cultura Política de la Democracia en Colombia, 2013." USAID, Vanderbilt University, May 2014.

Sapolsky, Robert M. *Behave.* New York: Penguin, 2017.

Schmidle, Nicholas. "Glenn Beck Tries Out Decency." *The New Yorker*, November 7, 2016.

Schrøder, Anne Cathrine Munch. "In the Wake of the Wolf." PhD diss., Aarhus University, 2018.

Shadid, Anthony. "Syrian Unrest Stirs New Fear of Deeper Sectarian Divide." *New York Times*, June 13, 2011.

Sharfstein, Daniel J. "Saving the Race." *Legal Affairs*, 2005.

Shellenberger, Michael. *Apocalypse Never: Why Environmental Alarmism Hurts Us All*. New York: HarperCollins, 2020.

Sherman, Ed. "Grit Turns Warehouse into School of Winners." *Chicago Tribune*, March 26, 1984.

Shultz, Susanne, Christopher Opie, and Quentin D. Atkinson. "Stepwise Evolution of Stable Sociality in Primates." *Nature* 479 (2011).

Simpson, Dick, Thomas J. Gradel, Marco Rosaire Rossi, and Katherine Taylor. "Continuing Corruption in Illinois." Anti-Corruption Report Number 10, University of Illinois at Chicago, May 15, 2018.

Smith, Katherine F., Michael Goldberg, Samantha Rosenthal, Lynn Carlson, Jane Chen, Cici Chen, and Sohini Ramachandran. "Global Rise in Human Infectious Disease Outbreaks." *Journal of the Royal Society Interface* 11, no. 101 (December 2014).

Singh Ospina, N., Phillips, K.A., Rodriguez-Gutierrez, R., et al. "Eliciting the Patient's Agenda—Secondary Analysis of Recorded Clinical Encounters." *Journal of General Internal Medicine* 34 (2019).

Smothers, David. "Jeff Fort: A Gangster Who Survives." UPI, November 12, 1981.

Sofield, Laura, and Susan W. Salmond. "Workplace Violence. A Focus on Verbal Abuse and Intent to Leave the Organization." *Orthopedic Nursing* 22, no. 4 (2003).

Stewart, Doug. "Expand the Pie Before You Divvy It Up." *Smithsonian Magazine*, November 1, 1997.

Stewart, Robert B., Andrea L. Kozak, Lynn M. Tingley, Jean M. Goddard, Elissa M. Blake, and Wendy A. Cassel. "Adult Sibling Relationships: Validation of a Typology." *Personal Relationships* 8, no. 3 (2001).

Storr, Will. "Mark Lynas: Truth, Treachery, and GM Food." *The Guardian*, March 9, 2013.

Swift, Art. "Americans' Trust in Mass Media Sinks to New Low." Gallup, September 14, 2016.

Tajfel, Henri, M. G. Billig, R. P. Bundy, and Claude Flament. "Social Categorization and Intergroup Behaviour." *European Journal of Social Psychology* 1, no. 2 (1971).

Taub, Amanda, and Max Fisher. "Why Referendums Aren't as Democratic as They Seem." *New York Times*, October 4, 2016.

Taylor, Matthew. "Wild Wolf Shot and Killed in Denmark." *The Guardian*, May 1, 2018.

Theidon, Kimberly. "Transitional Subjects: The Disarmament, Demobilization and Reintegration of Former Combatants in Colombia." *International Journal of Transitional Justice* 1, no. 1 (2007).

Todd, Tony. "French Farmers Take Park Boss Hostage over Wolf Attacks." *France 24*, September 2, 2015.

Torres, Wilfredo Magno III, ed. *Rido: Clan Feuding and Conflict Management in Mindanao*. Quezon City: Ateneo de Manila University Press, 2014.

Twain, Mark. *Adventures of Huckleberry Finn*. New York: Dover, 1994.

Ulrich, Allan, and Ray Delgado. "Symphony Musicians Don't Play, but Picket." *San Francisco Examiner*, December 6, 1996.

UNHCR. "Colombia." Accessed August 2020.

United Nations. "4 out of 10 Child Soldiers Are Girls." February 12, 2015.

UPI. "Swift Justice Sought for Wilson Attackers." *Daily Dispatch*, November 27, 1984.

Ury, William. *Getting Past No*. New York: Bantam, 1991.

———. *Getting to Yes with Yourself*. New York: HarperOne, 2015.

———. "2016 Dawson High School Graduation Talk." Speech to Dawson High School, June 12, 2016.

Valentino, Silas. "Muir Beach Faces Election Divided by Varying Opinions on Water Hike." *Point Reyes Light*, October 26, 2017.

Vezzali, Loris, and Sofia Stathi, eds. *Intergroup Contact Theory*. London: Routledge, 2017.

Voss, Christopher. *Never Split the Difference*. New York: HarperCollins, 2016.

Waller, Altina L. *Feud: Hatfields, McCoys, and Social Change in Appalachia, 1860–1900*. Chapel Hill: University of North Carolina Press, 1988.

Wallisch, Pascal. "Illumination Assumptions Account for Individual Differences in the Perceptual Interpretation of a Profoundly Ambiguous Stimulus in the Color Domain: 'The Dress.'" *Journal of Vision* 17, no. 4 (April 2017).

Wang, Zheng. "National Humiliation, History Education, and the Politics of Historical Memory: Patriotic Education Campaign in China." *International Studies Quarterly* 52 (2008).

Washington, George. "Washington's Farewell Address to the People of the United States." First appeared in the *Philadelphia Daily American Advertiser* and then in newspapers nationwide, September 19, 1796. (Accessed through www.Senate.gov on October 28, 2020.)

Wesselmann, Eric D., Fionnuala A. Butler, Kipling D. Williams, and Cynthia L. Pickett. "Adding Injury to Insult: Unexpected Rejection Leads to More Aggressive Responses." *Aggressive Behavior* 36, no. 4 (2010).

Wheat, Sue. "Crying Wolf." *The Guardian*, March 14, 2001.

Whiteside, Mary F. "The Parental Alliance Following Divorce: An Overview." *Journal of Marital and Family Therapy* 24, no. 1 (1998).

Whitesides, John. "From Disputes to a Breakup: Wounds Still Raw after U.S. Election." Reuters, February 7, 2017.

Widmer, Mireille, and Irene Pavesi. "Monitoring Trends in Violent Deaths." *Small Arms Survey Research Notes* 59 (September 2016).

Williams, Kipling D., and Kristin L. Sommer. "Social Ostracism by Coworkers: Does Rejection Lead to Loafing or Compensation?" *Personality and Social Psychology Bulletin* 23, no. 7 (1997).

Williams, Kipling D., Christopher K. T. Cheung, and Wilma Choi. "Cyberostracism: Effects of Being Ignored over the Internet." *Journal of Personality and Social Psychology* 79, no. 5 (2000).

Williams, Kipling D., and Steve A. Nida. "Ostracism: Consequences and Coping." *Current Directions in Psychological Science* 20, no. 2 (2011).

Wood, Gordon S. *Friends Divided: John Adams and Thomas Jefferson.* New York: Penguin, 2017.

Woodson, Carter G. *The Mis-Education of the Negro.* Washington: Associated Publishers, 1933.

World Economic Forum. "Outbreak Readiness and Business Impact," January 2019, http://www3.weforum.org/docs/WEF%20HGHI_Outbreak_Readiness_Business_Impact.pdf.

World Health Organization. "Pneumonia of Unknown Cause—China." January 5, 2020.

Yanagizawa-Drott, David. "Propaganda and Conflict: Evidence from the Rwandan Genocide." *Quarterly Journal of Economics* 129, no. 4 (2014).

Yong, Ed. "How the Pandemic Defeated America." *The Atlantic*, August 4, 2020.

Yudkin, Daniel, Stephen Hawkins, and Tim Dixon. "The Perception Gap." More in Common, June 2019.

notes

introduction

1 *Mark Lynas:* The details of Mark's story come from interviews he's done with me and other reporters, as well as his own writing over the years. I particularly recommend his 2018 book, *Seeds of Science*, which tells his own story and explains the widely misunderstood science of genetically modified organisms. I am grateful to Mark for having the courage not only to reconsider his assumptions but to talk openly about his own evolution.

2 *"In the great global genetic experiment":* Lynas, *Seeds of Science.*

3 *"I'm quite law abiding":* Storr, "Mark Lynas: Truth, Treachery and GM Food."

3 *High conflict:* A word on definitions. Traditionally, in family therapy, the phrase "high conflict" has been used as an adjective, to describe particularly difficult people or divorces. This book reinvents the term "high conflict" as a noun, referring to an entire system in which conflict becomes self-perpetuating and paralyzing. Some high conflicts would fall under the label "intractable conflict," which researchers use to refer to violent conflict that has lasted for generations and defies resolution. But high conflict in this book is more common than intractable conflict. It does not need to last for generations, nor does it need to be violent (although it can easily become violent). To read more about the fascinating research into intractable conflicts, check out Bar-Tal, *Intractable Conflicts,* and Coleman, *The Five Percent: Finding Solutions to Seemingly Impossible Conflicts.*

4 *"high conflict personalities":* In one survey of business leaders, nine out of ten said they'd had to deal with "toxic" high conflict personalities in their careers. See Kusy and Holloway, *Toxic Workplace!*

7 *frightening:* Pew Research Center, "Partisanship and Political Animosity in 2016."

7 *38 million:* This is an estimate based on a Reuters/Ipsos poll taken after the election. In that survey of 6,426 people, 16 percent said they had stopped talking to a family member or friend because of the election. Extrapolating from there, 16 percent of the population of U.S. adults is about 38 million. See Whitesides, "From Disputes to a Breakup: Wounds Still Raw After U.S. Election."

8 *Two out of three Americans:* Swift, "Americans' Trust in Mass Media Sinks to New Low."

8 *In Argentina:* Kaur-Ballagan et al., "BBC Global Survey: A World Divided?"

8 *Half of Europeans:* Ibid.

8 *"Germany shouts and screams":* This quote comes from a 2018 speech that I attended in Berlin at an event called My Country Talks, organized by Zeit Online.

10 *Everyone lost:* For more about Oak Park, check out Heather McGhee's excellent TED Talk entitled "Racism Has a Cost for Everyone" and Merriman, "Gilmore v. City of Montgomery."

11 *a supermarket sponge cake:* This incident can be found on YouTube. The professor, Bjørn Lomborg, was promoting his book *The Skeptical Environmentalist.* Mark has since apologized to Lomborg.

12 *Zambia:* Paarlberg, *Starved for Science.*

13 *nonviolent movements:* These movements, which include boycotts, strikes, and protests, succeed because they attract big and diverse followings, enough people to put sustained, meaningful pressure on the levers of power. Chenoweth and Stephan, *Why Civil Resistance Works.*

14 *a cluster of pneumonia cases:* World Health Organization, "Pneumonia of Unknown Cause—China."

14 *a Washington State resident:* Rabin, "First Patient with Wuhan Coronavirus Is Identified in the U.S."

14 *Chinese authorities downplayed:* Associated Press, "China Didn't Warn Public of Likely Pandemic for Six Key Days."

14 *the situation was under control:* Rauhala, "Chinese Officials Note Serious Problems in Coronavirus Response. The World Health Organization Keeps Praising Them."

14 *eleven thousand New Yorkers:* Carey and Glanz, "Hidden Outbreaks Spread Through U.S. Cities Far Earlier than Americans Knew, Estimates Say."

14 *"we're all in it together:"* More in Common and YouGov, "COVID 19: Polarization and the Pandemic."

15 *"Coronajihad":* Sahoo, "India: Infections, Islamophobia, and Intensifying Societal Polarization."

15 *Cutting funding:* BBC News, "Coronavirus: Trump's WHO De-funding 'As Dangerous as It Sounds.'"

15 *Schools reopened:* Hartney and Finger, "Politics, Markets, and Pandemics."

15 *a day and a half:* World Economic Forum, "Outbreak Readiness and Business Impact."

15 *12,012 recorded outbreaks:* Smith et al., "Global Rise in Human Infectious Disease Outbreaks."

16 *"moral proximity":* Allport, *The Nature of Prejudice.*

16 *George Floyd:* Fernandez and Burch, "George Floyd, from 'I Want to Touch the World' to 'I Can't Breathe.'"

16 *At least a dozen additional Americans died:* At the time this book went to press, this number was hard to pin down with any certainty. It was difficult to tell, in some cases, whether the shootings were related to the protests or not. A more meaningful number will, hopefully, become available in time. Al Jazeera, "Nearly a Dozen Deaths Tied to Continuing Unrest in U.S."

16 *At least 163,000 people:* Ortaliza et al. "COVID-19 Preventable Mortality and Leading Cause of Death Ranking."

17 *"run rampant and breed:"* Lynas, "GM Won't Yield a Harvest for the World."

18 *"Now my lords, ladies, and gentlemen":* Lynas, "Lecture to Oxford Farming Conference."

chapter 1: the understory of conflict

23 *Jay and Lorna:* The story of Jay and Lorna comes from my own interviews with Gary, along with two of Gary's books: Friedman, *A Guide to Divorce Mediation*, and Friedman, *Inside Out.* The real names of his clients have been changed to protect their privacy.

26 *La Brea Tar Pits:* Details on the Tar Pits come from a Tar Pits employee as well as news clippings and information from the totally captivating Tar Pits website (tarpits.org), which I recommend checking out.

28 *Two thirds of Americans:* Hawkins et al., "Hidden Tribes: A Study of America's Polarized Landscape." This report, conducted by the nonpartisan organization More in Common, labeled this group of Americans the "exhausted majority." The report is one of the most thoughtful and useful analyses I've seen on polarization in the U.S.

29 *staying home days before:* Mehari, "The Role of Social Trust in Citizen Mobility During COVID-19."

29 *three times that many signed up:* Butler, "A Million Volunteer to Help NHS and Others During Covid-19 Outbreak."

29 *adversarialism:* For an excellent book detailing the limits of adversarialism and the potential for mutualism, see Karlberg, *Beyond the Culture of Contest.*

30 *a contest:* Interestingly, business best practices may now be more sophisticated than political strategy when it comes to recognizing the limits of adversarialism. For decades, business schools have taught that collaboration in negotiation often leads to a better outcome than competition, for example. (There are many great books on negotiation including the classic *Getting to Yes* by Roger Fisher and William Ury. I also like *Getting Past No* and *Getting to Yes with Yourself,* both by William Ury.) A lot of interesting quantitative evidence undergirds this point, but the bottom line for our purposes is that an us-versus-them mindset tends to leave people worse off. In business, politics, marriage, pandemics, and almost every part of life that really matters.

30 *"battle and blood":* Margolick, "Burger Says Lawyers Make Legal Help Too Costly."

36 *the Legos:* Both the Legos case and the Hibachi grill story were described to me by professional conflict mediators in 2019.

37 *Mediation typically costs a fraction:* In 2007, a firm in Boston analyzed 199 of its recent divorce cases and concluded that mediation was by far the least expensive option, costing about $6,600 on average, compared to $26,830 for a divorce settlement negotiated by rival lawyers. Full-scale litigation, which is what happens in the traditional system when the parties can't reach a negotiated agreement, cost nearly $78,000 on average. So in this particular sample, going to court against a spouse cost almost twelve times what mediation cost. (Another option is collaborative divorce, which is sort of mediation plus. The husband and wife each have their own attorneys, along with other consultants as needed, but everyone tries to work together to find a fair agreement. In this particular firm at that time, collaborative divorces cost nearly $20,000 on average.) All of this assumes that both parties want to work out an agreement. If either person is not committed,

litigation might be cheaper, because someone else (a judge) decides on the result. Crary, "Keen Interest in Gentler Ways to Divorce."

38 *"unstrained, unlittered, Pacific isolation"*: Gold, "Easy Living in Marin."

41 *San Francisco Symphony orchestra*: Gary worked on a team of negotiators including Robert Mnookin from Harvard Law School and Joel Cutcher-Gershenfeld, a labor relations expert. Their efforts were funded by a grant by the Hewlett Foundation. For more details, see Mnookin et al., "A New Direction: Transforming Relations Within the San Francisco Symphony."

41 *"I'm sure there's a better way"*: Ulrich and Delgado, "Symphony Musicians Don't Play, but Picket."

42 *"A kind of desperation"*: Mnookin et al., "A New Direction: Transforming Relations Within the San Francisco Symphony."

42 *eleven seconds:* Singh Ospina et al., "Eliciting the Patient's Agenda."

42 *consequences to our bad listening:* For more on the research into the measurable effects of high-quality listening, see Guy Itzchakov and Avraham Kluger, "The Listening Circle: A Simple Tool to Enhance Listening and Reduce Extremism Among Employees."

43 *Customers who feel heard:* Bergeron and Laroche, "The Effects of Perceived Salesperson Listening Effectiveness in the Financial Industry."

43 *Workers who feel heard:* Guy Itzchakov and Avraham Kluger, "The Listening Circle: A Simple Tool to Enhance Listening and Reduce Extremism Among Employees."

43 *more likely to follow their doctor's orders:* Kim et al., "The Effects of Physician Empathy on Patient Satisfaction and Compliance."

43 *Among couples:* Gordon and Chen, "Do You Get Where I'm Coming From?"

43 *looping:* Looping for understanding is a technique developed by Gary Friedman and Jack Himmelstein, detailed in their book, *Challenging Conflict*. It is the kind of thing that sounds simple but is actually quite cognitively challenging to do well. (Gary and his colleagues at the Center for Understanding in Conflict offer training on looping, for anyone interested in learning more.)

43 *"to play alongside":* These quotes are based on Gary's memory of the symphony looping exercises, as well as my own observations, having watched, joined, or led about a dozen trainings in looping.

44 *"I came to understand":* Mnookin et al., "A New Direction: Transforming Relations Within the San Francisco Symphony."

45 *one of the best-paid symphonies:* It would be fourteen years before the San

Francisco Symphony went on strike again. That was a long period of peace, relative to the organization's track record. Over time, the musicians and management changed. New people arrived who had not experienced the mediation with Gary and his colleagues. The muscle memory for navigating conflict fades without practice.

45 *"Boy, has Muir Beach changed":* Most of the details and quotes from board events described in this book come from audio recordings, minutes, and meeting agendas, posted on the Muir Beach Community Services District website. Other details come from my interviews with some of the participants.

46 *"a tone of respect":* Liberatore, "Longtime Residents, Relative Newcomers Vie for Seats on Muir Beach CSD."

chapter 2: the power of the binary

48 *John Adams and Thomas Jefferson:* Wood, *Friends Divided: John Adams and Thomas Jefferson*; Duverger, "Public Opinion and Political Parties in France"; and Bober, *Thomas Jefferson: Draftsman of a Nation.*

51 *"His ambition and his cunning":* Wood, *Friends Divided: John Adams and Thomas Jefferson.*

51 *"Overcategorizaton":* Allport, *The Nature of Prejudice.*

51 *52 million years ago:* Shultz et al., "Stepwise Evolution of Stable Sociality in Primates."

52 *Under the influence of categories:* Categories aren't benign descriptors. They are created to solve problems for someone. In the nineteenth century, for example, American immigrants from Ireland were referred to as part of the "Irish race," generally considered inferior to the "Anglo-Saxon race." Then there was the "Italian race" and the "Jewish race," both of which were considered suspect for different reasons. An elaborate hierarchy of supposed racial differences, even within the category of "White," served to explain and preserve inequalities in American society. For a great, in-depth read on the science of identity, I recommend Berreby, *Us and Them.*

52 *Planet of the Apes:* Thank you to Robert Sapolsky, who flagged this in his fascinating book *Behave*, citing David Hofstede's *Planet of the Apes: An Unofficial Companion.*

52 *six paintings:* Tajfel et al., "Social Categorization and Intergroup Behaviour." I've included two paintings here as examples of both artists' style,

but I was unable to determine which specific paintings the researchers used in the original experiment.

53 *White American children:* Newheiser and Olson, "White and Black American Children's Implicit Intergroup Bias."

54 *binary referendums:* Taub and Fisher, "Why Referendums Aren't as Democratic as They Seem."

54 *"almost never":* Ibid.

55 *The Dress:* If you haven't already tried this out yourself, you can see an image of the dress here: https://en.wikipedia.org/wiki/The_dress. For the science behind this viral phenomenon, see Wallisch, "Illumination Assumptions Account for Individual Differences in the Perceptual Interpretation of a Profoundly Ambiguous Stimulus in the Color Domain: 'The Dress.'"

57 *Meditation:* For more on the research into the effects of meditation, see National Center for Complementary and Integrative Health, "Meditation: In Depth." If you're interested in trying meditation out, there are lots of free and low-cost apps to help guide you along. Personally, I recommend Headspace, which I've used ever since I came home from this training with Gary. It is way easier than trying to meditate for the first time on your own, and the short meditations include a lot of really practical lessons about mindfulness generally.

57 *changed how I work:* The project that came out of this initial reporting was commissioned by the Solutions Journalism Network, a nonprofit that trains journalists to rigorously report on what communities are doing to solve problems (rather than just reporting on the problems). See Ripley, "Complicating the Narratives."

61 *"He hated everybody":* Sharfstein, "Saving the Race."

62 *"oversimplified camps":* Friedman, *Inside Out.*

62 *$5,500:* Bridgeport Post, "Jury Awards $5,500 to Woman in Crash."

64 *testosterone:* Winning at just about anything tends to boost testosterone—as long as the vanquished is seen as an outsider. For instance, in a study of men playing dominoes in a Caribbean community, those who beat a member of another group experienced a surge of testosterone shortly after the match. Men who beat a friend from their *own* group exhibited no such hormonal change. Flinn et al., "Hormonal Mechanisms for Regulation of Aggression in Human Coalitions."

65 *just under 3 percent:* This experiment comes a 1990 dissertation by Stanford Graduate student Elizabeth Newton: "The Rocky Road from Actions to

Intentions." Interestingly, Newton found a gender difference in this tapping experiment. While both men and women offered up overconfident, unrealistically high estimates for how guessable their taps would be, male tappers were significantly more likely to give inflated estimates.

66 *"is the illusion that it has taken place":* This quote has been attributed to George Bernard Shaw, but the folks at Quote Investigator could not find any evidence he actually said it. It's hard to say for sure, but it appears to be based on a less pithy but similar point originally made by the journalist William H. Whyte in a *Fortune* article in 1950 about the need for better communication in businesses.

66 *People generally overestimate:* Gilovich et al., "The Illusion of Transparency."

67 *idiot-driver reflex:* This human tendency to judge others more harshly than ourselves is known in psychology as the fundamental attribution error. I made up the term "idiot-driver reflex" because I find the formal term to be hard to remember and understand.

69 *Marin Independent Journal:* Klien, "Muir Beach Election Pits Old Guard Against New."

69 *"I do not feel the comfort":* Valentino, "Muir Beach Faces Election Divided by Varying Opinions on Water Hike."

71 *Cyberball:* See Williams and Sommer, "Social Ostracism by Coworkers: Does Rejection Lead to Loafing or Compensation?"; Williams et al., "Cyberostracism: Effects of Being Ignored over the Internet"; and Williams and Nida, "Ostracism: Consequences and Coping."

72 *threats that are unexpected*: Wesselmann et al., "Adding Injury to Insult: Unexpected Rejection Leads to More Aggressive Responses."

72 *disrespected:* DeBono and Muraven, "Rejection Perceptions: Feeling Disrespected Leads to Greater Aggression than Feeling Disliked."

73 *the Red Hen:* Parker, "Lexington Came Together After the Red Hen Incident. Can America Do the Same?"

76 *hateful:* As of 2018, more than 80 percent of both Democrats and Republicans said their opponents were "hateful." Democrats said Republicans were "racist," and Republicans said the same about Democrats. Yudkin et al., "The Perception Gap."

76 *"Contempt":* Giles, "Maths Predicts Chance of Divorce."

79 *seventy-five times easier:* In 2019, Harvard had an acceptance rate of 4.5 percent, according to *The Harvard Crimson*.

79 *"You depend on each other":* This quote is from my interview with Buckey.

79 *"a crew without conflict":* Quotes are from my in-person interview with Binsted.

80 *forty-nine conflicts:* Basner et al., "Psychological and Behavioral Changes During Confinement in a 520-Day Simulated Interplanetary Mission to Mars."

81 *Ed White:* This exchange comes from an episode of the Gimlet podcast, *The Habitat.*

88 *peace plans:* Halperin, *Emotions in Conflict.*

89 *godless, gay, and radical:* Ahler and Sood, "The Parties in Our Heads."

89 *hold extreme views:* Yudkin et al., "The Perception Gap."

89 *the other side dislikes them:* Moore-Berg et al., "Exaggerated Meta-Perceptions Predict Intergroup Hostility Between American Political Partisans."

89 *votes were defensive:* Geiger, "For Many Voters, It's Not Which Presidential Candidate They're for but Which They're Against."

90 *three times as inaccurate:* Yudkin et al., "The Perception Gap."

91 *"most fatal disease":* Chernow, *Alexander Hamilton.*

91 *"cunning, ambitious, and unprincipled":* Washington, George. "Washington's Farewell Address to the People of the United States." I'd recommend reading this document in full. It is a shock to see our current political pathology foreshadowed so unblinkingly, so long ago. You can find it in many places including, ironically, on the website for the US Senate at www.senate.gov.

94 *Warfare:* Ferguson, "War Is Not Part of Human Nature."

95 *"If we took":* Christakis, *Blueprint: The Evolutionary Origins of a Good Society.*

96 *Ranked-choice voting:* Drutman, *Breaking the Two-Party Doom Loop: The Case for Multiparty Democracy in America.*

96 *proportional representation:* Ibid.

97 *fictional elections:* Fischer et al., "The Impact of Electoral Systems and Outcomes on Mass Attitudes: Experimental Attitudes."

chapter 3: the fire starters

100 *the Hatfield and the McCoy families:* There are many sensationalized accounts of the Hatfield and McCoy feud. I'm relying largely on the more evidenced-based version found in the book *Feud: Hatfields, McCoys, and Social Change in Appalachia, 1860–1900* by historian Altina Waller.

103 *"The war spirit":* Hatfield, "Letter to the Editor."

103 *Curtis Toler:* I originally met Curtis in San Francisco at an event orga-

nized by the Emerson Collective, a social impact firm that invests in journalism, education, and other issues. At the time, I was a fellow with the Emerson Collective, and Curtis was working for Chicago CRED, which is funded by the same organization. That fellowship has since ended, and I have never had any financial ties to Curtis or CRED, but I am deeply grateful that the Emerson Collective brought us together.

108 *national identities:* The scholar Benedict Anderson calls this sense of national identity an "imagined community," a collective of people to whom we feel like we have some bond. See Anderson, *Imagined Communities: Reflections on the Origins and Spread of Nationalism.*

110 *no apparent difference:* Sapolsky, *Behave.*

110 *Basketball fans:* Hirt et al., "Costs and Benefits of Allegiance: Changes in Fans' Self-Ascribed Competencies After Team Victory Versus Defeat."

112 *"standing by their father":* Carlson, "Nixon Daughters Bury the Hatchet."

113 *sibling:* Stewart et al., "Adult Sibling Relationships: Validation of a Typology."

113 *drive a wedge:* Carlson, "Nixon Daughters Bury the Hatchet." The Nixon Foundation did not respond to my requests to talk with the sisters directly, so I relied on the many news clippings about the dispute. I would be very curious to hear the story from the sisters themselves, should they ever wish to share it.

114 *"complete estrangement":* Martelle et al., "Bequest Leads to Deep Rift for Nixon Kin."

114 *"I love my sister":* Pfeifer et al., "Views Emerge in Rift Between Nixon Sisters."

114 *"a party":* Dahlburg and Pfeifer, "For Feuding Nixon Sisters, Finally a Peace with Honor."

114 *"and we always will":* Associated Press, "Nixon Sisters Debate Library Fund."

115 *Jeff Fort:* The Black P Stone Nation was founded by Eugene "Bull" Hairston and Jeff Fort in the early 1960s and has changed names multiple times. Details on Jeff Fort come from my interviews with Curtis, as well as news clippings and books, especially: Moore and Williams, *The Almighty Black P Stone Nation: The Rise, Fall, and Resurgence of an American Gang.*

116 *dope rings:* Smothers, "Jeff Fort: A Gangster Who Survives."

117 *Alawites:* Fisher, "The One Map That Shows Why Syria Is So Complicated."

117 *"forcing us to hate"*: Shadid, "Syrian Unrest Stirs New Fear of Deeper Sectarian Divide."

118 *"Ethnic wars"*: Bass, "What Really Causes Civil War?"

118 *released extremist prisoners*: Dagher, *Assad or We Burn the Country*.

118 *identity manipulation*: for more on how to be mindful of identity manipulation, see Klein, *Why We're Polarized*.

119 *"school of winners"*: Sherman, "Grit Turns Warehouse into School of Winners."

119 *loans*: Reardon, "Redlining Drains City, Aids Suburbs."

119 *vacant*: Greater Chatham Initiative, "History: Auburn Gresham."

121 *"random, senseless"*: Davidson and Recktenwald, "Bullets End Benjy's Fight to Be the Best."

122 *"A superstar is dead"*: Associated Press, "Rev. Jesse Jackson Eulogizes Ben Wilson."

123 *Humiliation*: Lindner, "Genocide, Humiliation and Inferiority."

123 *"addiction or dependence"*: Lindner, "Making Enemies Unwittingly."

123 *"The single most underappreciated force"*: Friedman, "The Humiliation Factor."

124 *"serious act of violence"*: Gilligan, *Violence: Reflections on a National Epidemic*.

124 *"people who thrive on humiliation"*: Lindner, "Making Enemies Unwittingly."

124 *Holocaust survivors*: Frijda, "The Lex Talionis: On Vengeance."

125 *"One man's transparency"*: CNN.com, "N. Ireland Process: Where Did It Go Wrong?"

125 *emotion*: Barrett, *How Emotions Are Made*. Also, for a powerful story about how humans interpret emotions, I recommend NPR's *Invisibilia* podcast, "Emotions," from June 22, 2017.

127 *Utku*: Briggs, *Never in Anger: Portrait of an Eskimo Family*.

128 *"Thanksgiving in the morgue"*: UPI, "Swift Justice Sought for Wilson Attackers."

128 *the Disciples*: Billy was a member of the Gangster Disciples, not to be confused with other rival organizations—like the Black Disciples. Curtis generally refers to Billy's organization as "the Disciples," and I've chosen to do the same throughout this book.

130 *"The enduring attraction"*: Hedges, *War Is a Force That Gives Us Meaning*.

130 *groups distribute the conflict*: The technical term for this is intergroup emotions theory, and it refers to the ways that humans experience emotions vicariously, on behalf of fellow group members. This theory was developed

by social psychologists Diane M. Mackie and Eliot R. Smith. See Mackie et al., "Intergroup Emotions Theory."

130 *a character named Buck:* Twain, *Adventures of Huckleberry Finn.*

131 *"They will never change":* Halperin, *Emotions in Conflict.*

132 *Polos and penny loafers:* The descriptions of how Stones and Disciples could tell each other apart come from my interviews with Curtis. Disciples (and other Stones) no doubt have different recollections about these details.

133 *"telling":* The section on the telling in Northern Ireland comes from a fascinating thesis by Meagan Anne McGuire: "Verbal and Visual Symbolism in Northern Irish Cultural Identity."

133 *White, middle-class, and heterosexual:* Ahler and Sood, "The Parties in Our Heads."

133 *eat, drive, and drink:* Lee, "How the Politicization of Everyday Activities Affects the Public Sphere."

135 *Revenge:* For a powerful essay on revenge, see Frijda, "The Lex Talionis: On Vengeance." "Revenge," Frijda wrote, "is the social power regulator in a society without central justice."

135 *"What America is tasting now":* Associated Press, translated statement.

136 *Never Forget Our National Humiliation:* Wang, "National Humiliation, History Education, and the Politics of Historical Memory: Patriotic Education Campaign in China."

137 *Parisians:* Rovenpor et al., "Intergroup Conflict Self-Perpetuates via Meaning."

139 *third parties:* Fearon, "Civil War and the Current International System."

139 *eight out of every ten violent deaths:* Widmer and Pavesi, "Monitoring Trends in Violent Deaths."

139 *St. Louis:* In 2018, St. Louis had a homicide rate of 60 murders per 100,000 people, according to FBI data; Chicago's homicide rate was 21 murders per 100,000 people. Global homicide rates come from El Consejo Ciudadano para la Seguridad Pública y la Justicia Penal, "Metodología del Ranking (2018) de las 50 Ciudades Más Violentas del Mundo."

139 *existence of groups:* For more on how diversity does or does not correlate with war, see political scientists James Fearon and David Laitin's analysis of 127 civil wars occurring between 1945 and 1999: Fearon and Laitin, "Ethnicity, Insurgency and Civil War."

140 *civilian-owned guns:* Ingraham, "There Are More Guns than People in the United States, According to a New Study of Global Firearm Ownership."

140 *homicide rate:* OECD, "Better Life Index."

140 *GDP:* Roman, "The Puzzling Relationship Between Crime and the Economy."

140 *complicit state:* Kleinfeld, *A Savage Order.*

141 *White gangs:* Grossman et al., *The Encyclopedia of Chicago.*

141 *"Murder City":* Lesy, *Murder City: The Bloody History of Chicago in the Twenties.*

141 *aldermen:* Simpson et al., "Continuing Corruption in Illinois."

141 *federal political corruption charges:* This statistic refers to the period from 1976 to 2018. Simpson et al., "Continuing Corruption in Illinois."

141 *judges:* Cook County Judge Thomas J. Maloney was found guilty in 1993 of taking thousands of dollars to fix three murder trials and one other felony case. One of the bribes came from the El Rukn gang, an offshoot of the Stones (when Curtis was a relatively new member of the gang). Maloney served twelve years in prison and died in 2008. Jensen, "Thomas J. Maloney: 1925–2008."

142 *getting away with it:* Mitchell, "Chicago's Dismal Murder Solve Rate Even Worse When Victims Are Black."

142 *trust in state government:* Jones, "Illinois Residents Least Confident in Their State Government."

142 *personal beefs:* For more about the current state of gang violence in Chicago, see Hagedorn et al., "The Fracturing of Gangs and Violence in Chicago."

143 *addiction:* Details about the drug addiction of Walter Henderson, Curtis's stepdad, come from interviews with Curtis as well as court filings by Henderson on his own behalf.

144 *stabbed:* Details about the murder of Rita Henderson, Curtis's mother, come from her death certificate; Cook County court records regarding the prosecution of her husband, Walter Henderson; and Henderson's subsequent appeal attempts.

145 *"There is a sense":* Morrison, *The Bluest Eye.*

145 *feds raided:* Moore and Williams, *The Almighty Black P Stone Nation.*

146 *beat a man:* Details of this incident and the other two arrests described in this chapter come from interviews with Curtis as well as Cook County court records.

chapter 4: buying time

154 *"You're the inspiration":* Chicago, "You're the Inspiration."

156 *rido:* Torres, *Rido: Clan Feuding and Conflict Management in Mindanao.*

157 *Benjamin Rush:* Wood, *Friends Divided: John Adams and Thomas Jefferson.*

160 *Hitler:* Milbank, *Tears of a Clown.*

160 *"deep-seated hatred":* Beck, Interview on *Fox & Friends.* To read more about Glenn Beck's story from his own perspective, I recommend his book *Addicted to Outrage,* which came out in 2018.

160 *"I think I played a role":* Beck, Interview by Megyn Kelly, *The Kelly File.*

160 *"dangerously unhinged":* Schmidle, "Glenn Beck Tries Out Decency."

160 *"the African-American experience":* Ibid.

160 *Samantha Bee:* Beck, Interview by Samantha Bee, *Full Frontal with Samantha Bee.*

161 *Krista Tippett:* Beck, Interview by Krista Tippett, *On Being with Krista Tippett.*

161 *"Loyalty":* Beck, Interview by Peter Kafka, *Recode Media with Peter Kafka.*

161 *"sociopath":* CBS DC, "Glenn Beck Says Media Are 'Rat Bastards,' Obama Is a Dictator."

161 *"My audience":* Beck, Interview by Krista Tippett, *On Being with Krista Tippett.*

162 *"Remarkable!":* Leach, "Glenn Beck Dons MAGA Hat: I Will 'Gladly' Vote for Trump in 2020."

162 *off the air:* Bond, "Glenn Beck's TheBlaze to End on Linear TV."

164 *Georgia:* In her book *A Savage Order,* Rachel Kleinfeld describes how countries like Georgia find a way out of endemic violence. The first step governments take is to make bargains with warlords, literally buying time by giving guerrilla fighters money and political power in exchange for a little peace. She calls these "dirty deals," and like the "peace agreements" among the gangs in Chicago, they don't buy peace. "They purchase time."

165 *unusual solution:* Hoffman, "All You Need Is Love."

167 *The Mis-Education of the Negro:* Woodson, *The Mis-Education of the Negro.*

168 *the Reverend Michael Pfleger:* Father Pfleger is a fascinating Chicago character, worthy of more attention than I give him here. To learn more about him, check out Evan Osnos's 2016 *New Yorker* profile, "Father Mike."

169 *"Stop demonizing them!":* Butigan, "Chicago's South Side Rises Up Against Gun Violence."

172 *A Different Story:* The section on Billy's perspective comes from news accounts, my own in-person interviews with Billy Moore, and Billy's not-yet-published autobiography, *Until the Lion Speaks,* which he wrote in 2019 and shared with me that September. This is Billy's version of events based on his own memory. It is impossible to know for certain what really happened that day, as different witnesses have given different accounts. Benji's girlfriend testified at the trial that Omar Dixon had grabbed Benji and asked him for money, before telling Billy to shoot Benji—a claim that both Omar and Billy have denied.

175 *the prosecutor:* At trial, the prosecutor in question testified that the signed statement only included what Billy had told him. That prosecutor eventually became a judge. I was unable to check Billy's version of the story with him, as the judge is now deceased. See also Myers, "A Bump, a Taunt—then Death."

176 *"very unanimous":* Myers, "2 Teens Convicted in Murder of Ben Wilson."

178 *contact theory:* Pettigrew and Tropp, "A Meta-Analytic Test of Intergroup Contact Theory"; Vezzali and Stathi, eds., *Intergroup Contact Theory.*

179 *Muslims:* Abrams et al., "Does Terror Defeat Contact? Intergroup Contact and Prejudice Toward Muslims Before and After the London Bombings."

180 *"a tremendous honor":* Oxford Mail, "Science Writer Wins Award."

181 *"I now regret it":* Lynas, "Lecture to Oxford Farming Conference."

181 *summer camp:* Mussen, "Some Personality and Social Factors Related to Changes in Children's Attitudes Toward Negroes."

182 *scapegoat:* Ibid.; Allport, *The Nature of Prejudice.*

183 *apocalyptic narrative:* For more about the strange way we can get seduced by apocalyptic narratives around climate change, I recommend *Apocalypse Never: Why Environmental Alarmism Hurts Us All,* by Michael Shellenberger.

186 *two to three more hours a week online:* Pyrooz et al., "Criminal and Routine Activities in Online Settings: Gangs, Offenders, and the Internet."

188 *regulate their own emotions:* The psychologist James Gross has identified five strategies people use to regulate their emotions. For more, see Gross, ed., *Handbook of Emotion Regulation,* especially Chapter 1.

190 *Hugo Chávez:* Ury, "2016 Dawson High School Graduation Talk." See also Ury, *Getting to Yes with Yourself.*

191 *sixty married couples:* Finkel et al., "A Brief Intervention to Promote Conflict Reappraisal Preserves Marital Quality over Time."

chapter 5: making space

196 *disrupted:* In studying violent conflicts around the world, Columbia University's Peter T. Coleman has seen this pattern play out again and again. About three quarters of intractable conflicts end within ten years of a political shock, he has estimated. For instance, the last time America was as politically polarized as it is now was shortly after the Civil War. That epoch of polarization ended in the 1920s—after the shock of World War I reordered the world. For more, see Coleman, "COVID Could Be the Shock That Ends Our Deep Divisions."

197 *"the curse of humanity":* Sadat, "73 Statement to the Knesset."

200 *"magic ratio":* Gottman with Silver, *Why Marriages Succeed or Fail.*

200 *Antarctic:* Edholm and Gunderson, eds., *Polar Human Biology.*

202 *three questions:* These questions are not original to Gary. Author Justin Bariso included them in his book *EQ Applied,* attributing them to the comedian and TV host Craig Ferguson. But there may be other sources.

202 *the purity of nature:* Feinberg and Willer, "From Gulf to Bridge: When Do Moral Arguments Facilitate Political Influence?"

204 *a special meeting:* If Gary were a national politician, it's worth noting, he would have had every reason to call a special meeting. Doing so would have generated immediate campaign donations and social media followers. Right now, there are far too many incentives for higher-profile politicians to speak the moral language of their base rather than the language of all the people they were elected to serve.

205 *"Who's winning this marriage?":* Ury is quoted in Stewart, "Expand the Pie Before You Divvy It Up."

206 *"Anger is not transformative":* King, *Mindful of Race.*

chapter 6: reverse engineering

210 *Sierra Leone:* Humphreys and Weinstein, "Demobilization and Reintegration."

211 *quarter of a million people:* Felter and Renwick, "Colombia's Civil Conflict."

211 *Arab–Israeli conflict:* Jewish Virtual Library, "Vital Statistics: Total Casualties, Arab-Israeli Conflict."

213 *40 percent are girls:* United Nations, "4 Out of 10 Child Soldiers Are Girls."

214 *propaganda ad:* Fattal, *Guerrilla Marketing.*

215 *The military murdered:* The military's killing of civilians is known in Colombia as the "False Positives" scandal. See Parkin Daniels, "Colombian Army Killed Thousands More Civilians than Reported, Study Claims."

215 *refugees:* UNHCR, "Colombia."

217 *research paper:* Juan Pablo Aparicio's idea turned into a 2021 working paper, which he authored with Michael Jetter and Christopher Parsons: "For FARC's Sake: Demobilizing the Oldest Guerrilla in Modern History." He shared an advance copy, which had not yet been peer-reviewed.

218 *Rwandan genocide:* Yanagizawa-Drott, "Propaganda and Conflict: Evidence from the Rwandan Genocide."

219 *twenty extra guerrilla members:* Aparicio et al., "For FARC's Sake."

221 *"Reintegration Route":* The description of Colombia's reintegration website at the time of Sandra's demobilization comes from my interview with Sandra and from an archived copy of the site, accessed through the Internet Archive's Wayback Machine in 2020. When Sandra accessed this site, it was known as the Office of the High Commissioner for Social and Economic Reintegration of the Presidency of the Republic (Alta Consejería para la Reintegración Social y Económica de la Presidencia de la República). Within the next year, the office would change names, becoming a full-fledged agency. Unfortunately, the archive does not include copies from 2010, when Sandra accessed it. But it does include a copy from 2009, which should be very similar.

224 *"When a man is denied":* Mandela, *Long Walk to Freedom: The Autobiography of Nelson Mandela*

226 *drug trafficking syndicates:* McDermott, "Criminal Activities of the FARC and Rebel Earnings."

226 *more FARC members deserted:* Nussio and Ugarriza, "Why Rebels Stop Fighting."

226 *exhausting:* When anthropologist Kimberly Theidon interviewed 112 ex-combatants in Colombia, more than half told her they'd abandoned the war because they had grown "so tired" and "so sick" of the guerrilla life. They complained, Theidon wrote, about "gnawing hunger; days and weeks without sleep; falling sick without access to medical care or medications; living in fear and clandestinity; having to kill and watch others killing . . ." Theidon, "Transitional Subjects: The Disarmament, Demobilization and Reintegration of Former Combatants in Colombia."

229 *police and military records:* Kaplan and Nussio, "Explaining Recidivism of Ex-Combatants in Colombia."

230 *more predictive:* It's possible that finding a job was not as powerful as family ties because, in this case, ex-combatants were receiving money from the government through the reintegration program. It's also worth noting that families can sometimes push people toward conflict identities, rather than pulling them away. Some FARC members joined the guerrilla group as children in order to escape sexual or physical abuse in their own families. Nothing is simple.

230 *did not trust:* Nussio, "Ex-Combatants and Violence in Colombia: Are Yesterday's Villains Today's Principal Threat?"

230 *Half of Colombians:* Gibson, "Reintegration or Segregation? How Perceptions of Ex-Combatants and Civil Society Affect Reintegration (and Peace) in Colombia."

232 *Macedonia:* Brusset and Otto, "Evaluation of Nashe Maalo"; and Estes, "Radio Soap Operas Teach Conflict Resolution." Search for Common Ground has produced other popular shows in Burundi, Sierra Leone, Liberia, Congo, Angola, Indonesia, Ukraine, and the Palestinian territories.

235 *conflict at work:* CPP Inc., "Workplace Conflict and How Businesses Can Harness It to Thrive."

235 *nurses:* Sofield and Salmond, "Workplace Violence: A Focus on Verbal Abuse and Intent to Leave the Organization."

235 *Family estrangement:* Pillemer, *Fault Lines.*

235 *A quarter of divorces:* High conflict divorces are, according to one *American Journal of Family Therapy* article, "pervasive negative exchanges" in a "hostile, insecure, emotional environment." See Anderson et al., "Defining High Conflict," and Whiteside, "The Parental Alliance Following Divorce: An Overview."

235 *195,510 high conflict divorces:* The number of high conflict divorces per year is my own estimate, based on one quarter of all divorces in the U.S., using 2018 divorce data from the U.S. Centers for Disease Control and Prevention.

chapter 7: complicating the narrative

237 *B'nai Jeshurun:* I owe a debt of gratitude to Melissa Weintraub from Resetting the Table, who told me (with Roly's permission) that BJ might be a good model for how an organization can change its culture to be more

conflict resilient. You can learn more about Resetting the Table at www
.resettingthetable.org.

238 *"a great moment":* Matalon et al., "B'nai Jeshurun Leadership E-mail on
Palestine."

238 *"Synagogue Tests Its Members":* Otterman and Berger, "Cheering U.N. Palestine Vote, Synagogue Tests Its Members."

238 *"We regret":* Matalon et al., "Second B'nai Jeshurun Leadership E-mail on
Palestine."

239 *"We felt like outsiders":* Rosenblatt, "Fuel for Debate over Rabbis' Role."

239 *"unforgiveable":* Ibid.

240 *five hundred American rabbis:* Cohen and Gitlin, "Reluctant or Repressed?"

243 *Difficult Conversations Lab:* I originally did some of this reporting for a
feature article I wrote about journalism, with support from the Solutions
Journalism Network. Ripley, "Complicating the Narratives."

243 *"real-life, intractable conflict":* To read more about the Difficult Conversations Lab and the fascinating research by Coleman and his colleagues,
see Coleman, *The Five Percent: Finding Solutions to Seemingly Impossible
Conflicts.*

247 *really listening to them:* For journalists interested in how they can do a better job listening, I have two suggestions. First, consider inviting the Solutions Journalism Network to come to your newsroom to teach the skills of
Complicating the Narratives (go to solutionsjournalism.org). In remarkably little time, thanks to the brilliant work of Hélène Biandudi Hofer,
reporters can learn to loop and to cover conflict in a way that revives curiosity. Secondly, check out Hearken, a company that helps organizations
listen to their audiences in a systematic way. It was cofounded by Jennifer
Brandel (who was inspired by some of the principles of the Bahá'í faith,
mentioned earlier in this book). Hearken helps reporters shift to serving
the public rather than telling the public what to think. The motto is "journalism through a humble posture," which seems like what we need these
days. Check them out at wearehearken.com.

247 *the third paradox:* The third paradox of conflict is inspired by my conversation with the California mediator, teacher, and lawyer Catherine Conner,
who told me about recognizing a similar paradox in her own clients. It's
connected to the principle of Gestalt therapy known as the "paradoxical
theory of change," which holds that the more a person actively tries to
change herself to be something she's not, the more she stays the same. She
has to first accept herself as she is, according to this theory. Something

similar happens in conflict. We resist change unless and until we feel understood. To learn more about this, check out the chapter "The Paradoxical Theory of Change" by Arnold Beisser, which originally appeared in the 1970 book *Gestalt Therapy Now* by Joen Fagan and Irma Lee Shepherd.

248 *a complication, not a conflict:* Thank you to *Washington Post* journalist Elahe Izadi for pointing me to Jon Franklin, who expands upon this important point in his excellent book *Writing for Story.*

248 *Simplicity:* Be suspicious of simple stories, the economist Tyler Cowen warned in a 2009 TED Talk, "Be Suspicious of Simple Stories." I love this line in particular: "Imagine every time you're telling a good-versus-evil story, you're basically lowering your IQ by ten points or more."

249 *bring the mediators back:* Resetting the Table returned to do the initial design for this second series of programs and then handed off most of the project to organizational change consultant Adena Philips.

251 *"Clown Runs for Prez":* New York *Daily News,* "Clown Runs for Prez."

252 *"You're going to lose!":* Haberman and Lipton, "Nobody Waved Goodbye."

256 *Mindi Vroman:* I interviewed and observed Mindi Vroman during the exchanges, as I did all the participants in this chapter. I also benefited from a wonderfully honest (and funny) essay that Mindi wrote about the experience and shared with everyone in the group.

262 *the Republican Party:* There is some debate about whether the GOP was started two months earlier in Ripon, Wisconsin, but a lot of folks in Michigan insist it was in Jackson, where we saw the plaque. *Encyclopaedia Britannica* cites both locations in its entry about the founding of the party.

266 *politically mixed marriages:* In 1973, recently married couples shared the same political affiliation about 54 percent of the time. In 2014, recently married couples agreed 74 percent of the time. Iyengar et al., "The Home as a Political Fortress: Family Agreement in an Era of Polarization."

266 *Separation:* Pettigrew, "European Attitudes Toward Immigrants."

267 *People in politically mixed marriages:* Iyengar et al., "The Home as a Political Fortress."

267 *fuller, richer lives:* For an example of how political diversity can lead to fuller lives for everyone, see my 2019 *Atlantic* story, "The Least Politically Prejudiced Place in America."

270 *homicide rate:* The homicide rate of Lansing was 6.8 per 100,000 people in 2018. This is based on a reported 8 homicides in 2018 (Berg, "With Homicide Rates Down, Here's Where Each Lansing-Area Case Stands")

out of a population of 118,210 (U.S. Census Bureau). Meanwhile, New York City had 295 homicides in 2018 (NYPD, "Historical Crime Data: Seven Major Felony Offenses) out of a population of 8.3 million (U.S. Census Bureau). That's a homicide rate of 3.6 per 100,000 people.

272 *reading it aloud:* You can watch Andy Potter and his colleagues read this letter at BJ online. Search *B'nai Jeshurun November 10, 2018*.

appendix I: how to recognize high conflict in the world

281 *"like racism:"* Castle, "Wolves, Resurgent and Protected, Vex Swedish Farmers."

281 *"omnipresent and oppressive:"* Agence France-Presse, "Sheep Flock to Eiffel Tower as French Farmers Cry Wolf."

283 *sabotaging the hunt:* Wheat, "Crying Wolf."

283 *kidnapped the head:* Todd, "French Farmers Take Park Boss Hostage over Wolf Attacks."

283 *shot the animal:* Taylor, "Wild Wolf Shot and Killed in Denmark."

appendix II: how to recognize high conflict in yourself

290 *Wolf Dialogue Project:* I learned about this project through interviews with Hans Peter Hansen, who generously connected me to participants in the program. I also drew from a wonderful dissertation on the project written by Anne Cathrine Munch Schrøder titled "In the Wake of the Wolf."

293 *"As soon as you articulate":* Voss is quoted in Bernstein, "Worried About a Difficult Conversation?" For more, see Voss, *Never Split the Difference*.

index

about the author

Amanda Ripley writes stories about human behavior and change for *The Atlantic, The Washington Post,* and other outlets. She is the author of *The New York Times* bestselling book *The Smartest Kids in the World: And How They Got That Way,* and *The Unthinkable: Who Survives when Disaster Strikes—and Why.* Previously, she worked for *Time,* helping the magazine win two National Magazine Awards. To discuss her work, Amanda has appeared on ABC, NBC, Fox News, CNN, and NPR. But like all of us, she has many identities. She is also a trained conflict mediator, an undistinguished soccer player, a mother, a wife, and a neighbor in Washington, D.C.